# AN OLIGOPOLY

THOMAS GEER

# AN OLIGOPOLY

# The World Coffee Economy and Stabilization Schemes

## DUNELLEN

**New York**

To Marion

# Contents

List of Tables and Figures ix

1 Introduction 1

    Notes 9

2 A Critical Survey of
Established Findings 11

    Market Performance of
the Industry 11

    The Statistical Situation:
Surplus, Price Cycles, and
Excessive Fluctuations 11

    The Importance of the Industry
to the Producing Countries 20

    The International Coffee Agreement 20

    Methods of Establishing
the Agreement 27

    The Restrictive Character
of the Agreement 29

    Existing Rules for an International
Policy on Primary Commodity Markets 29

    Special Features of Production and
Consumption of Coffee 34

    Critique 42

    Notes 44

3 A Description of the World Coffee
Economy and Its Environment 49

    Characteristics of Production 49

    Agroeconomic Factors 49

    Economic Factors 52

    Characteristics of Industrial
Processing and End Consumption 65

The Final Product: Blends
and Solubles    65
Consumer Preferences    66
The State of the Processing Industry    67
Governmental Restrictions in
Importing Countries    67
Notes    68

4  **Market Performance as a Result
of Oligopolistic Competition**    71

The Market Structure    71
Product Differentiation and
Sectional Markets    71
Business Concentration of "Primary
Sellers" and "Buyers for Processing"    73
Production Policy of Oligopolistic Sellers    75
Market Price Assumptions: The Problem
of Stocks in Hands of "Primary Sellers"    75
The Market Organization on the
New York Coffee Exchange    76

The Conduct of Primary Sellers and
Buyers for Processing    77
The Creation of Surplus and
Excess Capacity    77
The "Excessive" Price Fluctuations
and Cycles    136
Notes    159

5  **An Evaluation of the
Competitive Aspects of the
International Coffee Agreement**    167

The World Coffee Market as
an "Exception"    167
The International Coffee Agreement
as an "Exception"    169
The Main Effects of the Agreement    171
The Secondary Effects of the Agreement    181
The Coffee Agreement — A Case of
Successful Economics?    183
Notes    187

**Appendixes**
International Coffee Agreement of 1962    191
International Coffee Agreement of 1968    249

**Bibliography**    313

# List of Tables and Figures

**Table**

1   Data on Export Concentration: Coffee
as a Percentage of Total Merchandising
Exports   **21**

2   Sectoral Coffee Markets   **72**

3   Money Prices for Santos 4 and Rio 7   **82**

4   Brazil's Coffee Area   **84**

5   Trends in Coffee Industry Data
in São Paulo   **93**

6   Trends in Coffee Industry Data
in Paraná   **98**

7   Prices, Acreage, and Output
Changes in Brazil   **106**

8   Postwar Trends in Coffee Production   **118**

9   End-of-Year Carryover Stocks of
ICO Member Countries   **119**

10   Brazilian Stocks at End of Year   **120**

11   Coffee Exports: São Paulo – Domestic
Average Price, Foreign Exchange Rate,
and Average Spot Quotations   **125**

**Figure**

1   Coffee: Production, Brazil and
All Other Areas   **13**

1a  World Supply and Demand for Coffee,
1946/47-1967-8   **14**

2   Coffee: Estimated Total Stocks
at End of Season   **16**

3   Short-run Fluctuations in N.Y.
Spot Coffee Prices, Santos and Milds   **17**

4   Coffee: Development of Exportable
Production, Apparent Consumption in
Importing Countries, and Price   **18**

5   Coffee: Spot Prices,
New York, by Types   **19**

6   Coffee: World Exports, by
Producing Areas   **51**

7   Colombia: Coffee Prices in U.S.
and Colombian Currency   **59**

8   Brazil: Coffee Prices in U.S.
and Brazilian Currency   **81**

9   Output: Brazil, Paraná, São Paulo   **86**

10  Acreage in Two Brazilian States   **87**

11  Brazilian Domestic Producer Prices   **89**

12  Price Ratio of Farm Products
to Coffee, São Paulo   **94**

13  Acreage Ratio of Farm Products
to Coffee, São Paulo   **95**

14  Price Ratio of Farm Products
to Coffee, Paraná   **100**

15  Acreage Ratio of Farm Products
to Coffee, Paraná   **101**

16  Price Indexes of Coffee, Fertilizers,
and Other Agricultural Products   **102**

| 17 | Real Coffee Prices | **103** |
|----|--------------------|---------|
| 18 | Ratio of Prices, Santos 4 - Rio 7 | **111** |
| 19 | World Exportable Production, Brazil, Other Latin America, and Africa | **116** |
| 20 | World Supply and Demand for Coffee, 1946/47-1969/70 | **117** |
| 21 | Brazil: Exportable Production, Exports and Prices | **123** |
| 22 | Monthly Average, N.Y. Spot Prices of Selected Coffees | **126** |
| 23 | Coffee: Shares of Import Volume, by Consuming Areas | **127** |
| 24 | Price Differentials Between Three Main Types of Coffee | **128** |
| 25a | Spot Price Differentials of Brazils in Relation to Robustas | **129** |
| 25b | Monthly Spot Price Percentage Differential of Selected Coffees in Relationship to "Mams" | **130** |
| 26 | Total U.S. Coffee Imports by Types; Total Consumption and Consumption per Head and U.S. National Income Index | **131** |
| 27 | Coffee: Shares of Export Volume, by Producing Areas, 1909-67 | **145** |
| 28 | Coffee: World Export Values | **146** |
| 29 | Exports of Coffee from the Developing Countries | **185** |

# 1 Introduction

Year-to-year movements of international coffee prices displaying erratic fluctuations as well as cyclical trends have been observed for a century. They have led to frequent endeavors of one or more coffee-producing countries to affect the world price and, in particular, to guarantee more stability in prices. Such action has normally been regarded as aimed at the exploitation of consumers, because the commonly used method has been a multilateral export restriction, with a distribution of quotas between producers.[1] The breakdown of agreements was therefore usually applauded by the consuming countries and by some economists. Since the boom of 1954, however, the leading importer, the United States, itself entered the producers' agreement in 1962 and led 90 percent of all importing countries to follow suit. It has frequently been argued that this was an entirely political move of the Kennedy administration and that the International Coffee Agreement (ICA) in its present form is not defensible on economic terms.[2] This statement recalls other writers who, after prolonged study of previous international commodity agreements, have concluded that those agreements are "restrictive per se"; that is, they restrict the play of competitive market forces because of their form.[3]

This restrictive feature is the core of the objection to the International Coffee Agreement as it is, because its form is alleged to prevent the achievement of a "long-run equilibrium price on a partial market." The importance of this school of thought in international commodity policy is fairly represented in a quotation of the United Nations Conference on Trade and Development: "It is a matter of fairly general agreement that international stabilization efforts should be directed at smoothing out the random fluctuations in price which tend to characterize the markets for primary commodities. As to whether international arrangements should go further than this and seek to influence the absolute level and trend of prices, opinions are much more divided."[4] Thus, opposition to this restrictive feature has been an argument frequently used by rich importing countries, which were committed to a national as well as an international policy of unrestricted trade. This opposition has been the main reason why in the postwar period only five international agreements have been concluded.[5] The importance of that idea in the scene of international trade policy between richer and poorer countries is thus evident and has had its bearing on the discussion of the relation between international trade and economic development.

It is the purpose of this study to examine the "per se restrictiveness" thesis in a critical fashion. Two general sentiments are included in this thesis: those economists and countries arguing against commodity agreements of the ICA type are not unaware of the special conditions that exist on world primary commodity markets, and they advocate remedial actions. They believe, however, that these remedial actions are undesirable if they restrict price competition on world commodity markets.

There are two lines of attack on this position. One is to use the arguments of those economists who have questioned the applicability to the poorer countries of the orthodox classical and neoclassical theory,[6] and hence the applicability of the laissez-faire approach in international trade.[7] (All the coffee producing and exporting countries are, in fact, relatively poor. The controversy centers around the implication of the classical principle of comparative advantage, according to which growth is promoted by specialization. The advocates of the classical theory assume that their theoretical model is applicable to the analysis of both rich and poor countries and that international trade leads, through the allocative function of an unrestricted market mechanism, to a partial equilibrium of markets and thus to a general equilibrium with an optimal allocation of resources and consequent promotion of growth.[8] Several facts have led the opposing economists to argue that the long-run equilibrium on a partial market of an export product, as achieved by unrestricted competition, is a necessary precondition neither for the optimal allocation of resources of the exporting country nor for the general equilibrium of world markets. In the opinion of these writers, international trade promotes the growth of poorer countries through the availability of foreign exchange for financing planned economic development. The theoretical basis of this theory of economic development, which involves as well elements of other policies, such as the balance of payments, domestic, financial, and taxation policy, foreign exchange policy, etc., lies in modern Keynesian and post-Keynesian economics. If the arguments of this macro-equilibrium approach were supposed to be generally valid, the conclusion that the regulations of the International Coffee Agreement are "restrictive per se" would not imply that it would be undesirable. Yet the use of this approach has not found universal acceptance, and different opinions about the application of the orthodox classical and neoclassical economic theory to the underdeveloped countries still exist.[9]

It therefore seems necessary to discuss the arguments of the critics of commodity agreements in their own terms. The emphasis these critics have laid on the unrestricted working of the market mechanism in international trade of primary commodities shows that they follow the classical approach. These critics believe that the price fluctuations on primary commodity markets are the result of imperfections in an equilibrium system, rather than of a fundamental disequilibrium.[10] This belief has led to the advocacy of compensatory finance schemes.

Of course, this *raisonnement* holds good only if the market is in a state of pure competition.[11] If, however, monopolistic market imperfections in the markets of primary commodities are producing the price instability and thus a distortion from the results, attributed to the working of competitive market forces on an unrestricted market mechanism, the argument would be invalid, as will be shown. To advance this proposition, we have to recall that it has been the task of the micro-economic price theory to analyze connections between market imperfection and the performance of a market. It is therefore necessary to inquire whether the findings of the theories of imperfect competition may be applicable to the analysis of price fluctuations in the international markets of primary commodities and of policies to regulate these markets.

One strain of the theory of imperfect competition, the theory of industrial organization, argues additionally that on markets with certain forms of monopolistic competition, "per se restrictive" regulations of prices and output may result in a better performance than that which results where competition is unregulated. Thus, if we describe the restrictive regulation of output and prices as a "per se restrictive" feature of an agreement, it does not follow that its results are also restrictive, i.e., preventing the economic performance attributed to workable competition. The character of the agreement can be seen only against the price formation on the market before the introduction of the agreement. This is the new "dual view" of this theory: it is thus on a model of the world coffee market in which the unrestricted competitive pricing produces a long-run equilibrium, on which the argument against a "per se restrictive" international coffee agreement can be based. Again, the basic concept of this argument is the recognition of the fact that certain markets within an economy may have such a market structure that the tendency toward a long-run equilibrium as defined on a market in pure competition cannot operate without additional measures, which are prima facie "restrictive."[12] The new concepts that have been added to identify such markets in an economy are the concepts of

4

"exceptions." These are "markets in which competition exists or could exist and has produced or may be expected to produce competitive results, but where in light of other policy considerations competitive results are unsatisfactory in one or more respect" and "markets in which active competition exists, but where because of imperfections in the market, competition does not produce one or more competitive results."[13] The first type of "exception" is a political one; the latter is called a "genuine exception," and it is this one in which we are interested for the rest of this study. The regulations to change the unwanted performance of competition are called "exemptions." The analysis of domestic markets in the United States has led to the regard of markets with *natural* monopoly or oligopoly as typical "genuine exception[s] to be regulated by control of production and prices"; that is, by means of being "restrictive per se." On international markets, situations comparable to such "genuine exceptions" have been said to exist if, by reason of private business concentration of enterprises or national policies of *different* countries, the price formation on the world market for a product has been transformed to one of oligopoly or oligopsony with discriminating and monopolistic conduct, or if national governments have discriminated against trading activities of non-nationals. Since they are not "national oligopolies" and from a point of view of a national government oligopolies cannot be dissolved by national antitrust measures, they have been termed "conditional genuine exceptions."[14]

The results of this theory have led to policy recommendations in the United States that were adopted to guide the U.S. antitrust policy. In those markets, analyzed as "exceptions to be regulated through a control of prices and outputs," "exemptions" of this "per se restrictive" type have been instituted on national markets by order of the government. But more important for our study, national "per se restrictive" exemptions to regulate "conditional genuine exceptions" on international product markets have been instituted too, in the form of national export cartel associations. However, this situation is regarded as unsatisfactory, and yet international policy measures to regulate trade in products with such forms of price formations have been unanimously demanded by representatives of this policy.[15]

These concepts, developed by the theory of industrial organization to analyze the performance of competition on national markets, may be a useful tool in analyzing what kind of market imperfection has been the source of the "excessive" price instability on the world coffee market. Also, the above concepts may serve as a basis for policy recommendations for an international economic policy on world commodity markets. It is thus the aim of this study firstly to establish whether the concepts that have been employed up to now for analyzing national markets in one country only can be used for analyzing an international (or world) coffee market as well. Secondly, it will be shown whether the world coffee industry* is a "conditional genuine exception" which needs to be regulated by a control of prices and output. This being established, the International Coffee Agreement of 1962 could then be regarded as an "exemption," i.e., as a regulation defensible even within the theoretical frame-work of arguments of those economists and countries, that are in favor of competitive international trade.

In order to decide whether such an "exception" exists, an investigation into "market structure" and "market conduct" must be carried out. Out of that type of research a certain model of competitive price formation on the world coffee market may be constructed,[16] which will explain the "performance."[17] This is a particularly important point in relation to the International Coffee Agreement, in that it is impossible to predict future performance of an oligopolistic industry from any observation of past performance, i.e., past price movements. And it is necessary to decide which form of "exemption" is applicable for such an "exception," insofar as the "exemption" should alter conduct

---

* As a manifestation of this approach the term "industry" will be used instead of the usual term "economy" — the latter we regard as a "nominal" obstacle to seeing the world coffee industry in a context comparable to any other industry and therefore as well disposed as any other (national or international) industry to an "industrial organization study."

and/or structure in such a way as to achieve the wanted results.

This leaves us to determine what will be understood by "market structure" and "market structure" in the context of this study. According to the theory of industrial organization, ". . . market structure means those conditions, external to the firm, which are relatively permanent or change only slowly and which affect, if they do not determine, the way the firm operates."[18] Or as I.W.L. McKie formulates: "Analysis of market structure involves at least the following elements: the number and relative size of sellers, technology, economies of scale in production and distribution, the proportion of fixed costs in the short run and the ease of exit from industry, the differentiation of the product, the elasticity of demand with respect to price and income, the . . . legal restrictions on competition and the number and size distribution of buyers."[19] "Market conduct on the other hand comprises aspects of the market, which are the result of specific decisions of firms and which are, at least conceivably, alterable in relatively short periods of time."[20] I.S. Bain[21] groups the conduct dimensions as follows:

"(1) The price policies of enterprises: These are effectively the principles, methods, and resultant actions that they employ in establishing what prices to charge, what output to produce, etc.

(2) The manner in which and devices and mechanisms by which the intrinsically rivalrous action of different sellers in an industry are coordinated, adapted to each other, or made mutually consistent in reacting to demand for products in the common market."[22] Examples quoted are: whether or not the price and output decisions of individual rival sellers are arrived at in a completely independent fashion, and if not, which of a variety of patterns of recognized interdependence, concerted actions, or collusion is followed by individual firms or by groups establishing selling prices and output.

(3)    The marketing or distribution channels utilized; again, whether there is independence of sellers, or whether interdependence, concerted action, or collusion is found.

(4)    The endeavors of established firms to maintain or enhance their established market position in rivalry with actual or potential competitors, the use of predatory tactics to weaken or eliminate established competition, and what sort of tactics are used.

Similar dimensions of market conduct for buyers may also be recognized.

We will use this approach in the following study, since we believe – as explained in more detail in the Critique of Chapter 2 of this book – that only through industrial organization analysis are we able to identify the importance of a significant feature of the world coffee industry since 1945: In all major coffee-producing countries, marketing boards or other semiautonomous statutory boards have been set up. Furthermore, the processing industry in the coffee-consuming countries has shown a tendency to large business concentration. The number of independent dealers and brokers on the world's leading coffee exchange in New York has decreased and the turnovers have become very small. Moreover, the statutory national organizations of producers have also followed an independent policy of price and output regulation on their domestic market. They have created a situation in which the domestic pattern of production has frequently been divorced from the world supply and demand situation. They also set export minimum prices and/or influenced the export price formation of their own exporting firms, both independently and collusively. It is probably these regulations and policies, that are now determining market structure dimensions, i.e., the number and relative size of sellers marketing or distribution channels utilized as well as the market conduct dimensions (price policies). The method used on the world coffee market in examination of market structure and conduct has already been used in other studies.[23]

Chapter 2 outlines the historical development of the world coffee industry and reviews the assumed "special conditions" on the coffee market. It also deals with the question of whether there is already a body of rules to deal with these problems in the form of an international economic policy. Chapter 3 discusses the structural characteristics of the coffee industry. Chapter 4 contains an analysis of market conduct as the cause of the excessive price fluctuations on the world coffee market. Finally, Chapter 5 considers whether the International Coffee Agreement is a suitable "exemption" to regulate world trade in coffee.

## NOTES

1. See, *inter alia;* J.S. Davis, *International Commodity Agreements: Hope, Illusion or Menace,* (New York: The Committee on International Economic Policy, 1947), p. 6.

2. V.D. Wickizer, "International Collaboration in the Coffee Market," *Food Research Studies,* IV, 3 (Stanford University Press, 1964), 301; C.P. Kindleberger, "The Terms of Trade for Primary Products," ed. M. Clanson, *National and International Development,* (Baltimore: Johns Hopkins, 1964), p. 21; especially, J.W. Rowe, *The World's Coffee,* (London: H.M.S.O., 1963), p. 190; R.F. Mikesell, "International Commodity Stabilization Schemes and the Export Problems of Developing Countries," AER, *Papers and Proceedings,* LIII (1963), 80; C.E. Staley, "An Evaluation," *op. cit.,* 245; Kindleberger, "Discussion," *op. cit.,* 106.

3. *Inter alia,* M. Ludwig, *Internationale Rohstoffpolitik* (Zurich, 1957).

4. United Nations Conference on Trade and Development, Staabilization of International Commodity Markets, E/Conf/46/8 (Geneva, March 1964), p. 34.

5. G. Blau, "International Commodity Agreements," paper presented at IER Congress on Economic Development (Vienna, Austria, 1962), pp. 2-3.

6. H.B. Chenery, *Comparative Advantage and Development Policy,* AER, Vol. LI, I (1961), p. 231. "The modern version of the comparative cost doctrine is essentially a simplified form of a static equilibrium theory."

7. H. Myint, "Economic Theory and the Underdeveloped Countries," *IPE,* Vol. 73 (1965), 477-481.

8. T. Megishi, "Stability of a Competitive Economy: A Survey Article," *Econometrica,* Vol. 30, 635-669.

9. Staley, *op. cit.,* pp. 336-339; Chenery *op. cit.;* Myint, *op. cit.*

9

10. R.M. Stern, "Fluctuations in Commodity Trade," *IPE,* LXXVII (1963), 258-273.

11. W.J.L. Ryan, *Price Theory,* (London: Macmillan, 1961), pp. 261-274. Here "pure" is used (according to Chamberlin, *The Theory of Monopolistic Competition,* Cambridge, Mass., 1962, pp. 12-29) in the sense that the market may be imperfect, but if competition is pure, i.e., *not monopolistic,* the supply and demand curves define the condition equilibrium. Also, M. Ezekiel, "The Cobweb Theorem," *QJE,* (1938), p. 258.

12. E. Hoppmann, *Wettbewerbspolitik und Exportkartelle,* pp. 380-421, or the dispute in the U.S. literature about the Webb-Pomerane Act, which allowed export trade associations to form in non-competitive markets.

13. C. Kaysen and D.F. Turner, *Antitrust Policy,* (Cambridge, Mass.: Harvard University Press, 1959), pp. 189-190, 194-198.

14. Hoppman, *op. cit.,* pp. 335-358.

15. *Inter alia,* C.D. Edwards, *Maintaining Competition* (London: McGraw-Hill, 1947), pp. 50-91.

16. S.H. Sosnick, "A Critique of Concepts of Workable Competition, *QJE* (1958), p. 410; J.S. Bain, "The Theory of Monopolistic Competition after Thirty Years: The Impact on Industrial Organization," AER, *Papers and Proceedings,* LIV (1964), 31.

17. E.S. Mason, Preface to Kaysen and Turner, *op. cit.,* pp. xviii-xix.

18. Kaysen and Turner, *op. cit.*

19. James W. McKie, *Tin Cans and Tinplate* (Cambridge, Mass.: Harvard University Press, 1959) p. 5.

20. Kaysen and Turner, *op. cit.,* p. 59.

21. Bain, *op. cit.,* pp. 9-11; Chap. 8, pp. 266-339.

22. Bain, *op. cit.,* p. 266.

23. *Inter alia,* C.F. Phillips, *Competition in the Synthetic Rubber Industry* (Chapel Hill: University of North Carolina Press, 1961); McKie, *op. cit.;* P.M. MacAron, *Price Formation in Natural Gas Fields* (Yale University Press, 1962).

# 2    A Critical Survey of Established Findings

## Market Performance of the Industry

### The Statistical Situation: Surplus, Price Cycles, and Excessive Fluctuations

The statistical development of the coffee economy can be described briefly. Broad and intensive investigations of the FAO and GATT preceded this study.[1]

Coffee production before World War II — which fluctuated at around 2.5 million tons per year — was highly concentrated in Latin America. The continent produced 90 percent of the world crop, Brazil alone accounting for more than 70 percent of Latin America's output and almost 60 percent of the world crop. Asia's share was 6 percent, and Africa's about the same.

In 1961-62 the total world production reached 4.5 million tons, an increase of about 85 percent. "Using quinquennial averages, the data indicate an advance in world production between the first and the second half of the 1950's by nearly 50 percent, followed by a much more moderate rise — less than 10 percent — in the first half of the 1960's."[2] But today the Latin American countries produce less than 80 percent and Asia only 2 percent, while the share of the African producers has risen to 18 percent.

The growth in coffee production has not been uniform. In the beginning the steady growth of production in the smaller producer countries of Latin America was accompanied by an extremely rapid extension in Africa, and a slow one in Brazil. In 1956 the picture changed completely: growth rates in the former countries were still positive, but became much smaller, whereas now Brazil and Colombia took the lead and increased their production steeply. Thus from 1955-56 to 1961-62 more than 80 percent of the increase in world production was harvested in Brazil, which doubled her output (Fig. 1). Two characteristics in this development should be emphasized:

(1)  There was an increase in production in Africa centers in those regions where coffee is grown by small peasant farmers: former French West Africa (Ivory Coast), Uganda, and Angola. The growth rates in African coffee-producing countries with large European plantations were much smaller.

(2)  The increase in Brazil was more or less exclusively a result of expanding production in the state of Paraná, which was opened for coffee production about 1950.

The volume of coffee trade could not keep pace with the rise in production. In 1941-45 it sank to some 1 million tons; a decrease of about 0.5 million tons compared with 1929-37. The previous level, however, was regained in 1944. Exports in 1950 exceeded 2 million tons and rose to 2.7 million tons in 1962. World coffee trade thus shows a steady increase, doubling the volume of transactions since 1945. It proceeded in two waves: the first steep advance of 1945-50 with a growth of some 0.5 million tons in the period, the second, from 1956 to 1960, amounting to 0.7 million tons. This increase, however, was insufficient to prevent the accumulation of surpluses, which have been entirely held by producing countries. The first sign of stock-building in Brazil appeared in 1954 and stocks have grown since then to 3 million tons. Since 1958, stock-building has also been taking place in

Figure 1

Coffee: Production, Brazil and All Other Areas
(million bags of 60 kg.)

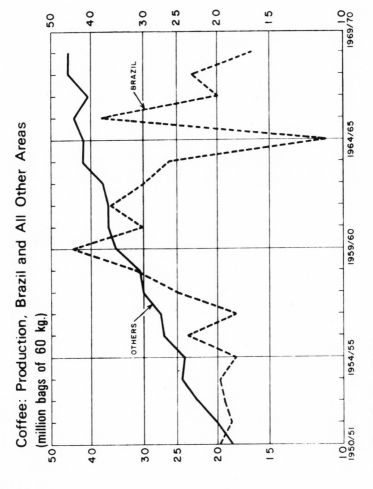

Source: Based on USDA data.

13

**Figure 1A**

## World Supply and Demand for Coffee 1946/47 – 1967/68
(million bags of 60 kg.)

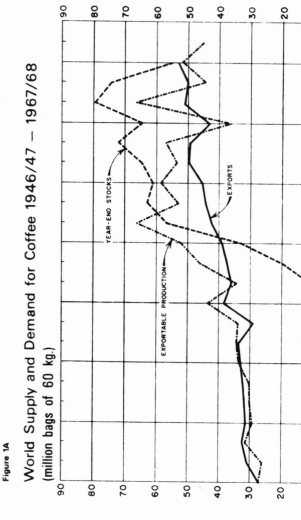

Note: In recent years some of the stocks were not of exportable quality.

Source: Based on USDA data.

14

Colombia, stocks rising to 400,000 tons, while African countries have also been stock-piling on a smaller scale, amounting to less than 100,000 tons.[3] (See Fig. 2.) Stocks in consumer hands were relatively stable and fluctuated around 400,000 tons.[4]

Prices and volumes have moved inversely. Owing to the efforts of the Inter-American Coffee Agreement, prices were fixed during World War II at around 13 cents per pound. The raising of the price ceiling on the New York Coffee Exchange induced prices to rise to 27 cents per pound. In the following three years on this exchange prices remained stable, then doubled and stayed at this level from 1950 to 1953-54. In 1954 the price accelerated again until it reached about 80 cts/lb. in the autumn. The collapse of the so-called coffee boom led to a decline in 1958 to the pre-1954 level of about 50 cts/lb. Thereafter prices were steady for two years, declining afterward to 30 cts/lb. in 1962-63. Besides those movements of yearly average prices, there were short-term price movements during each crop year.

During the period under review the development of prices and volumes on the coffee market their followed the typical pricing pattern, which is characteristic on many primary commodity markets:

(1) There were the usual excessive year-to-year average price fluctuations, making for "short-term price instability" (Fig. 3).

(2) Reviewing the whole period since 1945, we find the price movement displayed the typical course of a cyclical development which is well-known in economic discussions as the "coffee cycle."[5] (See Fig. 4). It was accompanied by the development of huge surpluses in stored coffee beans and of excess plant capacity. (Fig. 2).

Remedial action was contemplated and achieved with the signing of the International Coffee Agreement in 1962.

Figure 2

Coffee: Estimated Total Stocks at End of Season[a]
(million bags of 60 kg.)

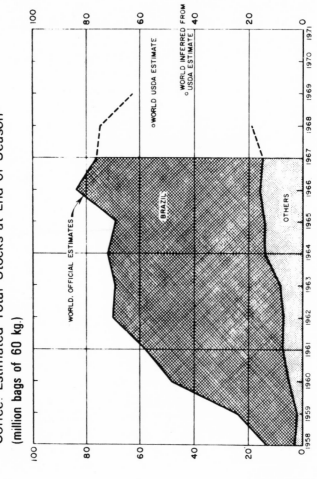

[a] End of June for Brazil and end of September others in calendar year as designated

Note: Dashed lines indicate preliminary figures

Source: Based on USDA data.

Figure 3

Short-Run Fluctuations in N.Y. Spot Coffee Prices, Santos and Milds
(U.S. cents per pound — monthly averages)

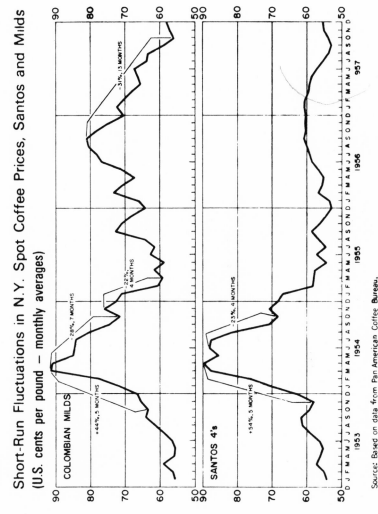

Source: Based on data from Pan American Coffee Bureau.

17

**Figure 4**

# Coffee: Development of Exportable Production, Apparent Consumption in Importing Countries, and Price (U.S. unit value)

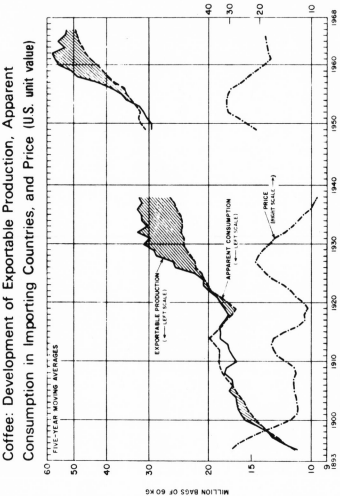

Notes: U.S. unit value, deflated by U.S. wholesale price. 1926 = 100.

Prices 1885 – 1938 refer to prices during crop years ending in year shown; 1949 – 1965 calendar years.

Production data throughout refer to crop years shown.

Source: Based on data from USDA and Pan American Coffee Bureau.

Figure 5

# Coffee: Spot Prices, New York, by types
## (U.S. cents per pound)

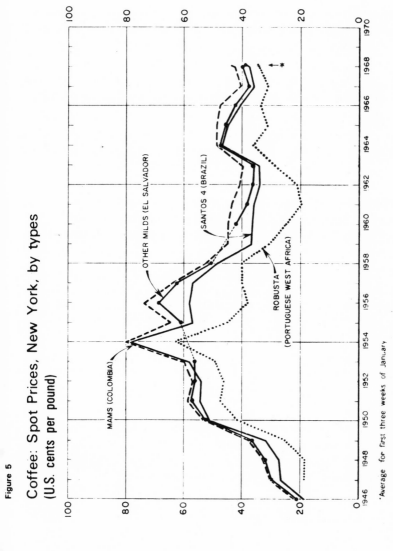

MAMS (COLOMBIA)

OTHER MILDS (EL SALVADOR)

SANTOS 4 (BRAZIL)

ROBUSTA
(PORTUGUESE WEST AFRICA)

*Average for first three weeks of January.

Source: Based on data from Pan American Coffee Bureau.

19

## The Importance of the Industry
## to the Producing Countries

"Coffee holds a peculiar position in the world economy. It is not one of the major agricultural crops and the value of world coffee production is small in comparison with that of rice, wheat, oils and fats, livestock products or sugar."[6] But coffee ranks first among agricultural commodities in terms of importance in world trade and is second only to petroleum among all primary commodities, with exports valued in excess of 1.75 billion dollars a year. Between 1947-49 and 1955-57, the volume of coffee exports increased only about 15 percent, but prices doubled, with the result that export earnings and the proportion represented by coffee also rose. Since 1957, when coffee prices began their most recent decline, the export value of coffee as a percentage of total exports has also tended to fall. During the period 1957-60, coffee exports from Central America ranged from 9 percent (Mexico) to 79 percent for smaller countries (El Salvador and Guatemala) of the total value of all exports from these countries.[7] In South America the range was from one percent (Venezuela) to 85 percent (Colombia) and in Africa from about 12 percent (Belgian Congo and Tanganyika) to 49 percent (Uganda) and 67 percent (Ethiopia).

The significance of coffee to the economic and political life of the producing countries can hardly be exaggerated. Almost all producing countries are poor single-crop economies, which rely heavily upon coffee exports for the foreign exchange they need to pay for imports for current consumption and particularly for economic development. Moreover, in some of these countries, taxes derived from coffee production and exports account for as much as 20 percent of total government revenues.[8]

### The International Coffee Agreement

The first International Coffee Agreement in which the governments of producer countries as well as of importer countries

# TABLE 1

Data on Export Concentration:

Coffee as a Percentage of Total Merchandise Exports

| | Percentages | | |
| --- | --- | --- | --- |
| | **1966** | **1960-62** Average | **1964-66** Average |
| Colombia | 65 | 68 | 67 |
| Ethiopia | 58 | 54 | 32 |
| Rwanda | 56 | 58 | 55 |
| Uganda | 53 | 43 | 52 |
| Haiti | 51 | 48 | 51 |
| Angola | 48 | 38 | 48 |
| El Salvador | 48 | 60 | 50 |
| Brazil | 44 | 53 | 47 |
| Guatemala | 44 | 60 | 46 |
| Ivory Coast | 40 | 46 | 40 |
| Costa Rica | 39 | 53 | 41 |
| Kenya | 32 | 29 | 32 |
| Madagascar | 32 | 31 | 31 |
| N. Guinea (Aust.) | 24 | 10 | 22 |
| Central African Republic | 24 | 27 | 22 |
| Cameroon | 23 | 20 | 23 |
| Togo | 22 | 27 | 25 |
| Nicaragua | 20[a] | 29 | 21[b] |
| Tanzania | 19 | 14 | 16 |
| Ecuador | 17 | 14 | 18 |
| Dominican Republic | 15 | 12 | 16 |
| Honduras | 14 | 15 | 17 |
| Guinea | 10[a] | 11 | |
| Mexico | 7 | 9 | 8 |
| Congo, D.R. | 4 | 9 | 6 |
| Dahomey | 4 | 6 | 4 |

[a]    1965.
[b]    1964-65 average.

**Sources:** *UN Yearbook of International Trade Statistics,* various issues; *International Financial Statistics,* various issues.

participated entered provisionally into force on July 1, 1963.[9] The importance of the coffee agreement in international commodity policy is well described by an author who states, "Its pattern may well form a principal model in future commodity negotiations, which will play an increasingly important role in the world economy."[10]

Attempts before World War II to regulate the world coffee market were mainly made by the unilateral action of Brazil, which at that time produced most of the world's coffee.[11] When these early attempts failed, Brazil tried several times to conclude agreements with other governments of producing countries.[12] The first regulatory scheme to be supported by an importing country occurred in 1940, when the United States and fourteen Latin American countries entered into the Inter-American Coffee Agreement coping with the problems created by the war-time closing of Continental European markets. The agreement was finally terminated in 1948.[13] The first steps and conferences toward creating a new agreement were taken in 1954, but it took three more years for one group of seven producing countries – Latin American ones – to sign an agreement to regulate marketing by withholding a portion of their exportable production on the basis of an allocation of quarterly export quotas to each participating country. This was the Latin American Coffee Agreement of 1958. In 1958 and 1959 the number of participants grew and the new International Coffee Agreement regulated about 90 percent of all exports. Export quotas were designed to regulate the U.S. market only.

The efforts to adjust the control scheme to the rules of the Havana Charter, the first attempt to formulate rules regarding restrictive practices in international trade, achieved success with the International Coffee Agreement of 1962.

In the preamble to the new agreement it is stated that there was "reason to expect a tendency toward persistent disequilibrium between production and consumption, accumulation of burdensome stocks and pronounced fluctuations in prices."[14] This situation on the world market in the opinion of the participating countries cannot "be corrected by normal market forces."[15] The agreement should therefore serve "to bring about long-term equilibrium between production and consumption."[16] Resolution No. 1, which was passed at the final conference as well, urges as "an aim of the agreement to realize free competition in the coffee trade."[17]

These objectives were to be attained principally through operating a system of variable export quotas to insure adequate supplies and remunerative prices; in the longer run, it was envisaged that policies directed toward diversification from coffee to other economic pursuits would relieve the pressure of oversupply. The agreement did not expressly define the long-term equilibrium level at which prices would be stabilized but implicitly set a floor price by recording that "the members agree on the necessity of assuring that the general level of coffee prices does not decline below the general level of such prices in 1962."[18] Contrary to other international agreements, no provision was made in the International Coffee Agreement regarding a corresponding price ceiling and subsequent obligations of member countries if the ceiling price is reached. At a later stage, i.e., beginning in 1965, the International Coffee Council adopted a flexible price stabilization system designed to mitigate short-term price fluctuations but adjustable each year to changing market conditions.

Thus, the operation of the agreement has revolved around the regulation of exports, incorporating the quota mechanism and pricing policies, and the longer-term objective of production controls and diversification. These fundamental aspects of the 1962 agreement had been essentially preserved under the renegotiated agreement of 1969, which is presently in force.

The basic quotas listed in Annex A to the agreement determine the basic percentage share assigned in any given year to each exporting member country in the aggregate export to the traditional market, i.e., all countries other than those listed as "new market" or "Annex B" countries. These basic quotas are expressed in the agreement in absolute terms, i.e., in terms of a specific number of bags of coffee for each country. However, the operational significance of each quota is not in its absolute value but in its implied ratio to the total basic quota since, as will be seen, the annual quota can differ substantially from the basic global quota in the agreement, and is prorated to each country in proportion to its percentage share of the basic quota in the agreement.

As noted above, the basic quotas do not cover exports to countries designated as "new markets." This is a measure to encourage increased coffee consumption in such countries. These "new markets," specifically listed by country in Annex B to the agreement, are defined as those "having a low per capita consumption, and considerable potential for expansion."[19] They comprise Japan, the Soviet Union, Poland, Hungary, Republic of South Africa, Thailand, countries surrounding the Persian Gulf, and a number of other smaller importing countries.

While the basic quota provides the basic guideline for sharing the market, the annual quotas reflect the Coffee Council's estimate of the market requirements from year to year. To arrive at the annual global quota the Coffee Council each year determines the total world import requirements (at an undefined "fair" price level).

This figure is then successively reduced by estimates for (a) probable exports from non-member countries, (b) shipments from dependent territories to their respective metropolitan countries, and (c) exports by member countries to non-quota markets and other reductions. The resultant global quota is then distributed pro rata among the member exporting countries.

The most important provision affecting the adjustment of quota was the price policy pursued by the council. The agreement had stipulated that prices should be "equitable" and if there were "marked price rises or falls occurring within brief periods,"[20] implying a period of a couple of weeks or so, the quotas might be adjusted by the council with a view to stabilizing the market. Accordingly, in 1963-64, the first full year of the coffee organization's existence, quotas were adjusted frequently, either upward or downward, with a view to maintaining stable prices at whatever levels were determined to be agreeable to the council. This system proved awkward, time-consuming, and impractical and at times raised uncertainties in world markets regarding possible council action, thereby destabilizing prices.

At a later date, with a view to streamlining the operation of the quota system and increasing market stability, a semiautomatic method of adjusting quotas was introduced in March, 1965, whereby the council established an indicator price range.

Thus if the indicator price remained below the floor for fifteen consecutive days, the global quota (and hence the pro-rated country quotas) was adjusted downward; if it stayed above the ceiling, the quota was adjusted upward. There were, however, limitations on the extent to which the quota could be adjusted in that manner. The system remained in effect for the coffee years 1964-65 and 1965-66. Although it was an improvement over ad hoc adjustments of quotas, the system nevertheless tended to treat coffee as a homogeneous commodity and desregarded differential price movements in the various types of coffee.

Demands for further rationalizing the price mechanism and to insure that the supply of the various types of coffee was made more responsive to changes in consumer demand were met by the council through the replacement of an indicator price range system with a new "selective price system." Under the selective price system, four price ranges were established for the four main groups of coffee — i.e., Colombian Mild Arabicas, other Mild Arabicas, Unwashed Arabicas, and Robustas — and member exporting countries were classified into the four groups. The ranges reflected historical price relationships among the four groups of coffee. If the daily average price of any group, taken over a period of fifteen consecutive market days, remained below the floor or above the ceiling, the quota for that particular group was adjusted downward or upward. There was, however, a limit on the extent to which the quota for any group could be adjusted downward, although no such inspection was applicable to upward revision. Thus, over the life of the 1962 agreement, the price policy of the council was gradually refined and increasingly differentiated.

The gradual shift to the selective adjustment of quotas has also represented, of course, a further modification of the strictly pro-rata principle of market sharing. A year-by-year comparison of the initial country quota fixed at the beginning of a coffee year and the final quota as it stood at the end of the year shows that quotas were modified during the course of various years. The differences between the initial figures and the corresponding final figures reflect changes resulting partly from price stabilization adjustments and partly from the grant of waivers, etc., authorized during the course of that year.*

The enforcement of quota control has remained a difficult problem throughout the life of the agreement. Production continued to exceed demand, and the attempts of some producing countries to unload their surpluses by using the existence of non-quota markets led to a sort of two-price system, one for the quota and the other for the non-quota market, with the prices considerably lower in the latter. As in some other instances, lower prices for non-quota exports could have led to the breakdown of the agreement.

This loophole in the quota system was closed, however, by cooperation from the importing countries, which instituted, under Article 45 (1), policies to restrict imports from member countries to Annex B markets. In order to be able to cut imports from member countries to Annex B countries, member importing countries had to apply stringent controls of domestic imports based upon regulations put into effect specifically for the purpose of assisting the International Coffee Agreement. In undertaking these measures, importing countries had been instrumental in maintaining the International Coffee Agreement despite the fact

---

* Article 60 of the agreement provided that the council might grant a waiver to a member country which, on account of exceptional or emergency circumstances, force majeure, constitutional obligations, et al., was likely to suffer serious hardship. The affected countries argued that even bumper crops came under that rule, contending that large unsold stocks would put an unbearable burden on their respective economies.

that exporting member countries did not always follow the rules of the agreement to the fullest extent.

Recognizing that as long as surpluses continue to accumulate, there could be no permanent solution to the coffee problem, the agreement had stipulated that "not later than one year after the agreement enters into force, the council shall . . . recommend production goals" for each member country and for the world as a whole. But the problem of controlling production on an internationally coordinated basis proved to be such a difficult and involved task that it has remained unresolved for the life of the 1962 and the present agreement.

Intertwined with the issue of production targets has been the question of assisting the surplus-ridden countries in diversifying out of coffee into other economic pursuits. It was felt that the availability of financial and technical assistance would facilitate the implementation of production controls. In 1966, the council approved, therefore, in principle, the establishment of a coffee diversification fund, but left the scale of contributions to the fund open. In 1966 and 1967, discussions on the establishment and management of this fund were continued. Finally, new guidelines for the diversification fund were embodied in the renegotiated agreement of 1968.

## Methods of Establishing the Agreement

The International Coffee Agreement of 1962 brings the actions of producers and consumers alike under the rules which the United Nations agreed on as terms of reference for international commodity agreements. These were part of the International Trade Organization (ITO), which never came into existence, but these relict chapters on trade with primary commodities have been adopted by the United Nations.[21]

The general framework for international commodity agreements after 1948 are the Rules of Chapter IV, Article 58, Parts 1 and 2 of the ITO. They are the basis for the creation and the duties of the Interim Coordinating Committee for International Commodity

Agreements (ICCICA). This committee serves the function of studying the problem of primary products trade, with its main task being the preparation of preliminary conferences to establish such relations that ultimate conferences for creating international commodity agreements along the line of the Havana Charter may become effective.

The Havana Charter distinguishes between special conditions, methods to regulate the markets, and aims and methods in establishing agreement. The rules of the coffee agreement, as far as the measures to regulate the market and aims are concerned, conform to the rules of this charter. Thus we have finally to deal with the latter points. They are twofold: one concerning the creation of an agreement, the other concerning the conditions of accession after the agreement came into force and its prolongation.

The first declares that an international commodity agreement has to be signed only in a conference under the auspices of the United Nations and that only the Secretary General of the United Nations can convene the first session of the administering council. Thus it is a condition that all countries interested in production, consumption, and trade of the commodity concerned will be invited to the conference. But there is no minority clause necessary to call ultimately for a conference. Secondly, the interests concerned are represented not by the industry or consumers but by the government of countries which declare themselves to be exporting or importing members. Nor is the entry of force of an agreement dependent on the univocal or at least on a prescribed majority vote of countries which have been represented at the conference. The last and most decisive part of these omissions has been a trouble spot in the U.N.-coffee conference.[22] "The major Latin American countries, supported by the United States, were anxious that the Agreement and its system of quota control should enter into force as soon as possible and thus favored a relatively low percentage of ratifications for this purpose. The European countries on the other hand were concerned about their obligations to restrict import from non-members and argued that the Agreement should not take effect until it had been accepted by a relatively high proportion of countries. The figure — eventually agreed upon — twenty exporting countries and ten importing countries accounting respectively for at least 80 percent of world exports and imports in 1961 — represented a compromise between these two positions."

The most important rule regarding the administration and the duration of an agreement is that which states that importing and exporting member countries should have equal voting power in the administration of the agreement and that the agreement shall not be "exclusive," i.e., it shall be impossible for member countries to prevent the entry of newcomers, it shall not last longer than five years, and an extension should be decided on at a new U.N. Conference. The coffee agreement does not exactly comply with these rules. It follows the rule on the participation of importing and exporting countries, but the accession to the agreement rests upon conditions of the council only, which are not agreed upon in the conference but are concluded by the member countries in the council. The same shadow of uncertainty rests upon the rule that the council — by fulfilling certain obligations on voting procedures — may have the power to extend the agreement. Both rules have been applied by the Council of the International Wheat Agreement. Their application aroused feelings of discrimination and they were afterward abolished because of strong pressure by ICCACA and non-member countries.[23]

## The Restrictive Character of the Agreement

Existing Rules for an International Economic Policy on Primary Commodity Markets

This section is concerned with the question of whether the International Coffee Agreement can be seen as a measure of an international economic policy aiming at competitively organized international trade. The control methods of the coffee agreement are examined in more detail and will furthermore be evaluated against the background of international rules concerning the form of international trade.

The International Coffee Agreement forms one of the export quota type agreements, a type providing for restrictive practices in international trade. It imposes restrictions on production and export, fixes prices, and allocates share of markets among the producing countries. If we look at it from the point of view of an instrument that influences the price formation on the market, its pattern follows closely that of a cartel in structure, methods, and policy.[24] It is an "association of producers (or their national representatives) in the same or similar branch of industry which has the purpose or effect of reducing or regulating competition."[25] The structure of the ICA resembles that of the cartel, with the ICO having the function of administering the agreement. The association undertakes to fix prices[26] in the manner of what is commonly called a "price cartel."[27]

The distinguishing characteristic of a cartel is the fact that it requires the substitution of independent policies for commonly agreed policies between cartel members in the determination of prices and production. It therefore restricts competition between its members on the world market, and thus disturbs the tendency of "long-run equilibrium" on the partial market inherent in competitive markets. On balance, this restricts the total volume of world trade and hampers the international division of labor.[28]

This charge had been put forward in two forms:[29] one line of thought argues that the main purpose of all cartels is to increase the profits of its members by using its market power so that sellers can set "their prices to a point where marginal revenue is larger than marginal costs."

The undesirable characteristics attributed to a private cartel are "the protecting of high-cost producers, the raising of prices above the levels necessary for reasonable long-run prosperity in the industry and seeking the maximum profits for the producers without regard for the interests of the consumers."[30] The monopolistic price being higher than the price in competition, and thus giving to the last marginal producer a monopoly rent, "fosters improper investment of productive resources." This occurs in at least two ways:

(1) By underinvestment through exclusion of investment funds which should go into cartelized fields for the employment of productive factors which are used elsewhere effectively or not at all;

(2) By overinvestment through the protection offered the cartel-membership by means of controlled price/cost relations.[31]

The same applies if the production is particularly labor-intensive – the labor force that remains unused as a result of the smaller output of the industry will probably remain unemployed if other lines of employment are not available. These two facts illustrate that two results may follow:[32] "an uneconomical allocation of resources among various lines of production in the industry" and an "uneconomical rate of utilization of resources for production in general."

Another school argues that "cartels are a means of softening the rigors of competition"[33] – or "a restriction to some degree of unlimited competition between the firms involved,"[34] and "could exist independently of any design to increase profits or raise prices."[35] This implies that prices will be set so high that there is no monopoly rent to the marginal producer in the industry – or that the price is set at a level which was the level of competitive pricing in the situation when the cartel was put into action. But it has been shown that under these conditions also the long-run price of the cartel will be higher than the long-run price under competitive conditions.[36] This is so because cost-saving machinery or new techniques normally produce an additional output which is proportionally higher than the reduction in expenses for the new machinery (e.g., the new techniques produce at about 5 percent cheaper but the output will be raised at optimum machinery efficiency by 12 percent). Under a fixed quota cartel, where each member has a fixed output, he is allowed to put this new technique into action only if he is granted a larger quota. If the marginal producer eventually sells his quota the new technique will be employed, but only after a struggle for quotas between the different members of the cartel who would like to employ the new technique. This struggle will lead to a price fixed by bargaining between the marginal producer and the buyers of his quota. The price will be included in the costs which the new owner of the quota of the marginal producer will calculate when he fixes his new price. The additional costs will then keep the new cartel price higher than the price which would have resulted — given the demand elasticity — under competitive price formation. It is, therefore, generally agreed that the "per se restrictive" regulations determine the character of the International Coffee Agreement. The main effect of the participation of importers is not a change in the character of the agreement, but bargaining power for their interests.[37] This may result in lower prices according to the theory of bilateral monopoly, but it does not prevent the impairment of the allocative function of the price mechanism.

After this examination of its restrictive character, we will now consider the standing of the International Coffee Agreement against the established rules of international trade. Since international commodity agreements are agreements between governments about internationally traded commodities and are designed to affect the flow of commodities in international commerce, they may be regarded as a form of trade agreement. A master agreement dealing with trade in all kinds of goods was the Havana Charter for an International Trade Organization. It was consummated in March, 1948, by the United Nations Conference on Trade and Employment and set forth a comprehensive body of international rules governing trade policies and practices. It was never ratified.

Instead, two relict agreements came out of ITO. One was the General Agreement on Tariffs and Trade (GATT). This body of rules covers all foreign commerce on all goods except primary commodities. The rules seek to abolish discrimination among sources of supply, whether in the form of preferential duties, closed bilateral deals, quotas, or otherwise, to dismantle administrative controls and other managerial devices calculated to substitute trade-distorting governmental decisions for trader discretion. In the ideal, these rules aim at a competitive world market which induces "long-run equilibrium tendencies" on all markets.[38] In connection with the theory of comparative costs in international trade, "these rules are framed in light of a design to stimulate international trade and promote the efficient international distribution of production by diminishing and removing the interferences that prevent the play of market forces from determining the volume and direction of exports and imports."[39]

The second relict agreement was the rules of the ITO on trade regulations concerning trade in primary products that became the chapters on international commodity agreements. These were agreed upon in the ECOSOC of the United Nations as terms of reference for the conclusion of international commodity agreements between members of the United Nations. They prescribe the special conditions that must prevail on world markets in order for a commodity agreement to be contemplated, four different types of market regulations, and methods in establishing commodity agreements. Besides one type – the buffer-stock type – all commodity agreements were quantitative limits on imports and/or exports as well as quantitative allocations among suppliers and takers, accompanied by restraint upon the freedom of importers to procure or exporters to sell outside these quantitative prescriptions. All agreements of these types thus have restrictive regulations that hamper the functions of market forces; that is, they are "restrictive per se."

The compilation has two important aspects. The first is that the international agreements urge the participating countries to change their national policy in their domestic market for the exported and/or imported good. They constitute and demand a change in the domestic economic policy of member countries.

They secondly prescribe the forms of regulations which may be applied by governments.

From the first aspect it follows that the rules concerning the forms of international commodity agreements are in effect prescriptions for ECOSOC member countries to institute a certain domestic policy and to form by accepting them an international economic policy. The second aspect reduces the numerous forms of restrictive regulations dealing with the special problems on primary commodity markets. By these two aspects the rules of the ECOSOC concerning international commodity agreements constitute an international policy toward restrictive practices with governments as contracting parties.[40]

In relation to the competitive model, implicit in the GATT trade agreement, the restrictive regulations are, in terms of the theory of industrial organization, "exemptions" from a general policy to create competitively organized international trade.

### Special Features of Production and Consumption of Coffee

The case for a commodity agreement of the export quota type is well known and it has been put forward in most of the articles that deal with the coffee agreement in scholarly reviews as well as by officials of various coffee exporting and importing countries.[41] The "coffee-problem" argument has as its basis the assumption that the price performance of the coffee market indicates such conditions on the supply as well as on the demand side that an institution like the "restrictive" coffee agreement does not hamper the approach to long-run equilibrium, which they still believe to be economically desirable. Instead, it regulates the competitive process on the coffee market in which certain conditions lead to a misallocation of resources, in such a way that an optimum allocation of resources in terms of comparative advantages can be achieved.

In a detailed manner this case for an agreement is stated as follows: "Consumption habits are such that demand increases slowly and gradually with population and income in importing countries, but reacts only slightly to price changes; substitution by or for other beverages . . . in response to a widening margin between prices is negligible. Being insensitive to business recessions or booms in importing countries, demand has shown very minor year-to-year fluctuations."[42] V.D. Wickizer draws the conclusion that "year-to-year market requirements tend to be relatively stable,"[43] assuming market requirements and consumption are of equal size.

On the supply side the conditions stem from two facts:

(1) Coffee is a tree crop.

(2) Coffee is an industry with high fixed costs.

Most coffee trees have a gestation period of some four to five years and subsequently live for twenty years or more. Therefore short-term adjustments in planting in periods of high prices are not feasible, and the resulting period of high prices induce planting far beyond the level required to meet demand. Wickizer describes this process as an inducement to "excessive" new planting, which leads to the problem of surpluses a few years later.[44] The obvious inability to scale down the current production in response to reduced prices is partly attributed to the fact that "the principal cost of cultivation to the grower arises from the cost of purchasing and clearing land and planting trees rather than in harvesting, and a crop will generally be harvested regardless of market prices."[45] Apparently if prices decline it pays to continue production as long as variable costs are covered. Or it is assumed that "if trees are once in production they are not readily abandoned or destroyed by their owners."[46] This might be due to an inverse supply reaction of the farmers. This is assumed to be a particular problem in coffee and mainly in Africa, where in contrast to Latin America, "where labor costs are now higher than before the war and more alternative uses exist for the resources at present employed, there are no or little profitable uses for the labor employed in coffee cultivation, so that the prices have to fall drastically before production will be seriously affected."[47] Partly this slight reaction is said to exist because the adaptation is "confined as a rule to lessened care or abandonment of older plantations which is not sufficient to bring output into line with demand."[48]

Superimposed on the conditions described are changes in available supplies which are "highly variable, owing to frequent and wide fluctuations in crop yields caused by a complex of factors, chief of which are weather, frosts, and droughts and the nature of a coffee plant. The effect on available supplies in this crop has been usually pronounced, especially in view of the concentration of such a large proportion of world production within a relatively small area in Southern Brazil."

In addition to local weather conditions which affect the yield of all crops, the coffee tree has a yield cycle of its own, bearing less immediately after a large output and more following a period of rest. The sharp fluctuations in yields evident in all coffee-growing countries are specially noticeable when weather conditions reinforce the up-and-down phase of the yield cycle.

A further group of difficulties is noted by R.B. Bilder: "Coffee producers are also subject to a so-called 'seasonal marketing problem,' resulting from the fact that a substantial part of world production is harvested at about the same time of the year. Since a number of Latin American producers, particularly in Central America, do not have the storage facilities or financial resources to hold such crops for orderly distribution throughout the year, a great deal of this coffee tends to flood the market at the same time, resulting in sharp price drops with price increases in non-harvest seasons."[49] The tendency to instability is increased by the fact that, if inventories have been built up, speculative elements can display further important influences.[50]

A third condition, prevailing especially in the period under review, is "simply that coffee cultivation has consistently tended to outpace the normal growth of world consumption. The comparative ease of coffee cultivation, the many areas of the world suited to its production and the high yields and returns possible for the successful grower per unit of area cultivated as compared with other tropical crops have led to a rapid and continuing expansion of productive capacity and to a disequilibrium."[51] "The disequilibrium has been further aggravated by the fact that some traditional producer countries, i.e., Brazil and Colombia, adopted national support policies ... which tend to maintain and increase production in the face of falling coffee prices on the world market."[52]

This statement is contradictory to the results of G. Lovasy's investigations and the finding of the FAO that the prices received by the producers have been kept well below the market price[53] "and have been falling since 1954, thus following the development of world market prices for coffee." But as Lovasy put it, "there has been no indication so far that prices received by exporters in any country have become unprofitable and production has continued to increase."

On the basis of these causal factors the price performance of competition in the world coffee market has been interpreted as another example of the well-known cobweb cycle.[54] This price formation process was assumed to exist because conditions one and two create the typical case of a "time-lagged" response of supply, in which the elasticity of a short-term supply curve out of existing capacity is low and the one of the long-run supply curve is high.

The initial disturbance needed for this form of interpretation has been a demand shift that started in 1949. Stocks in producing countries were then almost exhausted, and output fell short of demand. Because of the low short-run price elasticity of supply prices rose sharply till 1957-58. The statistical data show that the output — at least of Brazil and Africa — rose with the typical "time-lag" that produced the first part of the cycle. The price development since 1958 can then be interpreted as a second phase. In this the excessive output meets a demand with a low price elasticity, the world demand reacted on the price fall only by small increases in consumption. Surplus capacity and low elasticity of demand were therefore the reasons for the price gyrations on the coffee market. "Furthermore, these changes in supply and demand may not only bring about price changes, but also induce further changes in demand and supply."[55] These "induced price movements" may be helpful in restoring equilibrium, but otherwise may sometimes intensify fluctuations rather than damp them down.

In analyzing the existing situation on the coffee market, using the distinction that is common in regard to the performance of raw material prices, Wickizer and Lovasy and the FAO regard the price instability, caused by condition two as "short-run fluctuations," and the surplus development and price decline induced by condition one as structural maladjustment with "chronic surpluses and declining price trends,"[56] which is not a result of a cobweb cycle. Against this it is Bilder's opinion that conditions one and two create problems of "short-run market instability" and only condition three creates what he calls "a problem of long-run over production in terms of what the market will absorb at remunerative prices."[57]

The different terminology, which makes for confusion whether the problem is one of cyclical or short-term fluctuation or of long-term or secular trend character, cannot be maintained. The length of a cycle from one equilibrium point to the new one is described by "how long high (or low) prices must prevail (or must be expected to prevail) and how large price increases (or declines) must be to induce producers to change fixed-factor inputs."[58] In the production of tree crops it will take several years, depending on the gestation period of the tree and on the high fixed costs, because it is likely that the decision to plant may be delayed until the producers are convinced that the favorable cost-price constellation will persist for a considerable time until the first half of the cycle has been surpassed. If then prices are persistently low and trees are producing, it takes a long period of time to bring about a curtailment of production through the failure to replant. Thus the time between a change of demand and the necessary adaptation of supply can last for several years, being "long-term" in regard to the absolute time the adjustment process lasts, but "short-term" in an economic sense,[59] because the conditions lead to excessive cyclical movements in quantity and prices that do not represent a trend.[60] If so, the result of this cycle must be twofold:

(1) The price gyrations induce excessive reactions (over-reactions) on the supply side so that productive factors are allocated or removed on a larger scale than that necessary to reach the long-run equilibrium price in a frictionless world.[61]

(2) Price and quantities sold are the sources of foreign-exchange incomes of the producer countries. If these countries are underdeveloped the frequent changes in the foreign exchange available disturb a smoothly plann-ed economic development, and lead to foreign exchange bottlenecks that may lead to governmental measures that discourage private investment. In fact, it is just when prices are low that the country needs an especially large amount of foreign exchange to help the coffee producers to switch into other occupations, thus per-mitting a diversification of exports. These foreign-exchange fluctuations are greater than those which would prevail under long-run equilibrium conditions and serve no useful purpose; they would represent a struc-tural problem because of the length of a price cycle in coffee.

It is thus the conclusion of these writers that the free play of market forces produces an unsatisfactory result by being unable to produce a "long-run equilibrium" on the partial market. The recent literature reveals that everyone who has been concerned with problems of primary commodity trade shares this view.[62]

If we assume that the adaptation of the ITO rules by the United Nations created an international policy toward restrictive practices on primary commodity markets,[63] there seems to be a general understanding that primary commodity markets are "markets in which active competition exists but where because of imperfections in the market competition does not produce one or more competitive results," that is, world markets of primary commodities are an "exception" from international trade competitively organized. There is as well general acceptance that these imperfections are characteristics inherent in the production or consumption processes. It seems to be a fair representation to say that in terms of the theory of industrial organization primary commodity markets — and here the world coffee market — are assumed to be an "unconditional, genuine exception."

There is as well general agreement that measures must be taken to achieve remedial results.[64] Most recently this case has been put clearly by Meade, who argued: "The prices of primary products, when they are traded freely on uncontrolled world markets, are subject to violent fluctuations. It is for these reasons that steps should be taken to offset the damaging effects of sharp fluctuations of prices. If no alternative action is available a restrictive arrangement may often be better than doing nothing."[65] It is argued: The aim of the export quota agreement type with an appropriate stock policy is to prevent short-term fluctuations in output causing short-term price fluctuations. As far as the over-capacity situation is concerned, it provides time and foreign exchange, the amount of which is foreseeable to a certain extent. The lessened burden of uncertainty should enable producers to bear the burden of an artificially distributed reduction of output to the calculated long-run demand at a historically given price. Every country should adjust its production to accord with its basic export quota, to be produced by its lowest-cost producers. Where overinvestment has occurred, alternative employment should be provided for redundant producers. Such provision will be assisted by the greater certainty concerning foreign exchange receipts, which can be used to import the machinery necessary for new industries. The adjustment in production and the destruction of stocks then adapt output to the desired level and lead to the desired change in production structure. This should enable the industry to stand up to a new trial of competitive market forces on the coffee market without an agreement. Following this reasoning, the advocates of commodity agreements argue that the agreement may be a temporary measure designed only to mitigate the problems and hardships of adjustment and not to become a persistent instrument of undue price-raising. They also insist that besides export quotas, all exporting countries must agree on an effective production control, since it is only for the agreed change in production that the "long-run equilibrium" on the partial market may be reached.[66] Their third point is the participation of importing countries, which should insure bargaining power for consumer interests.

It is on this point that micro-economic writers see an insoluble dilemma: "The postulate of non-interference with long-term trends implies that prices resulting from an agreement should not differ in the average over a number of years from what they would have been in the absence of an agreement. Since the future is unknown, this 'neutral' price can be definitely ascertained only ex-post, whereas the technical solution of the problem presupposes that it is known ex-ante."[67] This dilemma has led some economists (e.g., Kindleberger and Machlup) to attack the whole concept of commodity agreements. Kindleberger argued: "We lack techniques for determining and applying the equilibrium price in commodity markets. Intervention in the price formation process then leads directly to the disequilibrium system in which incentives are created to undermine the pegged price, stocks pile up (or shortages develop) and ultimately the support price collapses or explodes."[68] In the view of this author the stabilization problem is therefore "not soluble in economic terms."[69]

Machlup, Swerling, et alia see the results of the inability to forecast the long-run equilibrium price on the partial market in that the "appropriate canons of economic adjustment, or social equity and of efficient administration are required to work at cross-purposes. Unsaleable current output is overt evidence that a commodity is already overpriced; yet the marginal incentive to expand output continues, while there is depending on demand elasticities some tendency to discourage consumption."[70] In his view, "international commodity agreements like the Coffee Agreement have the result that the enormous advantages of price signals for coaxing rather than coercing needed adjustment are lost."[71]

The price system as the major organizational mechanism of a free economy is disturbed. Shortly, in the view of these authors, the inability of economic science to forecast the long-run equilibrium price on the partial market makes the International Coffee Agreement an agreement with a "contradiction in the statement of objectives since it includes achieving equitable prices which will bring about long-term equilibrium between production and consumption." The charges recall those levelled against the cartel, which we mentioned earlier.[72]

## Critique

The writers using the micro-economic approach have argued for the ability of unregulated competition, supported through non-restrictive means, to achieve the wanted partial long-run equilibrium. The arguments against the International Coffee Agreement questioned whether the ICA would be a device to achieve the same results. Reformulated in terms of our approach, the discussion reveals the world coffee market as a genuine "exception." Against this background, the "dilemma of the micro-economic writers" finds full backing. The assumed model of a "genuine exception" does not allow for "per se restrictive" regulations.[73]

Yet, of course, the "dilemma" would not recur if the "exception" would result from such imperfections, which must be regulated by "per se restrictive" regulations, i.e., in the form of a natural or a conditional international oligopoly, mentioned earlier. It is only on the opposite assumption that the a priori case against the International Coffee Agreement in its present form can be constructed.

We have already stated above that this model of "genuine exception" stems from the assumed causal factors. Analysis to prove these assumed causative factors generally consisted of one methodological approach only:[74] the quantitative analysis of supply and demand reactions to changes of coffee prices and vice versa. The analysis of supply reactions consisted of time-series calculations; for demand reactions the same method has been used, supplemented by an analysis of family budget data and intercountry comparisons of per capita incomes and consumption. A further form of research has been to establish the coffee price movements since 1950 as a price cycle that revealed the typical feature of a cobweb cycle with a time lag of some 6 to 8 years.[75] This cobweb cycle was supposed to prove the time-lagged response of production as a result of the agroeconomic features of coffee production as well as the low elasticity of demand.

The theory of industrial organizations allows for criticism against these statements of a causal chain between the assumed factors and the performance of competition on the market. The aforementioned structure and conduct dimensions determine the elasticity of competitive supply and demand only.[76] Or vice versa, the measurement of low elasticity coefficients using quantitative analysis reveals only production processes or consumption habits as causative factors of the supply or demand reaction if it is assumed as a further necessary condition that the market has a price formation of pure competition.[77] The same criticism applies to the "cobweb cycle analysis." A cobweb cycle determines time-lagged responses of production and/or consumption as causative factors only under the further condition that the market is in a state of pure competition.[78] This form of analysis, therefore, tests neither the influence of monopolistic market structure nor conduct as causative factors for the market performance, i.e., the observed "excessive price instability."

It is thus on an assumed and not a tested model of a purely competitive world coffee market on which the assumption of all writers rests, that the assumed causative factors have created the price instability and thus created an "exception" on the world coffee market not to be regulated with a control of prices and output. These writers, therefore, have not answered the question of how price instability on the coffee market actually comes about.

# NOTES

1. GATT, *Trade in Tropical Products*, p. 35; FAO: *The World Coffee Economy*, Commodity Bulletin Series No. 33 (FAO-*CBS 33*), p. 6.

2. ICO: *Production Forecasts and Their Implication* (staff paper), ICC-2-4, p. 1.

3. FAO: *Commodity Review 1961*, Table 20, p. 98.

4. *Ibid.*, p. 69.

5. FAO: *CBS 33 passim.*

6. *Ibid.*, p. 1.

7. U.S. Senate, 87th Congress, *Hearings Before the Senate Commission on Foreign Relations on International Coffee Agreement 1962.*

8. Wickizer, "International Collaboration in the Coffee Market," *Food Research Studies*, IV, 3 (Stanford University Press, 1964), p. 277.

9. HMSO: International Coffee Agreement, (ICA) Cmnd. 1841, (London 1962); see Appendix A.

10. R.B. Bilder, "The International Coffee Agreement," *Law and Contemporary Problems*, Vol. 28 (1963), p. 328.

11. V.D. Wickizer, *Coffee, Tea and Cocoa*, Food Research Institute (Stanford University Press, 1945), p. 171.

12. Bilder, *op. cit.*, pp. 335-337.

13. HMSO, *op. cit.*, p. 6.

14. Wickizer, *International*, pp. 279-280.

15. ICA, *op. cit.*, p. 6.

16. *Ibid.*, p. 7.

17. ICO Resolutions, London 1963.

18. International Coffee Agreement, 1962, Article 28, Clause 2.

19. *Ibid.*, Article 40, Clause 1.

20. *Ibid.*, Article 34, Clause 5.

21. UN, *Review of International Commodity Problems 1949*, IBRD; *History of Commodity Agreements*, p. 4.

22. Bilder, *op. cit.*, p. 365.

23. ICCACA, *Review of International Commodity Problems* (1954), p. 8.

24. Department of Economic Affairs, League of Nations, *International Cartels*, pp. 48-49. It is for this reason that Stocking and Watkins, in *Cartel or Competition*, (New York: Twentieth Century Fund, 1948), pp. 68, 318, call intergovernmental commodity agreements "government-sponsored cartels" against "voluntary cartels," which are those forms of "loosely knit

association" that are concluded by private businessmen. Also, Wickizer, *Collaboration*, p. 291.

25. F. Machlup, Essay, ed. C.O. Edwards, *A Cartel Policy for the United Nations,* (New York: Columbia University Press), p. 5.

26. Clair Wilcox, *Public Policies Towards Business* (Chicago: Richard D. Irwin, 1955), p. 34.

27. Machlup, *The Political,* p. 94. In German literature the special term *Preis-Mengenkartelle* is used, which shows that in order to fix a price, a quota for all members is set and percentages of it or the absolute quotas alloted to all cartel members. It seems that "quota cartels" or "output syndicates" have the same meaning in American literature.

28. *Ibid.,* p. 96.

29. C.R. Whittlesey, *National Interest and International Cartels,* (New York: Macmillan, 1946), pp. 19-22.

30. B.F. Haley, "The Relation Between Cartel Policy and Commodity Agreement Policy," AER, *Papers and Proceedings,* XXXVI, 723.

31. M.L. Lindahl and W.A. Carter, *Corporate Concentration and Public Policy,* 3rd. ed. (Englewood Cliffs, N.J.: Prentice-Hall, 1959), p. 305.

32. Machlup, *op. cit.,* pp. 31-32.

33. Whittlesey, *op. cit.,* p. 20.

34. E. Schneider, "Real Economics of Integration and Large-scale Operation Versus Advantages of Domination," ed. E.H. Chamberlin, *Monopoly and Competition and Their Regulation* (London/New York: Macmillan, 1954), p. 205.

35. Whittlesey, *op. cit.,* p. 30.

36. Erich Carell, *Allgemeine Vokswirtschaftslehre,* 11th ed. rev. (Heidelberg, 1964), pp. 205-206.

37. G. Blau, "International Commodity Agreements," paper presented at IER Congress on Economic Development (Vienna, Austria, 1962), p. 3.

38. J. Bain, *Price Theory* (New York: Holt, Rinehart and Winston, 1963), pp. 173-174.

39. H. Walker, *The International Law of Commodity Agreements, Law and Contemporary Problems,* Vol. 28 (1963), p. 393; S. Curzon, *Multilateral Commercial Diplomacy, passim.*

40. Frequent remarks (Hoppmann, *op. cit.,* pp. 355-356, and other authors mentioned here) that "in the post-war period international policy towards restrictive practices failed" obviously overlook that intergovernmental commodity agreements are restrictive practices. The assumption that such practices with governments as members instead of private enterprise do not create international restrictive practices in the sense the authors normally use

the words is not justifiable, if not legal but economic terms of reference are used. Cf. H. Walker, *op. cit.,* pp. 392-415, and IBRD, *History of Commodity Agreements* (Washington, D.C., July 1959), p. 4: "Considering the supply and demand characteristics of most of the primary commodities may give rise to exaggerated price declines and severe distresses to producers, the ITO Charter permits the member governments to enter into agreements regulating the trade in such commodities. The possibility of concluding and operating such agreements has been construed as an exception to the general principle of free trade, justified by the special character of primary productions."

41. For a review of this interpretation before 1950, see Wickizer, *Coffee and Cocoa,* and the literature mentioned here. More recent publications are FAO, *CBS-33;* Adler, "Comments on Professor Nurkse's paper," *Kyklos,* Vol. XI (1958), pp. 155-168; G. Lovasy, "The International Coffee Market, A Note," IMF Staff Papers, Vol. X (1962), pp. 226-242.

42. Lovasy, *op. cit.,* p. 227.

43. Wickizer, *op. cit.,* p. 275.

44. *Ibid.*

45. Bilder, *op. cit.,* p. 331.

46. Wickizer, *op. cit.,* p. 275.

47. *Ibid.,* p. 94; FAO, *op. cit.,* p. 30.

48. Lovasy, *op. cit.,* p. 227.

49. Bilder, *op. cit.,* p. 334; Wickizer, *op. cit.,* p. 283, Footnote 8.

50. Federal Trade Commission (FTC), *Economic Report of the Investigation of Coffee Prices,* p. 153; H.W. Gerhard, "Commodity Trade Stabilization Through International Agreements," *Law and Contemporary Problems,* Vol. xxviii (1963), p. 283.

51. Bilder, *op. cit.,* p. 334.

52. *Ibid.*

53. Lovasy, *op. cit.,* p. 232; FAO, *CBS-33, op. cit.,* p. 14; O. van Teutem, "Coffee in Latin America: The Producers' Problem," UN, *Economic Bulletin for Latin America,* Vol. iv (1959), p. 35.

54. Wickizer, *op. cit.,* p. 279; Gerhard, *op. cit.,* p. 283.

55. J. Adler, *op. cit.,* p. 157; GATT, *Trends, op. cit.,* p. 29.

56. Wickizer, *op. cit.,* p. 275; G. Lovasy, "Discussions," *AER* (1962), p. 108.

57. Bilder, *op. cit.,* p. 334.

58. Adler, *op. cit.,* pp. 157-158.

59. O. Anderson, Jr., "Trend," *HdSW,* X, 405-408; GATT, *Trends, op. cit.,* p. 38; Bain, *op. cit.,* p. 181: ". . . very long life of fixed plants. . .which makes the 'short-run' last a long time."

60. Obviously Lovasy, *op. cit.*, would agree with this interpretation of the "trend" usage, insofar as she writes on pp. 233-234 that through reaction of supply on a lowering of the price at which all the production could be sold "would sooner or later reduce output and prices would rise again. A long-run equilibrium price which would induce output to keep in line with demand and would no doubt be considerably higher," and p. 227. Also, Kaysen and Turner, *Antitrust Policy* (Cambridge, Mass.: Harvard University Press, 1959), p. 197: "Excess capacity is not a sign of structural maladjustment but may exist for a variety of reasons—seasonal swings, cyclical ups and downs or permanent overcapacity because of overbuilding or shifts."

61. The main criticism here is the influence the price has on the optimal allocation of resources. Insofar as an excessive reaction invokes a "surplus" situation, this surplus is excessive because it induces a price fall that is such that "efficient producers whose capacity is only temporary in excess may then be a eliminated along with producers who are genuinely superfluous. The sacrifice of capital equipment and technical skills, which later must be replaced—and a considerable part of employment in these plants—constitute an economic loss to society." Whittlesey, *op. cit.*, pp. 30-31. In this way the problem of (short-term) price instability and "surplus" are connected and an economically meaningful interpretation of the term "surplus" can be arrived at. F. Schmits, *Regulierungsprobleme auf den Weltrohstoffmaerkten*, p. 58; H. Stackelberg, *Grundlagen der Theoretischen Volkswirtschaftslehre*, p. 172.

62. "Problems of International Commodity Stabilization" AER *Papers and Proceedings*, Vol. LIII (1963), p. 147.

63. See Note 40, above.

64. Stackelberg, *op. cit.*, p. 177: "Um solche Wellenbewegungen der Mengen und Preise auszuschalten kann die staatliche Wirtschaftspolitik in die Preisbildung eingreifen. Sie kann z.B. nach erfolgter Nachfrageausweitung eine Preiserhoehung auf po verhindern und den Preis auf einen neuen Gleichgewichtspreis p' festsetzen. Sie kann zugleich das gegenueber der neuen Gleichgewichtsmenge zu kleine Angebot auf die Nachfrage direkt verteilen (rationieren) und die Umstellung der Betriebe foerdern, bis ihre Produktion die neue Gleichgewichtskapazitaet erreicht hat und die staatliche Intervention nicht mehr notwendig ist. Wir erkennen sofort, daB die Wirkungen einer solchen staatlichen Wirtschaftslenkung sehr wohltaetig sein koennen. Aber diese Politik setzt sowohl eine genaue Analyse der jeweiligen Marktvorgaenge als auch ein schnelles Handeln der zustaendigen sachlichen Stellen voraus." Using the terminology of antitrust or "workable competition" theory the ICA is an "exemption."

65. UNCTAD: Doc. E/Conf. 46/P/1/Rev. 1, Geneva (June 15, 1964), p. 3.

66. Wickizer, *Collaboration, op. cit.*, pp. 287-289.

67. Blau, *op. cit.*, p. 3.

68. C.P. Kindleberger, "Discussion," AER, *Papers and Proceedings*, LIII (1963), p. 105.

69. *Ibid.*, pp. 105, 106.

70. B. Swerling, "Problems of International Commodity Stabilization," AER *Papers and Proceedings*, Vol. LIII (1963), p. 70.

71. *Ibid.*

72. Staley, "An Evaluation," AER, *Papers and Proceedings*, LIII (1963), p. 345.

73. C.D. Edwards, pp. 62-66; Kaysen and Turner, *op. cit., passim.*

74. *Inter alia*, FAO *CBS-33, passim.*

75. *Inter alia*, FAO, *CBS-33, passim*, especially the chapter entitled "Economic Factors. . . ."

76. F. Machlup, *International Payments, Debts and Gold* (New York: Scribner's, 1964).

77. H.R. Edwards, *Competition and Monopoly in the British Soap Industry* (Oxford: Clarendon Press, 1962), p. 27: "Fitting correlations do only indicate that such a quantitative price volume relation exist, but must not *a priori* be accepted as indicative of a causative relationship between the hypothetical assumption of a model and the performance of a market. Willingness to accept a correlation as a causative factor rests not upon the statistical evidence, but upon the implicit assumption, which forms then part of the interpretation of the datas."

78. A further discussion of this point is not necessary, sinnce this contribution of Ezekiel has found general acceptance: cf. *op. cit.*, p. 255.

# 3 A Description of the World Coffee Economy and Its Environment

## Characteristics of Production

Agroeconomic Factors

Coffee is a tree crop. Coffee beans are the contents of coffee cherries, which are picked at harvest time, cleaned, dried, and fermented. Coffee in this production stage — green coffee — is a subject of international trade.

It is by no means a homogeneous product. Due to strong differences in taste, three main kinds of coffee — each with a very wide range of varying qualities — are distinguishable. The trade terms them Milds, Brazils, and Robustas. Putting them into order according to their bitterness of taste, Milds hold last place. They have a mild, very full flavor. They are preceded by the stronger tasting Brazils. There is a rough division in this category between "soft" and "hard" Brazils. Generally speaking, coffees from São Paulo are regarded as the best "soft" Brazilian coffee; coffee from Paraná is typically "hard." The latter is inferior to the former and is quoted as "lower grade coffee."[1] In the third category, Robustas, have a high acid content, creating their very typical bitter taste. Robustas are grown from a different variety of coffee trees than Milds and Brazils. It is a much more vigorous tree. It can grow in tropical conditions, as opposed to the subtropical conditions that suit the Arabica variety, which produces the Milds and Brazils, and it also bears more heavily.[2]

Production of the different categories is not evenly distributed in all the coffee-producing countries; there is a very high degree of geographical concentration. Milds are grown in all Central American countries except Brazil and in some African countries like Ethiopia, Kenya, and Tanganyika. Brazils are grown in Brazil − as their name implies − and in Ethiopia. Robustas are grown in Africa in the formerly French and Portuguese territories, that is, mainly the Ivory Coast and Angola, Cameroon, Madagascar, and to a certain extent Uganda.[3]

As has been mentioned, certain production cycles may emerge from the agronomic characteristics of the crop.[4] The first arises because of the growth period between planting and the first time the tree bears fruit, a period of four to six years.[5] After that, under constant conditions an average crop can be expected for 15 to 30 years before the productive life of a coffee tree ends.

Normally a decrease is expected in the year following a good harvest. This is described as a biological gestation cycle, which lasts two years. Other variations in output are due to the sensitivity of the coffee tree to weather conditions.

Doubts exist as to the importance of these agronomic characteristics for the development of production, for they depend on the state of agricultural technique applied. For instance, the time-lag of some four to five years is relevant only if trees are grown from seeds and not planted as seedlings − which is the common form nowadays. The same applies to the gestation cycle, which can be strongly influenced by cutting down processes and other weeding methods and which exist only when no husbandry and care is being taken.[6] There are also contradictory statements on the mature life of trees. Wickizer reports that good care can prolong the life of a tree up to a hundred years. Empirical investigations about the influences of new techniques on the production development are rare and done by small sample

**Figure 6**

# Coffee: World Exports, by Producing Areas (million bags of 60 kg.)

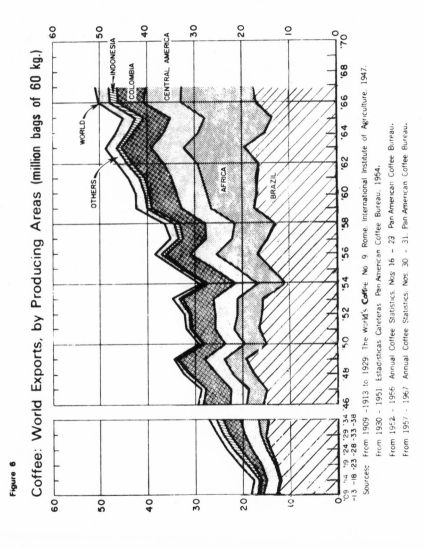

Sources: From 1909 –1913 to 1929 The World's Coffee No 9. Rome. International Institute of Agriculture. 1947.

From 1930 – 1951 Estadísticas Cafeteras Pan American Coffee Bureau. 1954.

From 1952 – 1956 Annual Coffee Statistics. Nos 16 – 23 Pan American Coffee Bureau.

From 1957 – 1967 Annual Coffee Statistics. Nos. 30 – 31. Pan American Coffee Bureau.

methods only, but it is generally agreed that the use of fertilizer is fast increasing. A similar precaution is offered in regard to statements about the weather sensitivity of a coffee tree. Frost is regarded as the most important cause of yield changes, and it is stated that two different results are distinguishable:

(1) Light frost may damage the yield of trees without interfering with their ability to grow a normal harvest in the following year.

(2) Severe frost may damage the tree altogether.

Yet the decision whether such complete destruction occurs lies with the farmer. Normally, if additional labor is employed and the frost-bitten tree is cut back just above the ground, even trees damaged completely will start bearing again after a time-lag of about two years.[7] Thus it can reasonably be argued that trees do not produce without care; an abandonment rate of about 40 percent in ten years exists when no care is taken at all. In areas with an additionally high probability of frost, like Paraná, the abandonment rate may be still higher. This is of great importance because, in economic terms, this means that the capacity of coffee production in Brazil, as given by the amount of input of fixed factors of production, i.e., of land and capital, does not exist for a longer period of time. It needs a continuous input of variable factors to keep the capacity at the starting level, and the fixed costs of a given coffee plantation are thus not just the costs of land and capital invested. This may be of great importance in the case of a coffee price policy, designed to influence output over a period of time in which a frost might occur. In such a case, the capacity can be influenced by influencing the relation between current returns and current costs of variable factors, especially of labor force and fertilizer.

## Economic Factors

*Estate and Peasant Cultivation.* Three types of production units exist: units with less than two hectares producing about 17

52

percent; units between 2 and 30 hectares producing about 50 percent; and larger plantations producing about 33 percent of the total world crop.[8] Normally the coffee economy of a single country contains all three types. Empirical investigations on cost distribution have been made on sample methods in some departments in Colombia and Brazil and others in research stations in Africa. They show that statements about an unusually high fixed capital-cost relation obviously cannot be well generalized; they "vary greatly by size of holding, by country and even by region."[9] New empirical evidence suggests that variable costs have increased greatly, due to the increase in labor costs[10] and machinery costs. It seems that the situation where the costs of labor can be disregarded because picking and weeding is done by the peasant proprietor and members of his family, whose labor has no monetary value, is no longer typical. It would not apply to about 80 percent of production − that is, all plantations of ten hectares or over.

Coffee beans must be processed before entering international trade in the form of green coffee. Processing varies from country to country. This variation can be due to different techniques of processing or to the size of the processing plant. In Brazil it takes place on the larger farms themselves, whereas the smaller farmers in Latin America and in Africa bring their crops to co-operative societies.

Structure and competitiveness in the processing industry and middlemen trade would be of great importance in determining the price formation process and thus the price for the producer. But as will be shown in the following pages, this process is now guided by governmental marketing schemes rather than by free market forces.

**National Marketing Schemes on Domestic Markets in Producing Countries and Policies since 1945.** The various national marketing schemes and policies of the producing countries represent the "market form" as well as the "conduct" of the "primary sellers."

Since these policies have differed greatly from country to country, and methods have changed in almost every year, no historical study is yet available covering these features of the world coffee industry. The present investigation attempts no such coverage. We can, however, examine the various current policies in order to provide a picture of the market form and some information on the conduct of primary sellers. An exception to this method is made in the case of Brazil, whose conduct is the most important in the world coffee industry. This chapter analyzes only the structural aspects of her marketing policy, the aspect of conduct being separately analyzed below.

In all producing countries, governments or semiautonomous statutory organizations founded by governments in accordance with producer and middlemen organizations interfere with the price formation process on the domestic market. Besides this, there are in many countries specially fixed exchange rates and/or export taxes for coffee exports. The interventionist measures can be divided into direct measures to fix the domestic price for coffee and indirect ones, which do not interfere with the competitive process, but influence the data and thus result in a change of prices.

Indirect interventionist measures appear in two forms: the fixing of exchange rates, thus creating a special rate of foreign exchange earned in coffee exports, and/or the leveling of an export tax, which the exporting merchant has to pay in foreign exchange to the national bank of the country concerned. A twofold distinction can also be drawn within direct interventions: the intervention may be restricted to provide only for a fixed floor price for the domestic producer, thus eliminating price competition between domestic producers, but leaving competition between middlemen unhampered. If government policy does not concern itself with the next stages of production, then the amount produced is determined by the difference between the foreign exchange equivalent of the domestic floor price and the trade margin plus the world market price. If the volume of output is

---

* Rowe terms this stage of marketing "primary marketing."

larger than the demand at the foreign exchange equivalent of the domestic floor price, any surplus production has to be taken off the market. Another form of market regulation is to subsidize the domestic producers by subsidizing export so as to eliminate any difference between the domestic price and world market price. In this case no part of the production will be retained.*

Some countries fix the export price in terms of foreign exchange as well as the domestic price. Here the competition between export traders is restricted, and no exports are allowed if export prices fall to the minimum level. Some countries stop the middlemen trade altogether or control their export trade. In most countries these different devices have been combined. Furthermore, they have changed in the period under review.

*Angola, Ethiopia, and FEDECAMA States.* In Angola, Ethiopia, and several Latin American countries the government intervened only by introducing export taxes and/or fixed exchange rates for coffee dollars.[11] When they joined the International Coffee Agreement of 1958 and the subsequent agreements, however, these countries accepted the obligation to regulate the volume and price of exports directly. Data is lacking as to how these measures affected the producers' domestic price; but they probably damped price fluctuations without divorcing the domestic price from the world market price.

*CFA Countries.* All the former French territories adopted the method of fixing the price for domestic producers only. Since 1956, prices have been regulated by a Caisse des Stabilisations des Prix in each territory. This guarantees the producer a floor price for his crop in advance, without guaranteeing the grower an option to sell to the Caisses if he is unable to sell to private exporters. Domestic middlemen are obliged to pay the minimum price.

---

* This part looks only into the set-up of regulations and means to influence the price to the domestic producer as a feature of market structure. The actual results are analyzed as conducts of the oligopolistic sellers in Chapter 4.

If the world market price is higher than the c.i.f. price, constructed on the basis of the fixed floor price, then the Caisse charges a levy equal to the difference between the two prices. Conversely, if the world market price stays below the indicated c.i.f. price, the difference is equalized by a subsidy paid to the exporting middlemen.*

Besides possible proceeds from the sort of export levy described above, the Caisse can draw a credit from a special support bank of the French Government. Loans of this kind have to be repaid after a certain time, without regard to the financial situation of the repaying Caisse. Because exports on the Metropolitan French Market fetched a supported higher price than the c.i.f. price *"indicatif,"* these exports were generally liable to an export tax in the period under review. Since 1959 the funds had to be used to finance the price *"indicatif."* Furthermore, since 1959, a further 5 million French francs had to be drawn from the French Government Bank.[12] Since 1959 domestic prices have been supported and exports, which are still traded by private exporters, subsidized.[13]

*Marketing Board Countries.* Governmental regulations in British and former British territories are not uniform.[14] A distinction has to be made between the productions of European-owned plantations and those of the peasant African small holder. The total production of the latter has to be sold at set prices to a governmental marketing board that controls the actions of all middlemen. The board sells the crop on the world market. Its scheme regulates about 70 percent of the total production.

The residual 30 percent of European-grown coffees were exported directly by European farmers or exporters outside the regulations of the marketing board. There is no intervention in the price-making decisions of the single exporter.[15] The European

---

* Prior to 1956 the same effect had been achieved through a distribution of export licenses to France, whose export charged higher than world market prices, which were bound with preceding exports to the world market.

farmer, also, is allowed to sell his coffee to the marketing board at the official coffee price for peasant producers.* Funds collected by the marketing boards were partly — only in West Africa — transferred to governmental budgets and used for general development purposes.[16] Private exporters had to pay a small export tax. Contrary to that experience there was no transfer of funds in Uganda, where no payment had to be made for general development purposes. Instead, until 1961-62 a further 8 million pounds were spent to finance domestic coffee production.[17]

*Colombia.* The export and middlemen trade has not been nationalized in Colombia and Brazil. Intervention and regulation in the price-formation process of coffee at the domestic market consisted of a combination of direct and indirect measures, i.e., of marketing schemes and intervention in the foreign exchange market.

In Colombia this task is delegated to an autonomous statutory body, the Federation Nacional de Cafetoras,[18] which is connected with the National Bank of Colombia.[19] It announces floor prices at which it is prepared to buy, if the farmer cannot sell his output at this price.[20] Trade in coffee at prices below the minimum levels set by the federation is prohibited. Storage capacity has been built up since 1930 all over the country and purchase agents placed in all important domestic trading places, parallel to the already existing warehouses owned by private middlemen and exporters. Similar developments were instituted in the ports. Furthermore, the federation maintains buffer stocks in trading centers in Europe and the United States and acts as an exporter, and "it is said that the federation goes further than this and that some exporting firms are now virtually acting as commission agents for the federation in U.S. trade."[21]

The federation uses two methods to enforce its marketing policy. Firstly, it is given authority by the government to prescribe production, stocks, and quotas.[22] Secondly, it has unusual

---

* The coffee has to be sold to middlemen, licensed by the marketing board as its agent. Prices and profit margins of dealers and processors are set by regulations of the board. Since 1955, they may change three times a year.

financial resources.[23] They consist of an effectively unlimited credit fund with the Colombian National Bank (Banco de Republica), which can be drawn upon on very favorable terms. It also receives the whole amount of export taxes raised from exporters both in kind[24] and in cash. The activities of the Colombian National Bank in connection with the federation was to set the *reintegro* or surrender price, a price which had to be paid by every exporter on every sale to the national bank in U.S. dollars and for which a specially fixed exchange rate applied. If the *reintegro* price exceeds the export market price, the exporter is free to sell his foreign exchange surplus for more pesos than the official rate would have brought; if it is lower[25] the exporter must purchase the requisite dollars at the higher free market rate. These methods have been used throughout the period under review and continuous changes have taken place, setting the amount of *reintegro* prices, taxes, etc.

According to a detailed study by the United Nations on the use of those instruments, prices for domestic producers from 1953 to 1958 were determined by a slow increase in the fixed coffee rate up to the level of the free market dollar ratio. This policy influenced the domestic prices in Colombia in such a way that between 1952 and 1958, when the world market price was declining, the peso equivalent for Colombian coffee actually increased.

By 1957 the domestic price already exceeded the peso equivalent of the world market price in the boom period year of 1954, but in February, 1958, a new coffee price policy was adopted. Its main features were the abolition of a floating coffee rate, the setting of a minimum export price as well as a minimum domestic price designed to keep the peso equivalent of the export price below the actual world market price, and an additional export tax for coffee. The UN study concluded that "the measures adopted in connection with coffee were partly responsible for the fact that domestic prices for this commodity followed the same trend as New York quotations from the first quarter of 1958 onwards."[26] By the same measures the financial burden

Figure 7

## Colombia: Coffee Prices in U.S. and Colombian Currency (semi-logarithmic scale)

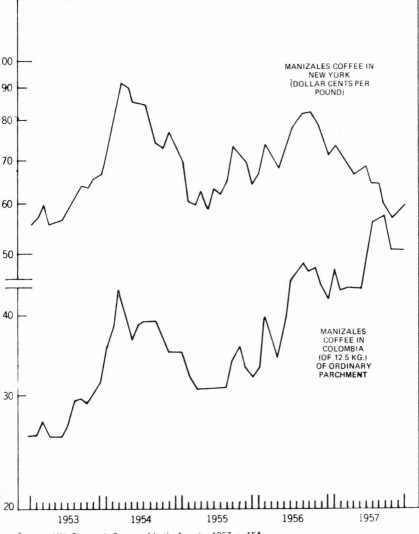

Sources: UN, *Economic Survey of Latin America 1957*, p. 154,
and UN, *Economic Survey of Latin America, 1958*, p. 118.

represented by the building up of coffee reserves was transferred from the government exchequer to the coffee industry itself.[27] The impact of the federation's policy from 1956 to 1962 is covered in Rowe's investigations; he comes to a contradictory conclusion actually showing that "up to 1956 the federation's minimum price [paid to producers] was lower than the experters; it acted in fact as an effective floor price, but the federation had . . . little to buy. Since then its minimum price was above parity with the export price."[28] Besides its impact on producer prices, the federation "exercised a general control over export prices by regulating the prices at which it sells to exporters when they have to come to it for their supplies."[29]

Furthermore the new price development for domestic producers represented the price for high-class export qualities, which are specially cleaned coffees, the difference between the normal output and this grade being up to 30 percent of a whole crop. As small farmers are not able to clean and process their coffee by themselves, the prices received by the smaller domestic producer, normally producing poor-quality parchment, may still be lower by as much as 150 pesos than the fixed minimum price.[30]

This setting of the domestic structure influenced the structure of export trade. Private exporters became to a large extent unable to compete with the federation in getting supplies and, whereas in 1955 the greater proportion of coffee exported as sold by private traders,[31] now more than 70 percent is handled by the federation itself and more than 30 percent of all exporters buy from the federation. The federation obviously regards the European and U.S. markets for coffee as segmented markets and has followed a discriminatory price policy. On the former it acted as a single seller and sold aggressively, by barter deals, and cheaper than the export prices maintained to private exporters to the U.S. markets,[32] which is lower than the price received by the producer. This presumably had a strong impact on the sales figures of Colombia in Europe, which have risen since 1958.[33] The fact that the federation holds stocks is interesting in regard to the volume of stocks, published in records of international organizations. The federation publishes no statistics, thus all figures about stocks are guesses, which are made more uncertain by the fact that there seems to be disagreement as to whether these stocks are export qualities and saleable.[34]

*Brazil.* The market interventions of the Brazilian government are in principle similar to those in Colombia. Brazil also has a joint government-industry agency with statutory power, the Instituto Brasiliero do Cafe,* whose activities are strongly connected with the National Brasilian Bank (SUMOC).[35] The measures taken consist of a foreign exchange control** and a marketing scheme for coffee.

(1)   The IBC has been given authority to fix minimum prices on the domestic market and has declared itself ready to buy all supplies at that price. Since 1933 purchasing agents and storage capacity have spread over the whole country. This allowed for a price-support scheme, similar to that practiced by the Commodity Credit Corporation in the United States, consisting of a minimum purchase price and fixing the support loan level at which the farmer could surrender his crops. The loans were granted by the national bank.

(2)   There was also a specially fixed exchange rate for coffee dollars. Both the national bank and IBC worked hand-in-hand to raise the wanted foreign exchange. A "conversion price" similar to the "surrender price" in Colombia had to be paid by the exporter. It was equivalent to the domestic minimum price times the existing coffee rate, or a minimum export price in U.S.

---

* The institute has five presidents, appointed by the President of Brazil, and ten administrators who have voting powers as well and are voted for by the producer and the export trade.
** Until 1960 the Brazilian government was debarred by constitutional law from levying export taxes. It aimed for the same result through exchange rate manipulations.

61

dollars. The exporter was obliged to exchange this sum in dollars at the given coffee exchange rate in order to be allowed to export his coffee. Thus the transaction obtained the character of an export licensing arrangement, preventing coffee from being sold cheaper by traders if they did not want to lose. The surrender price became in turn a de facto export minimum price. The enforcement of the control mechanism was based on a control of coffee movements between domestic producers both inland and at the ports. The output of each producer was registered, storage of coffee was permitted only in the warehouses of the IBC, and a certificate from the IBC was necessary to transport coffee from these warehouses to the export ports. Exports from ports other than those designated by the IBC were thus illegal and exports were concentrated in a few ports. Every shipment of coffee from the country needed a document from the Brasilian National Bank.

(3) Since 1960 an export tax has been levied which is handled by the national bank but given to the IBC and a contribution in kind (coffee of lower quality) was demanded to be given to the IBC (expurgo).

It is possible to group the several market interventions of the Brazilian government during the period under review in regard to different methods applied. Three periods are distinguishable:[*]

(1) In 1949[36] there were already two separate foreign-exchange markets. In relation to the unregulated (free) black market the cruzeiro on the legal market was overvalued. Taking account of this situation special coffee exchange rates were instituted and enforced by the surrender technique. The new Law 1807, or Free Exchange Law, in 1953 legalized those practices and

_____

[*] The results of the policy, as observed statistically, are given and analyzed in Chapter 4, which analyzes the price policy of the IBC, because of the great importance of this country in the world coffee industry.

provided for a system of multiple exchange rates, which were lower than free market rates but at premiums to other export rates. Thus an indirect export taxation took place. During that time until 1954-55 the exchange rate rose by 35 percent, and at the end of 1955 again by 100 percent,[37] the domestic incidence of which was offset through a rise in the minimum price paid to domestic producers. The export price also remained high, because in August, 1955, the government set an export minimum price, not meant to be adjusted daily to serve as a surrender price only, but fixed for a longer time in order to stabilize the price for Brazilian coffee on the world market.[38] In December, however, this method was abolished, and the daily fluctuating surrender-price quotation renewed. This change was accompanied by a change in the coffee rate and an offsetting higher minimum price. In 1956-57 the government followed its established policies, keeping the domestic price stable by large purchases at the fixed minimum domestic price in 1955-56 and small sales out of those stocks in 1956-57.[39]

(2) With the start of the crop year 1957-58, the Brazilian government introduced a new premium scheme for coffee. Besides the established fixed exchange rate, for each dollar by which the f.o.b. price of any grade exceeded 42 dollars per 60 kg. bag, a premium of 1 cent was paid. This premium was flexible and amounted in effect to an immediate devaluation by nearly 30 percent of the applicable exchange rate.[40] Applied to the newly set minimum export price of 58.5 cts/lb. in U.S. dollars, the effect on the domestic price was the equivalent of a rise in the price of Brazilian coffee on the New York Exchange to over 70 cents a pound.[41] In order to keep the world market price in line with fixed minimum export price, that is, the price to domestic producers, the government had to bear the financial burden of

63

storing the coffee in excess supply at ⟨...⟩ the
following years[42] higher domestic mini⟨...⟩
set in such a way that the domestic pro⟨...⟩
steady increase in the domestic cruze⟨...⟩
products. This line of policy was continu⟨...⟩
of the crop year 1960-61.

(3)  The crop of 1961-62 as well as the following ⟨...⟩
     harvested under different market regulations:

   A.  All coffee receipts in foreign exchange were ⟨...⟩
       by an export levy of $22 per 60 kg. bag of co⟨...⟩.
       This had been done in order to offset the increase
       in cruzeiros due to the fact that the special coffee
       exchange rate was abolished, allowing thus for the
       exchange of all coffee receipts to be handled on
       the free market.[43] The coffee exchange rate as
       published in the financial statistics since May,
       1961, represents the resulting effective rate after
       the deduction of the export levy.[44]

   B.  Only coffee of good quality was to be exported.
       Exportable coffees were split into two series: the
       "fine quality" coffee, which was to be exported
       freely, shipped directly and without cost to port,
       and the "lower quality" direct-quota coffee, which
       was subject to a retention in kind of 40 percent
       (i.e., four bags out of ten bought by the exporter).

   C.  Non-export coffee was purchased at a maximum
       price below 1,700 cruzeiros per 60 kg. bag, that is
       about 50 percent lower than the price received for
       export grades.[45]

As in Colombia, the IBC started to become more and more
important as direct sellers on the coffee market in the consuming
countries. Thus both the IBC and the federation founded agencies
at all coffee exchanges and constructed storage capacity in
importer countries. The agencies were only partly under their own
name. Some old, well-established exchange traders and brokers

were taken over or started to become commission agents for the IBC or the federation. The same obviously applied to the marketing boards of former British territories and several coffee producers' corporations of Latin American states (FEDECAMA). The effect of this general move of producers as firsthand sellers is an impact on the price formation on the New York Exchange, which will be dealt with below.

## Characteristics of Industrial
## Processing and End Consumption

### The Final Product: Blends and Solubles

Coffee is used mainly in the form of a coffee brew, other industrial usages being of minor importance. Coffee as a drink can be brewed out of coffee beans or obtained from instant coffee. From an economic point of view the two forms can almost be treated as distinctive industries.

Until 1949-53 the only method widely used in preparing coffee was to use coffee beans in blends. Today the share of coffee blends has declined to about 80 percent of world consumption. This figure also applies to the United States,[46] whereas in several European countries it is higher (about 90 percent in Germany) or lower (some 35 percent in the United Kingdom).[47]

Before coffee beans enter final retail trade in the form of coffee blends, they are roasted and different types of coffees are mixed. The taste of a coffee-bean blend is determined by the different types of coffee used. The taste-determining type need not make up to 100 percent of the blend. We can thus distinguish between "blending types" and "fillers." The taste depends then on the proportion between blending coffee and fillers. Falling back on the already discussed typical features of the three generic types of coffee in international trade, it is stated that blends, qualifying as of mild taste, can consist — besides the blending types of Milds — of a changing percentage of Brazils of the soft grade, that is, the Santos 4 type. The more bitter tasting grades of Brazils (Hards) as well as the similarly qualified Robustas cannot be blended for such quality blend, as they would destroy the mild flavor of the coffee blend. Coffee blends aiming for a stronger – that is, a more bitter – taste can be mixed from pure Brazils of the type Santos 4. A mixture of that type and of Robustas or Hards will increase the relative bitterness of the coffee brew.

The share of instant coffee in world consumption of green coffee rose from 1949, when it reached about 2 percent, to about 20 percent in 1955-56. It then declined slightly in the following years and nowadays is about 18 percent.[48]

It is a most important economic characteristic of this form of coffee processing that the taste of the instant coffee is not impaired by the bitter taste of the non-mild coffees. New production processes neutralize the acids, responsible for the bitter taste of a brew of bitter type coffees.[49] On the other hand, these types do not contain those additional flavors that create the typical mild taste. Thus a brew of instant coffee of bitter types of coffee beans tastes different from a brew made of Milds.

An additional difference is the fact that instant coffee produces more cups per pound of green coffee than does roasted coffee.[50] Further improvements in the last years reduced the amount of green coffee in instant coffee to 60 percent, the additional 40 percent being supplemented by chemical ingredients (stretchers). These are sprayed with coffee flavor and kept under vacuum package.[51]

Consumer Preferences

Consumer preferences for the various coffee brew flavors are influenced by several factors; including that of changes in income. Without giving the causative factors, generally the literature[52] agrees that consumers in the United States and several western European countries regard the mild flavor, attributed to blends containing Milds, as superior to the blends of bitter taste. Opposite tastes are established in southern and northern Europe, where consumers prefer the stronger taste of the more bitter types of coffee.

## The State of the Processing Industry

The coffee processing and retailing industry shows considerable concentration. Market concentration can be found in the roasting industry[53] on national levels, and to a lesser extent internationally. Concentration on the international level is very much higher in the instant-coffee industry, the largest producers being international concerns, like Nestlé with its trademark Nescafé and General Foods with its trademark Maxwell.[54]

## Governmental Restrictions in Importing Countries

The import of coffee is generally unhampered. One important[55] exception is the European market, where France, England, and Portugal assured their former dependent colonial countries market access through preferential tariffs. In 1959 France changed this control into import restrictions against imports of third countries but abolished it again in 1965.

The import control of the French market proceeded in two steps: from 1949 to 1958 the regulation consisted of an import tariff of 20 percent ad valorem; since 1959 France has entered into a price-quota guarantee with a fixed price, independent of changes in world market prices. The former price has exceeded the latter by about 30 percent in the last two years.[56] The guarantee quota increased from 80,000 tons in 1958 to 150,000 tons in 1961,[57] that is, about 75 percent of the French coffee imports and 60 percent of the exports of the CFA countries. Similar volumes were traded in the controlled eastern European markets. These markets together accounted for no more than 8 percent of world imports and the eastern European markets were based on direct dealing agreements between marketing boards and statutory import monopolies.

## NOTES

1. PCB: *Annual Coffee Statistics,* 1962, p. 72.

2. O. van Teutem, "Coffee in Latin America: The Producers' Problem," UN, *Economic Bulletin for Latin America,* Vol. IV, No. 1 (1959), p. 36.

3. FAO, *CBS-33,* p. 8.

4. Federal Trade Commission, *Economic Report of the Investigation of Coffee Prices,* pp. 48-59; FAO, *CBS-33,* pp. 10-12.

5. FAO, *CBS-33,* Chapter: Economic Factors . . .

6. A.E. Haarer, *Modern Coffee Production,* (London: Leonard Hill, 1962), p. 417.

7. J.W. Rowe, *The World's Coffee* (London: H.M.S.O., 1963), p. 34.

8. FAO, *CBS-33,* p. 9.

9. *Ibid.*

10. Especially, PPA – State of Paraná: *Investment Program 1966-71,* p. 74.

11. U.S. Department of Agriculture, *Coffee Situation, Programs and Policies in Producing Countries,* Foreign Agricultural Service (FAS-M-148), pp. 11-12.

12. FAO-UN, *Commodity Stabilization Funds in the French Area,* p. 32.

13. U.S. Department of Agriculture, *op. cit.,* p. 10.

14. FAO-UN, *The Role of Marketing Boards for Export Crops in Developing Countries.* No. E/CN 13/50: "Those territories now independent are Uganda, Tanganyika and Kenya. Our description refers mainly to Uganda, the largest producer of Robustas between those countries. In Kenya, the influence of European coffee producers is more, in Tanganyika less, important."

15. *Ibid.,* p. 5.

16. J.M. Clark, "Export Taxes on Tropical Products," FAO, *Monthly Bulletin of Agricultural Economics and Statistics,* Vol. XII, No. 5 (1963), p. 11.

17. IBRD, *The Economic Development of Uganda,* p. 37.

18. UN, *Economic Survey of Latin America 1958,* pp. 118-119; FAO, *Coffee in Latin America,* Vol. I, pp. 87-94.

19. UN, *Economic Survey . . . 1958, op. cit.,* p. 9.

20. U.S. Department of Agriculture, *op. cit.,* p. 10.

21. Rowe, *op. cit.,* p. 74.

22. U.S. Department of Agriculture, *op. cit.,* p. 7.

23. UN, *Economic Survey . . . 1958, op. cit.,* p. 7.

24. Rowe, *op. cit.,* p. 24.

25. UN, *Economic Survey of Latin America 1957,* pp. 114-115.

26. UN, *Economic Survey . . . 1958, op. cit.,* p. 118.

27. *Ibid.,* p. 119.

28. Rowe, *op. cit.,* p. 24.

29. *Ibid.,* p. 76.

30. *Ibid.*

31. FAO, *Coffee in . . ., op. cit.,* Vol. I, p. 89.

32. Rowe, *op. cit.,* p. 76.

33. UN, *Economic Survey of Latin America 1963,* pp. 200-201; Rowe, *op. cit.,* pp. 73-75.

34. Rowe, *op. cit.,* p. 72.

35. For a description of the relations between SUMOC and the Bank of Brazil, which acted partly as Central Bank as well, see UN, *Economic Bulletin for Latin America,* Vol. IX, No. 2 (Nov. 1964), p. 214, footnotes 97, 98.

36. FTC, *Report, op. cit.,* pp. 97-119.

37. IMF, *Financial Statistics 1956,* Vol. IX, No. 1, p. 55; UN, *Economic Survey . . . 1957, op. cit.,* p. 132.

38. FTC, *Report, op. cit.,* p. 93.

39. UN, *Economic Survey . . . 1957, op. cit.,* p. 124.

40. *Ibid.,* p. 124.

41. *Ibid.,* p. 138.

42. *Conjunctura Economica,* Vol. VI, No. 2 (March 1959), p. 5; Vol. VII, No. 2 (Feb. 1960), p. 35; Vol. VII, No. 1 (Jan. 1960), p. 4; Vol. VII, No. 10 (Oct. 1960), p. 4.

43. GATT, Document L 1656; UN, *Economic Bulletin for Latin America,* Vol. IX, No. 2 (Nov. 1964), p. 209; IMF, *Financial Statistics, Supplement 1962-1963,* p. 23.

44. IMF, *Financial Statistics* (March 1965), p. 61.

45. FAO, *Commodity Review 1962,* pp. 11-55.

46. FAO, *CBS-33, op. cit.,* p. 34; O. van Teutem, *op. cit.,* p. 35.

47. *Review of the Federation of British Industries* (June 1964), p. 1; *Deutsche Zeitung und Handelsblatt,* 13, 4 (1965), p. 5.

48. FAO, *Commodity Review 1962,* pp. II, 53.

49. *Review of the Federation of British Industries, op. cit.,* p. 4.

50. FTC, *Report, op. cit.,* p. 45; UN, *Economic Survey . . . 1957, op. cit.,* p. 79.

51. *Neue Fuercher Zeitung.*

52. A.E. Haarer, *op. cit.,* p. 429; U.S. Senate, Subcommittee on Banking and Currency, Study of Coffee Prices, Hearing, Part I (Washington, D.C.: Government Printing Office), p. 125.

53. FTC, *Report, op. cit.,* Chapter II, pp. 127-246; G. Schmitt, *Einige Benerkungen zum Begriff und zur Theorie der vertikalen Integration in der Landwirtschaft, in "Agrarwirtschaft,"* Buchholz, *Der deutsche Kaffeemarkt,* pp. 93-94.

54. V.D. Wickizer, "International Collaboration in the Coffee Market," *Food Research Studies,* IV, 3 (Stanford University Press, 1964), p. 299: "General Foods claims to take 18 percent of all coffee trades in the world."

55. FAO, *CBS-33, op. cit.,* p. 34; FAO, Monthly Bulletin, Vol. X, No. 11 (Nov. 1961), p. 14; GATT, *Trade in Tropical Products,* p. 37.

56. FAO-UN, *Commodity Stabilization, op. cit.,* p. 11, map 11.

57. FAO-UN, *Commodity Stablization, op. cit.,* p. 39; GATT, *Trade in, op. cit.,* p. 37.

# 4     **Market Performance As a Result of Oligopolistic Competition**

## The Market Structure

For an analysis of the typical features, or performance, of the price formation[1] we shall now single out those aspects of the empirical material that can be regarded as market structure dimensions.

### Product Differentiation and Sectional Markets

Considering the different types of coffee and their different usages, it is possible to regard coffee as a non-homogeneous product and the coffee market as a market with product-differentiated goods. If we take the differentiation induced by demand as a criterion for different markets[2] two of those can be established. Both sectoral markets can be supplied with three different types of coffee. The first sectoral market is that for soluble coffee. The elimination of the difference in bitterness between the different types of coffee in the production of solubles eliminated consumer preferences between the various types of coffees in this market. Milds, Brazils (soft and hard), and Robustas are here substitute products, the substitution gap between them being very small. In such cases the substitution depends on the price differential between the different coffee types; the price elasticity of demand for the product of a single producer is very high.

The second sectoral market is that for blends of roasted coffee beans. Here, there is high cross-elasticity of demand between the flavoring type and the filler type of one blend, but it can be only of such an amount that the taste of the blend will not change distinctively. The price elasticity of demand for a single producer may be considerably smaller than in the market for solubles. The substitution possibilities can be shown in Table 2.

### TABLE 2

#### Sectoral Coffee Markets

| Markets | Blends of Roasted Coffee Beans | | Soluble Coffee |
|---------|-------------------------|-------------------------|-----------------|
| Type | Mild Tasting (Quality 1.) | Bitter Tasting (Quality 2.) | |
| Milds | x | | x |
| Brazils | x | x | x |
| Robusta | | x | x |

Under given conditions and habits of consumption, the demand for Brazils in roasted coffee depends on the price differential between Brazils and Milds on the one hand, and of Brazil and Robustas on the other. A shrinkage in the price differential between Brazils and Milds will lead to a reduction of Brazils in a mild blend.[3] A widening of the price differential will promote a substitution of Brazils for Milds, but only to such an extent that the taste barrier will not be crossed. If the price differential between Brazils and Robustas narrows, then a substitution of Brazils for Robustas may take place. It would raise the quality of the cheaper blends of roasted coffee beans, and thus further induce a shift of demand between roasted and soluble coffee, creating an increase in demand for Brazils instead of those Robustas used for the production of soluble coffee. But a substitution in the soluble coffee production itself will not take place as long as any price differential between Brazils and Robustas exists.

Thus, if blends of first quality are consumed regardless of price, then Milds will continue to have a market of their own in the first quality blend market, regardless of the magnitude of the price differential with Brazils. The share of Brazils in this market, as well as in the second quality market, will be maintained only as long as there is a price differential between both types of coffee.

This is not so in regard to the price differential between Robustas and Brazils. If there is none at all, Brazil will have a market of its own, on the second quality market and on the market for soluble coffee. If there is one, the share of Brazils in the second quality blend market will depend on the differential between Robustas and Brazils, the competition of Robustas being restricted by the taste barrier in the second quality market. But it will displace Brazils on the market for soluble coffee and reduce the share of the second quality market in end consumption through substitution of end products.

## Business Concentration of "Primary Sellers" and "Buyers for Processing"

The result of market or exchange regulations of producing countries are twofold: over time they constitute conduct and influence structure of the world market. Here we are only concerned with the latter. An influence is easily discernible where market regulations take the form of direct market interventions, i.e., the formation of marketing boards which become the intermediary monopolists for national production or "single sellers" for a national product. In contrast to this device we have mentioned two other forms of intervention which we may classify as indirect interventions, i.e., the setting of a domestic floor price or the manipulation of the foreign exchange rate for coffee. But these measures do not only influence the price on the domestic market; they also influence the price formation on the export market for the domestic good. If the country concerned fixes a special foreign exchange rate for coffee export proceeds, then this leads to export subsidies or export taxation. Insofar as this applies to the whole export trade of a producing country, a change of policy influences the cost data on which export traders base their price policy. If there is competition between them, a change in cost data will induce a uniform price change.

This common reaction of coffee traders of a producing country to a change in the domestic policy of the country allows us to regard its total exports as the supply of one seller on the world market. The only exception to this is the supply from the former French countries, now the CFA-zone states, where there is no fixation of an export subsidy in advance, so that traders are still free to settle their supply on their own terms. The structure of the "primary" supply side of the world coffee market shows thus an oligopoly in Milds coffee, the largest oligopolist being Colombia with about 50 percent of all supplies concentrated in its hand, and a monopoly for those of the Brazils type. The sellers' concentration for all coffees of Robustas is quite different. It is one of oligopoly or at least "teiloligopol," where several traders of the CFA countries compete with the "single seller" marketing boards of the former British countries like Uganda.

Several forms of concentration can be detected on the different markets.

(1) On the submarket for roasted coffee blends of first quality we distinguish a highly concentrated structure of differentiated oligopoly, faced by a less strict oligopsony, mainly in the United States, but also to a lesser extent in Europe and the rest of the world.

(2)  The same buyers' concentration and product differentiation applies to the market for blends of the second quality. The sellers concentration on this market is much smaller, tending to a polypoly.

(3)  On the market for soluble coffee we find parallel sellers' concentration and product differentiation — comparable to that on the second quality market — but here the concentration of buyers seems to be considerably higher, even on the international level and reaches a form of clear oligopsony.

## Production Policy of Oligopolistic Sellers

As indicated earlier, it is evident that the powers of the marketing boards or other statutory agencies were considerable. We distinguished direct interventions, i.e., fixing of prices for domestic producers, or indirect interventions in form of a special coffee rate. Both measures insure that domestic prices can be developed differently from the world market prices. (See the later discussion in this chapter under "The Effects of the Domestic Price Policy of the IBC on Brazil's Domestic Output.") Thus the output of domestic farmers in more or less every coffee-producing country — the output of the oligopolistic seller — need not be a function of the world market price, but may depend on the domestic price policy of the single national marketing board, that is, the principles and methods of the single seller in deciding what output shall be produced in one country.

## Market Price Assumptions: The Problem of Stocks in Hands of "Primary Sellers"

A further evaluation of national market schemes allowing for a stock policy, is needed in regard to the effects of direct as well as indirect inventories into the volume of exports in those producing countries. It applies to Brazil and Colombia as well as Uganda. As marketing boards were able to sell from or hold for inventories, we cannot assume that the full quantities of yearly crops were released for sale in a given market period. To understand the price formation on the world coffee market involves, not "output," but "market-price" hypotheses[4] in a market with differentiated oligopoly in both sides of the market. Weintraub mentions that "Firms can sell from or hold for inventory, if carrying costs are prohibitive they can destroy part of their output if to do so is more profitable than enlarging sales .... If both firms are of approximately the same size, there appears a new motive for inventory holdings, to ward off a rival's price-cutting propensities with the retaliatory weapon of sizeable inventory carry-over may be less than the costs of acquiescence to downward price revisions."[5]

### The Market Organization on the New York Coffee Exchange

Turnovers in green coffee are dealt with wherever coffee is grown, but only the price quotations of the New York Coffee and Sugar Exchange are regarded as world market prices and New York is the dominant world market. Here large merchandise firms, brokers, and agents of large roasters come together to fix a daily quotation for immediate delivery as well as for contracts for delivery months ahead. Thus the exchange has both a "spot" market and a "futures" market.

The "spot" or "actual" market is not a unified market at all. It is used here as a term for the sum of transactions to buy and to sell actual (physical) coffee, and for the agencies involved in these transactions. Transactions on the actual markets are not necessarily public. Ideally, the spot market consists of principal intermediaries between the coffee producers and the roasters who buy the green coffee, that is, of brokers and dealers. They buy c.i.f. from the producing countries coffee for which they have not yet found a customer, or contract supply for coffee which they have not yet bought, hoping to make a profit.

The price formation on the "terminal" or "future" market takes place under conditions of an organized exchange. It should consist firstly of the same people as those who do the actual trade. Ideally, under those conditions trading practices are such that several imperfections in the competitive price formations on actual markets are overcome. Insofar as information is worldwide, geographical inequities do not exist, and in the "ring" there are no personal preferences between single buyer and seller, the market structure is regarded as atomistic, and a highly standardized grading system is established.[6] Thus prices or price differentials between different types of commodities are market-determined prices and reflect competitive market influences. Disregarding speculative influences for the moment, the price formation is such that the price equates total supply with total demand. Futures trading also equates supply and demand for some time ahead. By using the price spread between several future prices, a technique developed — hedging, which allowed merchants and other stock-carrying people to shift the burden of risk to special risk bearers, the second group of people trading on the market, the speculators. The volume of transactions should then exceed the actual tonnage of coffee actually changing hands on the market and by doing so is said to broaden the market and strengthen its atomic structure.[7] It also increases the short-run price elasticity of both supply and demand.[8] A very strong connection between both markets must exist, because the "future" markets settle as well a price for coffee as a cash market quotation for that day for the various contracts as they do dealings in futures.

### The Conduct of Primary Sellers and Buyers for Processing

The Creation of Surplus and Excess Capacity

The enormous surpluses stocked in two producer countries, Brazil and Colombia, form a large part of the "coffee problem" (Fig. 2).

(Brazil stores about 80 percent of the world surplus, and Colombia most of the rest.[9] These two countries share about 60 percent of total world production). The FAO has made two analyses of the "cyclical surplus" in Brazil. Its concept of a "cyclical coffee surplus" started from the assumption that the excessive output in Brazil was caused by price increases on the world market between 1949 and 1954, resulting from a rise in demand for coffee combined with a time-lagged response of production. The very low "short-run" price elasticity of supply induced prices to stay high and led to an increase of output after a lag of some six to eight years, which was much greater than that needed to restore the equilibrium at the price before the shift of demand occurred.[10]

In order to prove this argument, it needs to be shown that the surplus crop from 1958-59 to 1961-62 were results of the price increases in 1949-54. Secondly, it has to be proved that the high volume of output which did not shrink in spite of the declining world market prices since 1954, was a result of the low price elasticity of production in coffee. Furthermore a cyclical interpretation has to start off with some long-run equilibrium between production and consumption. (See Chapter 2 for a detailed description of this concept.) An analysis has thirdly to take account of the national market regulations schemes of the coffee producing countries as shown above in the analysis of market structure in the world coffee industry. They can influence domestic output independently of the development of world market prices if the contract in form of a domestic price policy does not follow the tendencies of the world market. It may also, if the market share of one country on the world market is large enough, influence the price on the world market for its own type of coffee, and hence the demand for it. In analyzing the development of the existing surplus and/or excess capacity, these two factors have to be kept apart and examined separately.

Since no time-series data are available to show the application of these policies for a number of producing countries it is inside the scope of this study — following the FAO studies — only to evaluate their impact in the creation of the surplus capacity in the Brazilian example, since Brazil's output increase represented a large part of the surplus and the market share of Brazil in the world market fluctuated around 40 percent. As will become evident, the policy analysis of this country has already proved to be difficult with the material available, but it allows for a presentation of the main imperfections in the world coffee industry, which made for the market performance of the industry in the period under review.

**The Effects of the Domestic Price Policy of the IBC on Brazil's Domestic Output.** The effect of numerous interventions on the domestic market in Brazil, as explained in the analysis of market structure, divided the course of domestic coffee prices in the Brazilian coffee industry into successive phases:

In a first phase from 1949 to 1954* domestic monetary prices followed the trend in world market prices; in the second phase from 1954 to 1964 they had a trend of their own. This statement about the latter development cannot be upheld unqualified after 1961, when a new price policy for different grades was intensified.

(1) If the 1949 price was an equilibrium value[11] as assumed, it can be shown that the domestic producer in Brazil received a price lower than the then equilibrium market price valued at free exchange rates. Therefore the world market price was not an equilibrium price in the sense that it balanced output and consumption. Nor was the world coffee economy in equilibrium in the proper sense between production and consumption, because the domestic equilibrium price of the Brazilian producers was taxed by the Brazilian Government.

---

* Actually, world market price held stable at a 1950-53 level till the end of 1957. It may be a matter of argument whether the downward trend of the coffee cycle did not start before 1957. The reasoning for our assumption that the world market price displayed the second part of the cycle after 1954 is put forward in a later section.

Instead, it was a situation of potential excess production over demand at the going world market price. The ability to prevent such an excess-output rested solely with the government of the largest producer on the world market which was normally influenced by the very strong representation of coffee growers.[12] If we analyze the development of domestic prices in the period from 1949 to 1954[13] taking special account of this problem, it can be seen that the domestic price followed the trend of world market prices, but the relative increase of the former exceeded the relative increase of the latter by 30 percent, due to several changes in the foreign exchange rate for coffee. The same happened in the year 1954 when the world market price for Brazilian coffee advanced about 80 percent and the domestic monetary price almost doubled.

(2) The second phase began with the peak of the coffee boom on the world market. Whereas the world market price fell by some 30 percent and stayed there for about three years and decreased again by about 40 percent till 1961-62, the domestic price in Brazil remained stable at the peak level of 1954, "because the internal impact of this decline was mitigated by changes in the exchange rates" (Fig. 8).[14] It advanced from 1957 to 1959 by about 30 percent, and from 1959 to more than 100 percent, continuing its increasing trend till 1966 (Fig. 11 and Table 3).

(3) In analyzing the development of domestic monetary prices to producers a third point of importance is the price differential between the various grades of coffee. A change was instituted in 1961-62. The several measures of the IBC, described earlier, "led to the introduction of high quality standards for exportable coffee and allowing for much lower prices for the substandard qualities."[15] (E.g., Rio and Riouy flavors

Figure 8

# Brazil: Coffee Prices in U.S. and Brazilian Currency (semilogarithmic scale)

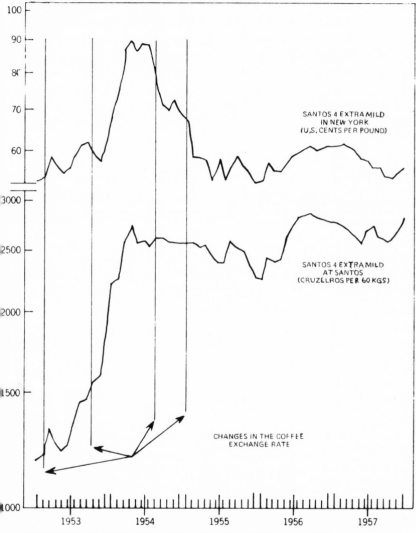

Note: From February 1953 to October 1953 and from August 1954 to January 1955, exporters were allowed to sell some foreign exchange on the free market, so the exchange rate fluctuated slightly in these periods.

Sources: UN, *Economic Survey of Latin America, 1957*, p. 154, and
UN, *Economic Survey of Latin America, 1958*, p. 118.

lower than cup quality 7/8.) This had in effect the result
that the prices for all coffees of grades inferior because
of bitterness or other imperfections declined sharply in
relation to the prices of exportable coffees and reached
comparatively low levels. This policy was intensified by
a change in the expurgo rate, which was observed by
Rowe. Till 1961-62 the fixed proportion of expurgo
coffee at 10 percent was larger than the yearly crop of

## TABLE 3

Actual Prices for Santos 4 and Rio 7[a]
(export ports in Brazil)

|      | Santos 4 | Rio 7 |
|------|----------|-------|
| 1950 | 184      | 141   |
| 1951 | 194      | 170   |
| 1952 | 198      | 173   |
| 1953 | 230      | 188   |
| 1954 | 416      | 310   |
| 1955 | 416      | 280   |
| 1956 | 437      | 300   |
| 1957 | 442      | 310   |
| 1958 | 460      | 280   |
| 1959 | 470      | 330   |
| 1960 | 542      | 450   |
| 1961 | 670      | 480   |
| 1962 | 900      | 480   |
| 1963 | 1500     | 950   |
| 1964 | 4925     | 3741  |

[a] Prices in cruzeiros per 10 kg.

**Source:** Instituto Brasileiro do café, *Anuario Estatistico do Café*

that quality and sellers of exportable coffee paid a higher price than the IBC minimum price for rights to expurgo and provided a direct stimulus to producers to expand the production of such a poor quality. From 1960-61 the poor quality was excluded from the expurgo surrender.

(4) "However, this policy of discrimination between various types of coffee was not maintained after 1964 and the difference in the effective price paid for coffee to be exported or to be stored became quite small."[16]

In setting out to analyze how coffee prices have influenced output and capacity in Brazil, certain preliminary distinctions should be made:

Firstly, one has to distinguish between the different prices for different types of coffee grown in Brazil. The two most important coffee producing states in this country are São Paolo and Paraná (Figs. 9 and 10). It is stated[17] that the output of São Paolo is of better cup quality and taste and that a very large percentage of the production of that state consists of beans of the Santos 4 type. We have thus regarded the price for Santos 4 as a representative price to producers in São Paolo. The quality of Paraná's coffee is considerably lower: it consists mainly of cup qualities No. 7 in a Hard or Rio taste. It seems thus meaningful to use the quotations of Rio 7 as an average representative price for the export production of that state.

Secondly, the reaction of farmers to price can be measured in output and capacity, the latter represented by the number of newly planted trees or acreage under coffee.

Thirdly, the rate of upkeep of capacity and capacity changes can be regarded as "long-run" reactions of production toward price changes; changes in output may reveal "short-run" reactions if one takes into account the effects of an increase in capacity toward output.

83

# TABLE 4

## Brazil's Coffee Area

| | (Million acres) | São Paolo | Paraná |
|---|---|---|---|
| 1945-48 | 6.0 | 3.2 | 0.3 |
| 1949 | 6.3 | 3.3 | 0.6 |
| 1950 | 6.6 | 3.5 | 0.7 |
| 1951 | 6.8 | 3.5 | 0.7 |
| 1952 | 7.0 | - | - |
| 1953 | 7.2 | 3.6 | 0.9 |
| 1954 | 7.4 | 3.6 | 1.0 |
| 1955 | 8.0 | 3.7 | 1.4 |
| 1956 | 8.4 | 3.8 | 1.6 |
| 1957 | 9.7 | 3.9 | 2.0 |
| 1958 | 10.7 | 4.0 | 2.6 |
| 1959 | 10.7 | 4.2 | 3.2 |
| 1960 | 11.0 | 4.2 | 3.4 |
| 1961 | 10.9 | 3.8 | 3.5 |
| 1962 | 11.1 | 3.4 | 4.0 |
| 1963 | 10.6 | 3.2 | 4.0 |
| 1964 | 9.1 | 2.8 | 3.0 |

**Source:** *World Coffee and Tea*, Vol. 6, No. 12 (April 1966), 20.

Table No. 4 reveals that the acreage in Brazil increased from 1948 to 1962 by 5 million acres, representing a rise in capacity of about 80 percent. The figures also show that the main extension of capacity took place between 1954 and 1960, with a further small extension in 1962, and acreage in production has since been falling. All investigations agree that the biggest increase in planting occurred between 1954 and 1960, a time of decreasing world market prices for all grades, whereas new planting after the introduction of the new Brazilian price policy has been much more selective.[18]

The changes in acreage planted with coffee in the two states São Paolo and Paraná respectively are shown in Table 4 and in Fig. 10. Coffee acreage in both states increased till 1959, but whereas a first sign of a change in trend occurs in São Paolo in 1960, such a reaction does not show up in Paraná till the year 1963. The second interesting feature of difference between both states is that in the period under review acreage in Paraná increased till 1962 by some 1200 percent against an increase in São Paolo of about 30 percent.

The second indication of production is output. It increased from 1946 to 1953, that is the year preceding the coffee boom, by some 300,000 tons, or 38 percent.[19] Output fluctuated around this figure in the early fifties, but by 1955-56 the production rose by 30 percent and culminated in the record crops of 1957-58 and 1959-60, the majority of which was produced in Paraná. The harvests of 1960-61 and 1961-62 showed a decrease of some 36 percent[20] and have fallen since then to about 60 percent of the record year 1959-60. Production trends in São Paolo and Paraná are not uniform (see chart 4).

In the analysis that follows comparisons of certain time series data have been made. We shall test the hypotheses of a casual relationship between the two variables looked into, even though evidence of association does not provide a causal explanation in itself.

Four different hypotheses of a causal relationship have been put forward. Some of them have already partly been tested by FAO:[21]

(1) comparison between trends in world market prices and output and capacity trends

(2) comparison between trends in the price paid to the domestic coffee producers, deflated by a cost-of-living index and output as well as capacity trends

(3) comparison between trends in monetary prices paid to coffee producers, and output as well as capacity trends

(4) comparison between the relative prices of coffee in relation to prices paid to producers for other crops, regarded as competitive to coffee.

**Figure 9**

# Output: Brazil, Paraná, São Paulo

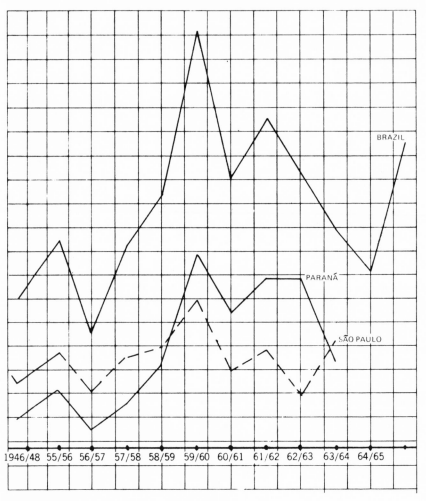

Source: Based on statistics from *Anuario Estatico do Brasil.*

**Figure 10**

# Acreage in Two Brazilian States

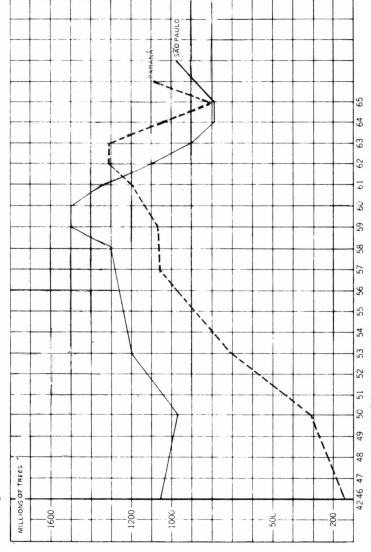

Source: Based on statistics from *Anuario Estatico do Brasil*.

87

In those studies it has been stated that "from the viewpoint of coffee growers, an extension of coffee cultivation either in the form of new planting or more intensive cultivation of old planting is worthwhile so long as the excess of coffee price over production cost is greater than the corresponding net returns from alternative uses of the same resources. The changes in relative profitability of coffee cultivation in relation to other alternative uses thus depends not only on the movement of coffee prices but also on that in prices of alternative agricultural activities, if any, and on the differences in cost in these alternatives compared with coffee growing."[22] Nonetheless, this analysis concluded, "evidence indicates that when coffee prices rise sharply, or by a substantial amount over a short period, the profitability of coffee growing also rises,"[23] giving a comparison of world market prices for Santos 4 and the output in Brazil as a whole.

Furthermore, comparison has been made of the development of a "real" price of coffee and output of Brazil as a whole.

These studies have been faced with the problem of allowing for the influence of a fast-growing inflation in Brazil, which was thought to be overcome by using deflated cruzeiro prices, obviously on the assumption that farmers would evaluate their coffee returns at comparable measures.

We can at this stage of our analysis begin to look critically at two of these approaches. It has been shown in the preceding chapter that world market prices for Brazilian coffee did not follow the same trend as that of the price received by the domestic producer. There is therefore no direct connection between output in Brazil and world market price for its product which would allow a comparison between these variables.

But a parallel movement existed between the world market price and the domestic price, defaulted by a cost of living index.

Two dominant features are discernible in the relationship between these two variables: "In relating production of coffee to price movements allowance has to be made for the lapse of time before newly planted trees approach full bearing. Quiquennial production may thus be compared to price developments in the

**Figure 11**

# Brazilian Domestic and Export Prices (in Brazilian cents per pound)

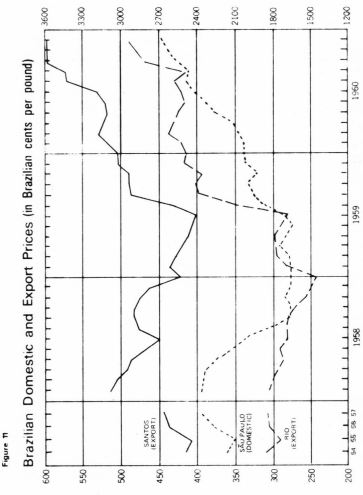

Note: There are no time series on prices paid to domestic producers in Brazil. Therefore, prices paid by exporters in export ports have been used. Producer prices in other states are assumed to have shown the same relationship to export prices observed in the case of San Paulo.

Source: *Agricultura Em São Paulo*, Boletim Da Divisao De Economia Dural, Vol. VII, No. 12 (1960), 67.

89

proceeding five years."[24] In doing this the study states: "the considerable expansion of coffee output in the second half of the 1950's reflects the sharp advance of prices, which started in 1949, but there was no visible reaction to the subsequent price decline," and this continues: "It is surprising that the considerable and protracted decline of real prices did not discourage a further increase of output."[25]

It can also be seen that acreage showed an increasing trend till 1963 (Fig. 10). A reaction of this kind is fundamentally different from the traditional concept of a "coffee cycle," which assumes an increase in capacity as long as prices are on an upswing, but no further expansion when prices are falling. Nor does it fit with the well-known concept of a backward-sloping supply curve which has been postulated by some economists. The latter assumes a tendency to study any reaction under the condition of farmers who do not evaluate their domestic labor costs. A fall in prices will induce those producers, aiming at a stable income, in monetary terms, to increase production regardless of those costs which they do not evaluate, by applying more labor force at the given capacity. In our case what actually did take place was a "long-run" extension, the establishment of which needs further capital and labor costs. (See discussion under "Economic Factors" in Chapter 3.)

There are two further approaches to explain the capacity increase in Brazil. One is to enquire into the trends of price ratios between competitive crops and the changes in acreage between competing crops, the other to follow up the trends of money prices paid to coffee producers. The former relationship will show the willingness of coffee growers to switch between different lines of production, provided that certain assumptions do apply to the situation as given. These assumptions are: that prices of inputs of all crops followed the same trend and magnitude; that technological changes in factor proportions have been more or less uniform in all crops concerned since the base years 1948-52, and that the price series supplied can to a significant extent serve as correct indicators for the prices received by the producers. The first condition can be assumed to be matched by the actual situation, since there has been no price discrimination in factor prices, i.e., for land, labor, and fertilizer for different lines of production, and land, labor, and fertilizer being completely substitutional between different uses. The second condition is almost impossible to observe. There is one study for the state of São Paolo, which states that technological changes of input in the competing crops have been almost uniform in relation to the application of fertilizers.[26] This study also states that yields per hectare on the basis of 1948-62 have been stable for coffee and corn, and slightly decreasing for rice and beans, while increases have been reported for cotton and sugar.[27] The last question needs further consideration since the data used are coffee prices paid by exporters at ports and the prices of all other crops are wholesale prices in capital towns of Brazil. It has been shown in Fig. 11 that the marketing cost margin between coffee prices paid by exporters and the prices received by producers kept almost stable. We have to allow as well for a similar margin between the wholesale prices for the competing crops and the prices received by the producers.

Given these conditions, a change in the relative prices for coffee should be the signal for farmers to shift resources, i.e., for the upkeep of capacity by pruning, weeding, etc. — by these methods changing the capacity of the neglected plantations without a deliberate effort to uproot — or actually to bring on a reaction by deliberate uprooting.

The trend of money prices is of importance if we assume a given capacity — that is, a number and state of health of trees — at the beginning of a crop year. Then costs of securing output in this crop year consists of the variable costs of picking only. Only so long as a profit between price and variable costs does not fall considerably lower than some normal profit per given unit of labor, will there be an incentive to producers to pick the crop. The "short-term" reaction of producers will thus depend on the development of money prices and costs for coffee. (This reasoning can be compared with the stock approach whereas the importance of the relative prices lies in the flow approach.)

Secondly, money prices may be an incentive if there are structural features in an economy which may induce producers to disregard their initial costs for labor and capital (i.e., as seen later). If so, the net profit position of a farmer consists of the difference between the current monetary prices and his current costs for variable factors. A comparatively large profit in relation to the "normal profit position" will then induce farmers to increase capacity.

Thirdly, domestic price policy of the IBC may be the cause for the relatively unfavorable price of other products compared to coffee. Figures 12 and 14 provide for a comparison between the price ratio of other agricultural crops to coffee of a grade going at São Paolo and Paraná respectively. Table 3 and Figure 18 show the trend of nominal prices for Santos 4 and Rio. Only if these two series are investigated separately can a price/output relationship be tested.

*The Long-term Reaction of Farmers: São Paolo.* To analyze the "long-run" reaction of farmers, data have been collected for São Paolo over a period of twenty years. They consist of money prices for coffee and other crops, the relative price for coffee and other crops, and the absolute as well as the relative coffee acreage in relation to other crops. The money prices for all crops can be found in a Study of the Rural Division of the State of São Paolo and will not be restated here.[28] An analysis of supply response to money prices is not possible here, since São Paolo is an economically developed state. The relative price of coffee has been expressed as an index, based on the average ratio of prices for certain crops and coffee in the period 1948-52 (Fig. 12). The trend of coffee acreage is given in Table 4 and Figure 10, and the trend in the relative changes of coffee acreages to that of competing crops is expressed in an index based on the average ratio of acreage in coffee and other crops in 1948-52 (Fig. 13). The crops selected have been stated to be competitive with coffee. Yet they give only an indication, since one major competing activity — breeding of cattle and livestock — has not been taken into account because of the lack of price series and figures of acreage in pasture. Further, the information on the trends since 1964 could not be spelled out in numbers, as they were not then available. That such a change in trend was persistent is stated in the latest reports available.

To allow for a comparison of trends, as discernible in the charts, these have been put together in Table 5.

### TABLE 5

Trends in Coffee Industry Data in São Paolo

(1948/52 - 1964)

| | Money Prices (1) | | Relative Prices (2) | | Coffee Acreage (3)      (4) | |
|---|---|---|---|---|---|---|
| | coffee | crops | coffee | crops | absolute | relative |
| 1948/52 - 1954 | rising | rising | rising | falling | rising | stable |
| 1954 - 1959 | rising | rising | falling | rising | rising | rising |
| 1959 - 1963 | rising | rising | falling | rising | falling | falling |
| 1963 - | rising | rising | rising | falling | rising | rising |

The comparison between the relative price of coffee (Column 2) and the absolute acreage of coffee (Column 3) should give a general picture of the "long-run" reaction of coffee farmers to a change in the relative price of coffee, that is, relative to prices for other agricultural products. This reaction should, given the existing condition in São Paolo, with all land cultivated, also show

Figure 12

## Price Ratio of Farm Products to Coffee, São Paulo
(index basis 1948 - 1952 = 100)

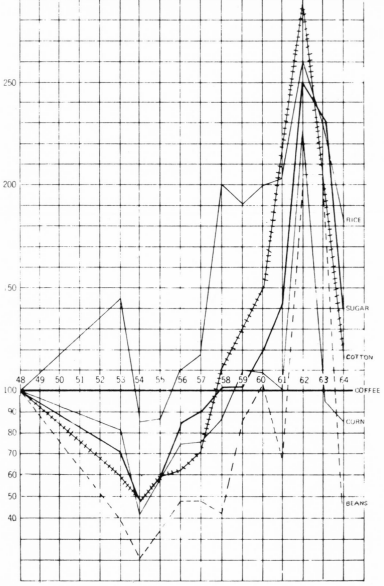

Source: Based on statistics from *Anuario Estatico do Brasil.*

Figure 13

## Acreage Ratio of Farm Products to Coffee, São Paulo (index basis 1948 - 1952 = 100)

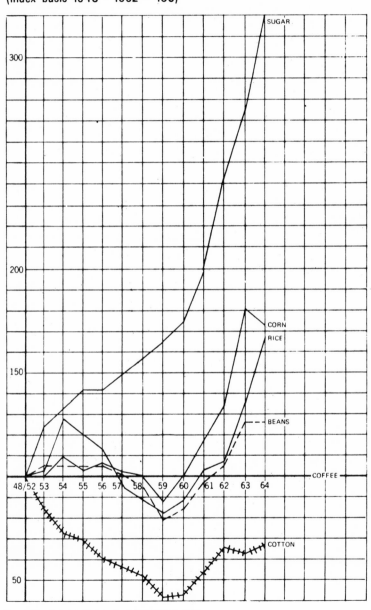

Source: Based on statistics from *Anuario Estatico do Brasil.*

the shifts between the various uses of land. That is illustrated in the relative ratio of coffee land to acreage of competing crops as displayed in Column 4. A comparison of Column 2 with Column 3 reveals an absolute decrease of coffee capacity when the relative price for coffee was falling and the opposite reaction to increases in the ratio. The same positive reaction of relative coffee area applies in these two periods. Thus the comparison suggests, that the "long-run" reaction of farmers in São Paolo to changes in the relative price of coffee was positive and that producers changed their acreage without a lag. This gives a general picture of the "long-run" adaptation to a change in the relative price of coffee, taking into consideration that certain lags in the response of acreage to changes in the price differential may represent statistical lags of one year.[29]

The observation based on the time series data is confirmed by GERCA,[30] which states: "Uprooting was particularly extensive in 1962-63 not only on account of frost, but also because domestic prices were relatively low. The 1964-65 rise in the domestic prices brought about a drop in the rate of uprootings in 1964 to 1963. In addition it would seem that the rate of replanting, which was especially low in 1962 and 1963, rose in the end of 1964 because of improvement in domestic prices; in 1965 a large increase in planting was observed in several of the main coffee growing areas."[31] This estimate of the capacity decrease due to low domestic prices to producers in São Paolo takes into account that frosts and droughts are a normal feature of coffee production in Brazil. It is therefore the rate of replanting and rehabilitation which shows the influence of relative domestic price changes to production in the "long-run." Under "no-frost" conditions the rate of replanting should be large enough to offset capacity losses because of age and diseases. With frost the ratio should rise because of additional frost rehabilitation to offset the loss, provided domestic prices remain remunerative and the farmers base their decision on the price ruling. It has already been stated that "the rate of replanting and rehabilitation was especially low in 1962 and 1963 and rose in 1964-65. . ." Since the figures used in Figure 10 show the net position of trees it can be assumed that the continuous decrease of capacity reflected the reactions of production — due to the special feature of coffee production — to relative prices in São Paolo. The picture of a positive "long-run" reaction of farmers in three of four periods observed is getting less clear for the period between 1954 and 1959, when, as shown in Table 5, the decreasing relative price of coffee was matched by an increase in coffee capacity or a decrease of competing crops respectively, which would make for an "inverse reaction" of farmers. To put this inverse behavior in the right perspective, it seems useful to look at Figures 12 and 13, and the development of monetary prices for all crops respectively. Monetary prices for all crops were increasing between 1954 and 1959. Yet the heavy price increase in 1954 for coffee without a following lowering of the price in line with world market quotations put the relative prices of coffee into a much better position in relation to the prices of all competing crops than was enjoyed in the previous four-year period (Fig. 12). As late as 1958-60 the previous position was regained by other crops, making in 1959-60 for an "equal net return position per unit of expenditure,"[32] between competing crops. It thus paid the farmer to go into coffee production, despite the slowly decreasing trend of relative coffee prices. It may be added, the equalization of net returns also backs the choice of 1948-52 as a basis of comparison. There are other strong points: firstly, there was no inflation in Brazil in that period and thus no distortion of the cost of production due to inflation. Secondly, all crops produced were sold at the going price and there were no leftover stocks. Lastly, Brazil's coffee capacity was reduced during World War II and the capacity for coffee production remained at that level for a considerable period of time.[33] All three points would lead to the assumption that net return to unit of expenditure were again equal. Taking these points into consideration, the "long-run" reaction of farmers in São Paolo seems to have been rational and relied upon an assessment of net returns per unit of expenditure in different crops.

*Paraná*. The development in Paraná is shown in Figures 14 and 15. As in the analysis in São Paolo, comparison is made between money prices for coffee and competing crops, their relative prices and the trends in absolute and relative coffee acreage. The trends as shown in these charts have been put together in Table 6.

| TABLE 6 | | | | | |
|---|---|---|---|---|---|
| Trends in Coffee Industry Data in Paraná | | | | | |
| (1948/52-1964) | | | | | |
| | **Money Prices** | | **Relative Prices** | | **Acreage Coffee** | |
| | **coffee** | **crops** | **coffee** | **crops** | **absolute** | **relative** |
| 1948/52 - 1954 | rising | rising | rising | falling | rising | stable |
| 1954 - 1958 | rising | rising | stable | stable | rising | rising |
| 1958 - 1961 | rising | rising | falling | rising | rising | stable |

Trends are distinguishable until 1961, but afterward there are changes from one year to the other covering more than one year, which cannot be put into a table. These developments may be followed on Figures 14 and 15. We are going to examine first the relationship between relative prices for coffee and absolute acreage of that crop: Reactions of farmers are positive in the period of 1948-54, and an increase of acreage is reported since 1964-65, which would accompany the increase in relative coffee prices since 1963, allowing for a one-year lag in statistics. No such positive reaction can be gathered for the period 1954-58, when the stable relative price for coffee did not discourage a further increase in coffee acreage. An inverse reaction occurs in the period 1958-62, due to capacity increase in Paraná. It may well be, that as in São Paolo the net returns were still more remunerative for coffee than the corresponding net returns from alternative uses of the same resources in the period 1954-58. And this proposition may hold good a further two years if, as in the case of São Paolo, the 1948-52 ratio of prices indicates a certain equlaization of net returns in Paraná. In this case a change of trend in 1962 would be due to the change in the net return position between different crops and imply a positive reaction of farmers to net returns. The statistical picture in Figure 14 would back up such reasoning. Yet no information concerning net returns comparable to the statement in São Paolo for the years 1958-59 could be obtained for Paraná. The hypothesis that the 1948-52 price ratio is an indication of an equilibrium over such a long period is highly improbable.

This picture suggests that the relative price has not been − at least till 1964-65 − the indicator of sole importance in regard to the agricultural production structure of Paraná. Analyzing other possible incentives, certain other structural features of the economy of Paraná may be helpful. It has been stated that (a) Paraná is a state in which at least until 1964 a considerable amount of land had not been cultivated at all[34] and (b) that the whole of Paraná was not connected to the marketing areas for domestic consumption of agricultural products in a way comparable to São Paolo till about 1962-63,[35] when further roads were opened up. Furthermore it is important in this case to note that Brazil was suffering from a heavy inflation in the period under review which, as has been observed in other countries, leads people to buy land as a means of hedging against the devaluation of their currency. Land free for this purpose was available only in the North of Paraná, the so-called Newest Zone, which is the region in Paraná most removed from centers of domestic food consumption and not fully connected with those regions. Costs of production (opportunity costs) of land were thus zero and the farmer's incentive not influenced by a comparison with net returns

**Figure 14**

Price Ratio of Farm Products to Coffee, Paraná (index basis 1948 - 1952 = 100)

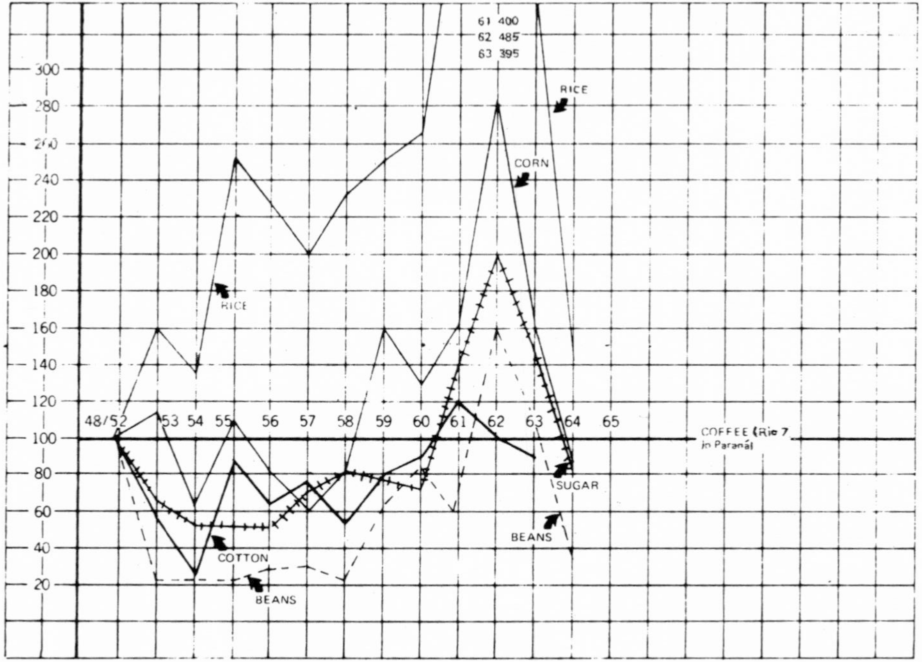

Source: Based on statistics from *Anuário Estatico do Brasil*,

**Figure 15**

# Acreage Ratio of Farm Products to Coffee, Paraná
## (index basis 1948-52=100)

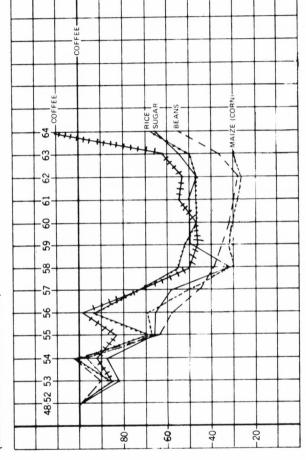

Source: Based on statistics from *Anuario Estatico do Brasil.*

Figure 16

# Price Indexes of Coffee, Fertilizers, and
# Other Agricultural Products (base: 1953=100)

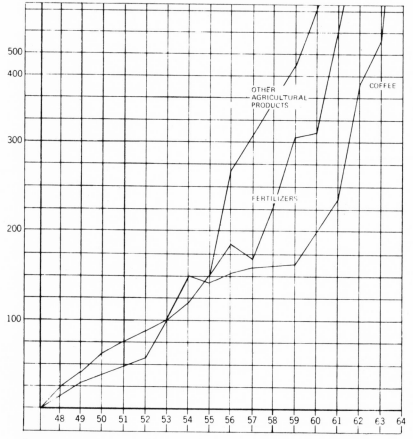

Source: Statistics from *Conjunctura Economica*.

**Figure 17**

# Real Coffee Prices

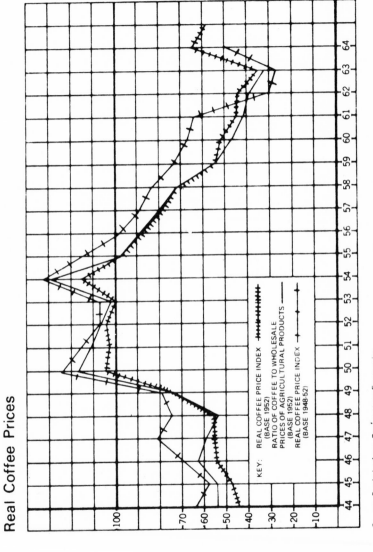

KEY: REAL COFFEE PRICE INDEX ++++++
(BASE 1952)
RATIO OF COFFEE TO WHOLESALE ——
PRICES OF AGRICULTURAL PRODUCTS
(BASE 1952)
REAL COFFEE PRICE INDEX +++++++
(BASE 1948-52)

Source: Statistics from *Coyuntura Economica.*

in alternative crops. Additionally, if the reaction of the planter to inflation fits the facts as well in Brazil then it is only the current variable costs which have to be taken into account to establish the net profit position of a coffee grower in the more remote "Newest Zone." It is then the trend of the money prices for coffee and of current variable costs which determine his profit position. No cost figures are available, but the development of acreage suggests that the yearly increases of money prices for coffee in Paraná have been large enough to secure a profit sufficient to induce owners of coffee land (acquired as a hedge against inflation) to take up production of coffee. It has been stated that the high capacity increases in Paraná were due to the planting in this region. Since no statistics for the different areas are available, in Paraná as a whole both influences need to be taken into consideration to come to a conclusive hypothesis in regard to the statistical picture presented.

The development since 1962 has to be evaluated in the light of the IBC policy change toward incentives for quality changes of output, and will be dealt with below. Putting all this together, the development of domestic money and relative prices to coffee producers suggest a positive relationship between the domestic money prices for coffee relative both to other crops and to the trend of capacity. A comparison between world market prices and/or real domestic prices deflated by either a general cost-of-living index or an index of fertilizer prices or wage levels (Figs. 16, 17) would suggest "perverse" reaction of producers to price decreases through an extension of capacity. Recalling the reasoning concerning these relationships it has been shown that such a relationship need not necessarily apply, and an alternative hypothesis can be formulated with equally logical support.

This leaves again, as in São Paolo, the question of price influence or weather conditions to be considered as causal factors. Using the same reasoning, the average reaction in cultivated acreage must include the average acreage decrease, due to the weather factors minus the amount of rehabilitating or replanting.

The whole of Paraná was hit by bad weather conditions in the years 1962-1964/65. Given the structural conditions in Paraná it is only the farmer in the still more remote area who would have tried to replant in these years, whereas the farmer in the older zones as well as in those opened since 1962, faced with deteriorating relative prices for coffee, did not feel the incentive to do so until the end of 1964. This reasoning is backed by the development of acreage in Paraná in 1954 and 1956.

In Paraná trees were usually planted which give a very high yield two or three years after they are set as seedlings.[36] Therefore, the exceptional increase in output from 1958 to 1960 must mirror the increase in planting over 1953-54.[37] Secondly, this state is considered marginal for coffee growing, because of the periodic occurrence of frost, but the quality of soils and the topography are especially favorable.[38] It was, in fact, exposed to several severe frosts in the marketing years 1954-55 and 1956-57. The increase of net existing capacity in 1954-55 and 1956-57 could only have been achieved by a very intensive rehabilitation of frostbitten trees. Coffee economists state that these processes are extremely labor-intensive.[39] They must have required very high expenditures, since wage costs in Brazil constitute by far the largest share in the total costs of an already established plantation and more than 60 percent of the crop in Paraná is raised in production units which need hired labor.[40]

**Short-term Reactions of Farmers.** We have now to discuss the nature of the short-term response of farmers. It should be noted that "short-term" is used here in the economic sense, that is not defined by the length of the time period between the change of price and the reaction, but by the adjustment of production through changes of variable factors from a given capacity in the form of more careful picking or more intensive cultivation. This concept can be meaningfully employed if the input of variables to keep capacity at a given level can be subtracted. The practical application of such a concept requires us to look into the different outputs at a given capacity during the period under review.

## TABLE 7

### Prices, Acreage, and Output Changes in Brazil

| Year | Coffee Prices | | Acreage | Output |
|------|------|------|------|------|
| | **Monetary** | **Relative** | | |
| 1946 - 1953 | rising | stable | + 18% | + 33% |
| 1953 - 1955 | rising | rising | + 5% | + 33% |
| 1955 - 1959 | rising | falling but more remunerative than other crops | + 30% | + 82% |
| 1959 - 1962 | rising | falling and not remunerative to other crops | + 4% | - 25% |

A comparison of output and acreage figures in Brazil, Paraná, and São Paolo is given in Figures 9 and 10. The changes are summarized in Table 7.

To determine short-term reactions appears to be a most difficult task with the information available. Output depends on various factors such as weather, acreage of trees, and the age composition of trees. The latter two may change capacity considerably, even if acreage remains stable between the years in which outputs are compared. The obvious higher increase in percentage output as opposed to capacity increases in the period between 1946 and 1960 may mirror changes in all these factors. It would thus be pure guesswork to argue that this trend explains short-term reactions of farmers, added to their long-term responses. Yet there are two examples that can be meaningfully exploited for a comparison.

One is the change of output in the years between 1952-54 and 1955-56. The price trend was one of doubling the monetary price and a steep increase in the relative price. Capacity stood at 7.2 million acres in 1952-54. In 1954, Brazil was hit by a frost. This even affected trees of all ages. The fast rate of replanting and rehabilitation increased capacity, despite the frost, to 8.0 million acres, that is, by about 10 percent, the age composition of which must have changed to relatively younger trees or trees not yet recovered to full bearing after rehabilitation. Both factors should have made for a lower output than in 1952-54, even if 1955-56 had been a good crop year. Yet despite that, output increased in 1955-56 by more than 33 percent in relation to 1952-54. Relying on these figures, one has to assume that the larger part has been a result of the price increase.[41] The influence of a relative slow increase in monetary prices for coffee and falling relative price is given in the changes in output between the years 1958-60 and 1960-62. Capacity increased since 1954 to 1960 by about 3 million acres − that is, about 35 percent of the 1954 capacity and in 1960-62 by a further 4 percent. In relation to this, one would have expected output to rise continually in 1960-62, if farmers were unresponsive in the short run to price changes. Yet output decreased by about 25 percent in relation to the crop years 1958-59 and 1959-60.

Both examples suggest that there is a short-term reaction of supply to prices and that the elasticity of supply in the short-run seems to be much higher than an analysis of trends in world market prices and Brazilian output as a whole suggests.[42]

Other reasons given as an explanation of the output trends between 1960 and 1964-65 are based on the bad weather conditions in the crop years 1962, 1963, and 1964. Reference is normally made to yield figures, based on IBC or FAO estimates. However, it has to be kept in mind that these figures are not obtained as actual yield figures, but are the statistical ratio between output and acreage. Since output can be influenced as much by price reactions of farmers as by weather conditions, the figures reported cannot be used to support either of the suggested causes that have been put forward.

As already explained in the long-term analysis, there is no doubt that bad weather conditions reduced output in these years. But certain indications as reported by observers in Brazil itself can be used to back up the hypothesis that the short-run reaction to declining monetary and relative prices did play a part:

(1) The comparative output between the crop year of 1959-60 and 1960-61 showed a decrease in the latter of some 25 percent despite the fact that acreage did increase and that the 1960-61 crop year was mentioned as an oustandingly good year.[43]

(2) Frequent reports of observers on the spot show that picking was not as complete as in the years before.[44]

(3) If we assume the differences between 1961-62 and 1960-61 and from 1962 onward as partly attributable to bad weather conditions and compare the average for 1956-57 to 1960-61 with that of 1960/61-1963/64, a decrease of 10 percent took place in spite of huge additional capacities which came into increasing or new productive stages.

**Policy Evaluation.** Concluding our analysis, the domestic price policy of the IBC has to be evaluated against the background of the "long-run elasticity of supply" hypothesis, which has been developed in the preceding pages, and also against the possibility of a positive reaction of farmers in the short run to price changes. Both hypotheses are important: Long-term decisions have increased coffee production in Brazil and have led to the accumulation of a coffee surplus. Short-term reactions, such as the rehabilitation of frost-damaged trees in 1953-54 and 1956-57 have added to the problem.

The development of the money prices is shown in Table 3. It is also obvious from Figures 12 and 14 that the increase of the relative price of coffee in Brazil has been the result of the IBC's decision to raise the price for domestic producers by comparatively higher amounts than the changes in world market prices allowed for and to stabilize the price on the domestic market at a level reached during the boom period of world market prices. It has been stated by a UN investigation[45] that, in order of importance, changes in the exchange rate,[46] the higher domestic minimum price for coffee, and the buying for coffee inventories by the IBC were causes of inflation till 1958. The high and stable monetary prices for coffee have thus been one cause for the steady increase of prices of other crops, which accelerated with the resulting domestic inflation. It follows that the coffee prices since 1953 were thus relatively too high in comparison with the relative level of other crops — prices attained before inflation started in Brazil. The situation after 1958[47] was again analyzed by the United Nations and it was stated that it was primarily through the financing of the inventory buying, which increased tremendously as a result of the larger crops after 1958-59 only in order to keep the domestic coffee prices up, that inflation was accelerated, which led to a faster increase in prices for other crops at this time. The effect of the rate of increase of inventory buying should then show itself in a higher rate of price rises for other crops in relation to coffee prices than between 1954 and 1959.

Relying on the United Nations results and our analysis, the excess capacity of the oligopolistic seller can thus be regarded as artificially created, not by the farmers' inverse reaction or induced through the upswing of world market prices until 1954, but as a result of his own — that is, the Brazilian Government's — price support policy on the domestic market. Both reactions of supply caused the larger part of the increasing capacity, which affected the record crops after 1958-59. Furthermore, it seems that the trends of the relative domestic coffee price in Brazil both for exportable and non-exportable grades until 1960 induced producers to utilize their capacity fully. The record crops in Brazil that created the surplus situation in the world coffee economy seem thus to be mainly a result of the domestic support policy of the Brazilian Government,[48] and the normal reaction of supply to these incentives. Thus the argument that the excess capacity as well as the excess output of the Brazilian coffee economy is an inevitable result of a coffee cycle does not appear to be defensible. We do not deny the existence of any such cycle, but stress the point that the surplus output in 1957-63 has obviously not been the result of a price development on the world market for coffee.

A second aspect of the price policy of the oligopolistic seller on the domestic market was that it applied to a particular product.

In order to consider the causative factors, one has to fall back on to the differences between the production in São Paolo and Paraná. Three factors are well established:

(1) Because of better soil, yields per tree in Paraná are on the average twice as high as in São Paolo.[49]

(2) "With higher yields the outgoings per bag tend to fall more than proportionally, unless higher yields are only obtained by proportionally increased expenditure, e.g., on fertilizer and better cultivation generally."[50]

(3) The difference in coffee types and grades depends on the quality of pruning and picking and further measures like wet-processing and more careful preparation during the drying process of the beans. The quality of green coffee is a function of factor inputs for these purposes.[51]

Against this it had been the price policy of the IBC to keep the price differentials between the more carefully produced São Paolo beans of good type and coffee of a Rio 7 type at about 20 percent to 30 percent (Fig. 18). The price of the lower grade coffee of a non-exportable quality was near the Rio 7 quotations. Furthermore "the IBC fixed the proportion of expurgo coffee [between 1958-61] at 10 percent of the crop whereas the grade really is only about 7 percent. In order to provide the retention quota of four bags for every six bags exported, sellers of exportable coffee paid by up to cr. 2000 for rights of expurgo and so with the IBC price to domestic producers it paid to produce the lowest grade, by this providing a direct stimulus to produce poor quality."[52]

110

# Ratio of Prices, Santos 4-Rio 7

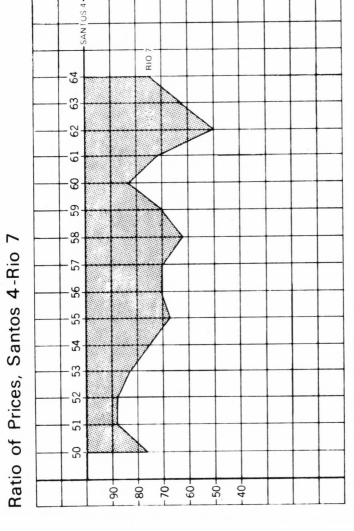

Source: Statistics from *Conjunctura Economica*.

Several other authors agree that the accent of the IBC's policy has been on quantity and not on quality.

Considering the difference in type and grade to be dependent on costs of processing and that yields per tree are also higher in Paraná one would assume that the price differential was too small to discourage production of higher grade coffee. This assumption has been backed by field research, which showed that costs of production in São Paolo were higher than in Paraná in 1961-62, at a given production structure of low grade coffee in Paraná and high grade in São Paolo. Correspondingly, the coffee production in Paraná yielded a higher profit than in São Paolo.[53] It thus seems a plausible hypothesis that the price policy of the oligopolistic seller Brazil on the world market induced an increase of output mainly in Paraná, with a crop regarded as inferior in world demand because of its bitter taste, which is again a result of a low quality picking and processing at the farm level. The policy thus created an excess capacity for a special type of production.

As indicated in the structural analysis, the IBC became aware of this problem and introduced a policy of discrimination against lower grade coffee with the beginning of the crop year 1961-62, as mentioned earlier. The output of Paraná, despite an increase in capacity in the years 1959-62, suggests — with the reservations described above — that the disincentives may have accounted for this development of output. But by 1963 this policy "was not maintained"[54] and "the differential in price paid for coffee to be exported or to be stored came again to be quite small."[55]

In line with this policy of a "weak government to the pressure of coffee growers,"[56] the nominal price for coffee was set again in 1964 and 1965 in such a way that the deflated price in coffee rose for the first time since 1954 and the relative price for coffee became as favorable to the producers as in the years 1958-60. As indicated already, an increase in net planting for coffee is taking place and the diversification of coffee land and other factor inputs to competitive uses has been slowed down.

**Brazil Since 1964.** In retrospect, the renewed record crop in

1965-66 bore excessive evidence of the changes in the incentive policy of Brazil. Production, however, from then on, declined constantly and has led to the beginning of an alleged shortage of world coffee supplies (Table 8; Figs. 19, 20). World market prices in late 1969 started to rise and since then have maintained a level approximately 20 percent above that of the first five years of the International Coffee Agreement.

It is a moot question whether this change in the Brazilian production pattern reflected a proper adjustment of farmers to a policy of disinvestment in coffee or the impact of unpredictable natural disasters, i.e., frosts and droughts. Official comments are unclear and do not provide sufficient comprehensive analysis for either views presented though from the former sources and others it appears that frosts and droughts have been the decisive factors. Early in 1969 an unofficial analysis of replanting rates predicted increases in yields from newly planted trees and in the total area under coffee in the four major producing areas of Brazil and indicated that replanting in all areas was sufficient to maintain output at approximately the 1966-67 level, if not slightly above it. On the other hand, in some 20 percent of all coffee farms, accounting for approximately 8 to 10 percent of the total Brazilian output, yields per acre were below levels necessary to carry costs of production. The study indicated that on account of these latter factors production under maintenance of the then existing price policies might decline by 10 percent as compared to the 1966-67 crop and then remain at approximately 18 million bags. If this estimate can stand up against further scrutiny it seems beyond doubt that natural disasters have been responsible for the downswing in production observed over the last ten years. The future potential in Brazil, therefore, would depend strongly not on the rate of replanting and new planting only but also on the additional abilities of farmers to rehabilitate trees damaged by frosts and droughts. As in 1954-57, the incentives provided may, however, be also sufficient to allow the rehabilitation of frostbitten trees. On the basis of the above analysis, an upswing in the Brazilian production within the next two to three years could be expected. An average production of 25 million bags, as planned by the Brazilian authority as a medium-term production goal would seem to be a realistic medium-term projection of Brazilian's output.

Stocks of a magnitude of 60 million bags estimated as existing in 1967-68 by the International Coffee Organization should have been sufficient to avoid any drop in the volume of exports of Brazilian coffee that might result from drought and frosts (Table 9). However, the question of quality as discussed in our earlier analysis has had impact on the stocks declared as "exportable surplus." We have argued that Brazil's stocks should, on the whole, contain a high percentage of low grade coffees, produced in Paraná and not of quality which could be sold on the world market at the common quality of Brazil's exports, i.e., Santos 4/5. Recently Brazil has announced that its stocks of "exportable" quality amounted to 36 million bags, or 40 percent below the calculated stock level of 59.3 million bags, calculated on initial stocks, production, and disappearances in the period 1964-65 to 1968. The key question that needs to be considered here is whether this reduction has been due to spoilage of beans while stored or due to the already low quality of beans at the time when purchased by IBC for storage. Brazilian authorities, as well as observers, have constantly claimed that coffee stocking in Brazil was done in storage facilities and under climatic conditions – i.e., in dry areas which should prevent any serious decline in the quality of beans while stocked. The new stock announcement as of early 1970 would, therefore, seem to support our hypothesis of low-quality surplus production in Brazil as of 1959 to 1964, though it is impossible at this time to ascertain this fact, because of lack of more precise information on the reasons why Brazil reduced its stock estimate.

**The Effects of the Brazilian Price Policy on the World Market.** An analysis of the impact of the Brazilian export policy has to be made in three steps. The first is to establish that it is possible to evaluate the statistical performance of the world market price quotations as a result of the export policy of the various producing countries. If it can be shown that such a causal relationship exists, the second step would be to deduce a meaningful "market price hypothesis" or conduct principle of the different "primary sellers," which can be used in the last step to explain the different price moves of "primary sellers" in regard to their parameters of action as oligopolists.

This chapter deals only with the first step. It examines the world market effects of the export price policy of the Brazilian authorities. The reasoning in relation to the first point has to fall back on the analysis of market structure in Chapter 4. Generally the performance of a market is the result of the conduct of competitors. Using the most simplified model, pure competition in a homogeneous market, the share of a single seller or buyer is so small that a change in his volume or selling price does not influence the supply to or the price in the market to a significant extent.[57] This is a unique model and other models of price formation, i.e., of imperfect competition, assume the market share of one producer or seller to be so large that his decision in regard to his conduct influences the price on the market.

The market structure of the world coffee industry showed three main imperfections, as has been said. The first is the fact that coffee is a non-homogeneous product and that the different types of coffee are each the products of one specific country: Brazil is the sole producer of Brazils, Colombia of Mams, while Milds of lower quality and Robustas are produced by more than one country. The second conclusion of our structural analysis was that all governments were able by using various devices to influence the export price of their domestic crop. The basic market structure of the first-hand sellers is therefore one of oligopolism on the supply side in a market with differentiated products, i.e, the market structure is a "differentiated oligopoly." In such a market it is the conduct of each oligopolist in relation to the parameters of action or reaction, i.e., the amount of the individual country's export volume at export price, the amount of the individual country's

Figure 19

Coffee: World Exportable Production, Brazil, Other Than
Latin America, and Africa (million bags of 60 kg.)

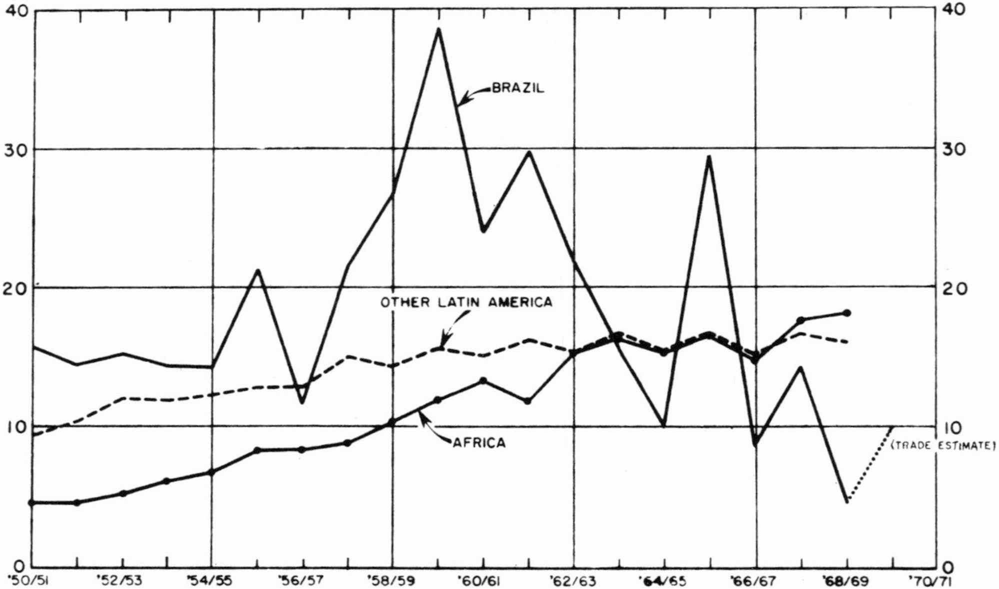

Sources: From 1950/51 to 1962/63, Pan-American Coffee Bureau Statistics; from 1963/64 to 1968/69, U.S. Department
of Agriculture Statistics; from 1957/58 to 1968/69, Brazilian figures shown in the above-mentioned sources have been
adjusted to agree with IBC and Brazilian trade figures resulting in adjusted world totals.

Figure 20

# World Supply and Demand for Coffee, 1946/47 – 1969/70
## (million bags of 60 kg.)

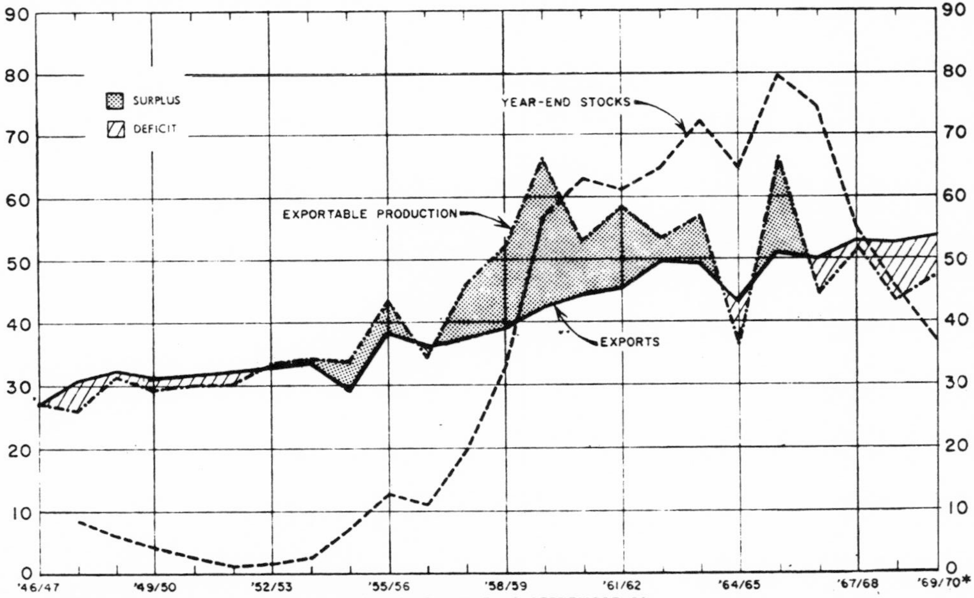

YEAR-END STOCKS

EXPORTABLE PRODUCTION

EXPORTS

SURPLUS

DEFICIT

90 80 70 60 50 40 30 20 10 0

'46/47 '49/50 '52/53 '55/56 '58/59 '61/62 '64/65 '67/68 '69/70*

COFFEE YEAR ENDING SEPTEMBER 30

Note: In recent years some of the stocks were not of exportable quality.
Source: Based on USDA data, supplemented by Net Exports estimates for 1965-69 and 1969/70 from ICO.
*Estimate

117

export volume or export price, which determines the world market price for his type of coffee. This applies unilaterally in the longer run (as a time period)[58] to the exports of Brazil and Colombia, whereas the price of lower quality Milds (FEDECAMA) depends on the collusive behavior of all FEDECAMA producers, and the price of Robustas on the collusive behavior of all African states. The only possible causal explanation of the world market

## TABLE 8

### Postwar Trends in Coffee Production

|  | 1946/47-<br>1968-69 | 1946/47-<br>1962/63 | 1962/63-<br>1968/69 |
|---|---|---|---|
|  | percent per annum | | |
| **Exportable Production** | | | |
| World (excluding Brazil) | 5.5 | 6.5 | 1.4 |
| World | 3.8 | 5.6 | -2.5 |
| **Harvested Production** | | | |
| World (excluding Brazil) | 5.3 | 6.0 | 1.9 |
| World | 3.8 | 5.2 | -1.1 |
|  | 1946/47-<br>1969/70 | | 1962/63-<br>1969/70 |
| **Harvested Production<br>by Types** | | | |
| Colombian Milds | 2.4 | 2.8 | 0.2 |
| Other Milds | 4.3 | 4.8 | 1.1 |
| Unwashed Arabicas | 1.9 | 4.7 | -4.8 |
| Robustas | 8.3 | 10.0 | 1.6 |

**Note:** Growth rates calculated from log Y = a + bt applied to a three-year moving average for columns 1 and 2; average growth rate from year to year change from column 3.

**Source:** Data from Pan-American Coffee Bureau.

# TABLE 9

## End-of-Year Carryover Stocks
## of ICO Member Countries
## 1964-65 to 1968-69

**thousand 60-kg bags**

| | 1964/65 | 1965/66 | 1966/67 | 1967/68 | 1968/69 |
|---|---|---|---|---|---|
| **Colombian Milds** | **3,966** | **5,065** | **5,832** | **5,727** | **5,386** |
| Colombia | 3,589 | 4,746 | 5,369 | 5,499 | 5,050 |
| Others | 377 | 319 | 463 | 228 | 336 |
| **Other Milds** | **2,922** | **2,774** | **2,790** | **2,995** | **2,680** |
| Ecuador | 400 | 506 | 105 | 149 | 202 |
| El Salvador | 413 | 521 | 201 | 481 | 346 |
| Guatemala | 484 | 44 | 298 | 139 | 79 |
| Honduras | 8 | 0 | 0 | 138 | 203 |
| India | 353 | 502 | 574 | 310 | 299 |
| Mexico | 309 | 418 | 722 | 1,002 | 933 |
| Peru | 484 | 672 | 482 | 477 | 417 |
| Others | 471 | 111 | 408 | 299 | 201 |
| **Unwashed Arabicas** | **56,074** | **68,512** | **64,453** | **60,936** | **48,365** |
| Brazil | 55,274 | 67,236 | 62,977 | 59,288 | 46,586 |
| Ethiopia | 800 | 1,276 | 1,476 | 1,645 | 1,771 |
| Others | 0 | 0 | 0 | 3 | 8 |
| **Robustas** | **6,928** | **6,337** | **5,231** | **7,089** | **6,793** |
| Congo (D.R.) | 534 | 329 | 478 | 350 | 551 |
| Indonesia | n.a. | n.a. | 500 | 1,100 | 400 |
| Cameroon | 262 | 304 | 246 | 230 | 350 |
| Ivory Coast | 2,005 | 2,527 | 207 | 1,592 | 715 |
| Portugal (Angola) | 2,804 | 2,304 | 2,490 | 2,890 | 2,000 |
| Uganda | 1,102 | 823 | 919 | 416 | 1,848 |
| Others | 221 | 50 | 491 | 511 | 929 |
| Total | 69,890 | 82,688 | 78,306 | 76,747 | 63,224 |
| Total (excluding Brazil) | 14,600 | 15,450 | 15,330 | 17,460 | 16,640 |

**Source:** International Coffee Organization.

# TABLE 10

## Brazilian Stocks at End of Year

|         | I.B.C. | Private |
|---------|--------|---------|
| 1953-54 | –      | 3.3     |
| 1954-55 | 2.9    | 3.3     |
| 1955-56 | 3.8    | 6.7     |
| 1956-57 | 3.7    | 3.7     |
| 1957-58 | 13.4   | x       |
| 1958-59 | –      | x       |
| 1959-60 | 34.9   | x       |
| 1960-61 | 42.9   | x       |
| 1961-62 | 55.1   | x       |
| 1962-63 | 60.3   | x       |
| 1963-64 | 57.6   | x       |
| 1964-65 | 55.3   | x       |

**Source:** UN Economic Survey 1957, *op. cit.,* p. 124; ICO: ICC-7-5, November 11, 1965, p. 4.

price quotations for Brazils and Colombian Milds is thus the conduct of the statutory agencies of the countries concerned. The price quotations on the New York Exchange are therefore the result of the export policy of these producing countries. It is important to understand that world market prices cannot be regarded as prices given to the producing countries at the oligopolistic market structure prevailing at the world coffee market.

This reasoning is not impeded by the fact that the world coffee market is one of differentiated oligopoly with various non-homogeneous products and varying degrees of price elasticity of substitution. In such a market structure, a change of one price differential due to either a deliberate change in the price of one seller or a change in the demand of this product is bound to affect not only the demand for the product whose price has been changed, but also the demand for all other types of coffee. But it is only demand which is affected, and a resulting change of price of all other types then depends on the reacting behavior of supplies of the other types. If there is no reaction the world market price of all types is bound to change. If there is a reaction, e.g., if supply changes, the price effect of a change in demand can be offset by a change in market supply.

The bases for determination for the IBC were the domestic minimum price and its dollar equivalent, due to the special foreign exchange rates for coffee receipts in dollars, and the domestic retention policy. It is possible to distinguish between two distinct periods, if we want to analyze the influence of the price policy of the primary sellers on the development of the world market price.

(1) If one compares the dollar equivalent of the domestic minimum price with the world market price for Brazilian coffees, it can be shown that the domestic export minimum price (that is, the domestic minimum price times the ruling coffee exchange rate) stood below the quotations announced at the New York Coffee Exchange.[59] Direct price maintenance for Brazilian coffee on the world market in the period before 1954 is not discernible using these instruments and stocks were non-existent.[60] An indirect result of the heavy export taxation or taxation of domestic producers may have been influential, reducing the output of the Brazilian coffee economy and thus increasing the price for those types on the Exchange.

(2) During the second period, 1954-55 until the present, Brazil employed its retention policy and built up stocks, buying directly from farmers in the interior as well as from exporters at ports (Table 10). The volume of exports flowing to the world market was thus artificially reduced and world market prices influenced.

A note regarding the method of analyzing this influence may be added. Given the market structure, the world market quotation must show the influence of the "retention-policy-conduct" of

Brazil on the quotations of Brazils. It is thus not meaningful to try to establish time series data for both the trend of domestic minimum prices, foreign exchange rates, and export prices and on the other hand world market quotations. Both series must move together, with small exceptions as analyzed later, and the statistical picture cannot reveal which price has been the causative factor for the development of the price series. Furthermore, whereas stock figures are available to prove that Brazil retained part of her production, there are no time series of domestic minimum prices, or detailed information on export minimum prices in those years when they were set by the IBC. Yet information, collected piecemeal from various sources, may give a tentative picture of the factual "export-minimum price." The latter was about 75 cents in 1953-54. A change in the exchange rate in 1955 let the equivalent export price decrease to 50 cents per pound, despite the fact that domestic prices to producers were improved.

In 1957 a direct export minimum was reinstituted for a time, but was soon abolished and the old system maintained. Since 1958 the exchange rate has been handled so as to maintain the world market price at about 40 cents per pound.

Price-fixing for primary exports of Brazils — that is, the setting of the export price in the form of a fixed "surrender" price or the domestic minimum price times the foreign exchange rate — influenced the magnitude of the price differentials on the world market as can be seen at Figure 22. The interesting feature here is that there were substantial changes in the price differentials in the time period under review, which are shown in absolute terms, in Figure 24. The percentage change between Brazils and Robustas is shown in Figure 25A, the percentage change between Brazils and Milds in 25B. It is interesting to note here the increase in the differential between Robustas and Brazils since 1954, some 25 percent against the differential of 1950-54, and the decrease between 1956 and 1958. Figure 25B shows the unusually small difference in 1954 and 1957-58 between Brazils and Mams (Colombian Milds) and the decrease in the price differential

**Figure 21**

# Brazil: Exportable Production,
## Exports and Prices (semi-logarithmic scale)

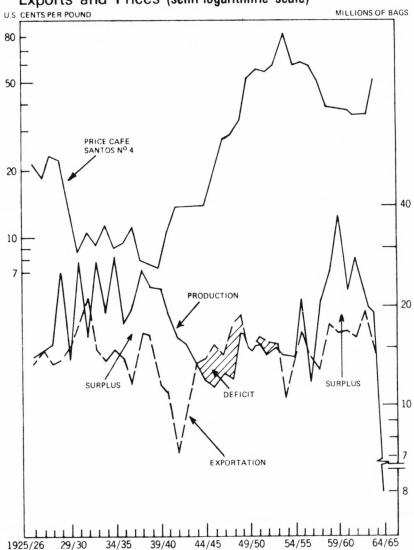

U.S. CENTS PER POUND

MILLIONS OF BAGS

PRICE CAFE
SANTOS Nº 4

PRODUCTION

SURPLUS

DEFICIT

SURPLUS

EXPORTATION

1925/26    29/30    34/35    39/40    44/45    49/50    54/55    59/60    64/65

Source: Pan American Coffee Bureau.

123

between Brazils and FEDECAMA Milds (Mexico Milds are a representative quotation) since 1961. If our structure of substitution on the three-sectoral market, described earlier, applies, these changes of the price differential should have changed the structure of imports and consumption of different types. No such information is available in regard to consumption, and for this analysis of the effect of changes in the price differential we have to use import figures.

The results will be investigated on the U.S. market, which is the main selling market for Brazilian coffees, competing with the substitutional types of African Robustas as well as Central American Milds.* It is meaningful to choose the U.S. market for such an analysis, because per capita consumption of green coffee remained stable from 1954 to 1960 and national income was almost stable, making for an increasing total consumption of green coffee at a stable rate (Fig. 26). In evaluating the changes in the import structure it is therefore possible to eliminate the effect of income changes, and changes in the consumption per head in the period after 1954, as causative factors of change in total consumption or imports into the United States. Structural changes in imports are thus completely dependent on changes in the general price level of all coffees as well as the structure of relative prices of different types of coffee.

The structure of coffee imports by types in the United States is described in Figure 26, which gives the imports by three main types: Milds, Brazils and Robustas. One interesting point emerges: there have been frequent and considerable changes in the structure, and yearly imports of Brazils vary by as much as 4 million to 10 million bags respectively. There have also been variations in Milds imports of between 9 to 13 million bags. Conversely, Robusta imports have been increasing steadily, with the exception of 1957-59.

If we compare the different types of coffee imported into the United States with the trends of price differentials, two tendencies

* The United States still dominates the coffee market as the main seller, though its share is constantly declining (Figure 26).

124

are clearly distinguishable. A change in the price differential between Robustas and Brazils was always accompanied by a change in the imports of Robustas, a change in the price differential between Brazils and Milds by changes in the imports of Brazils and Milds.

## TABLE 11

Coffee Exports: São Paulo — Domestic
Average Price, Foreign Exchange Rate, And
Average Spot Quotations

| Year | Producer Price<br>Cr/per 60 kg. | Export Price<br>Cr/per 60 kg. | Foreign Exchange<br>Rate<br>Cr: 1 US Dollar | Price/US Dollar<br>in New York<br>per 60 kg. |
|------|------|------|------|------|
| 1948 |  | 516 | 18.3 | 28.05 |
| " |  | 599 | 18.3 | 32.61 |
| " | 238 | 1104 | 18.3 | 58.34 |
| " |  | 1164 | 18.3 | 64.71 |
| 1953 |  | 1394 | 18.3/19.9 | 66.07/70.05 |
| 1954 | 2200 | 2496 | 26.1 | 86.84 |
| 1955 | 2130 | 2496 | 35.9 | 61.62 |
| 1956 | 2280 | 2622 | 36.6 | 61.27 |
| 1957 | 2360 | 2652 | 38.0 | 59.05 |
| 1958 | 1720 | 2760 | 44.7 | 53.32 |
| 1959 | 1930 | 2820 | 61.3 | 41.98 |
| 1960 | 2590 | 3252 | 83.8 | 42.38 |
| 1961 | 3570 | 4020 | 110.9 | 41.56 |
| 1962 | 6790 | 6000 | 166.3 | 39.24 |
| 1963 | 10,500 | 9000 | 259.1 | 38.28 |
| 1964 | n.a. | 29,550 | 751.7 | 50.84 |
|  | n.a. | n.a. | 795.6 | 54.16 |

**Source:** IBC, *Anuario Estatistico Do Cafe* (1964), p. 18, and *Relatorio Da Directoria 1959,* p. 18; IBCE, *Anuario Estatistico Do Brasil,* (1964), p. 5 (Preos).

It should be noted that these quotations are for coffee without any export restriction or retention.

125

Figure 22

## Monthly Average, N.Y. Spot Prices of Selected Coffees

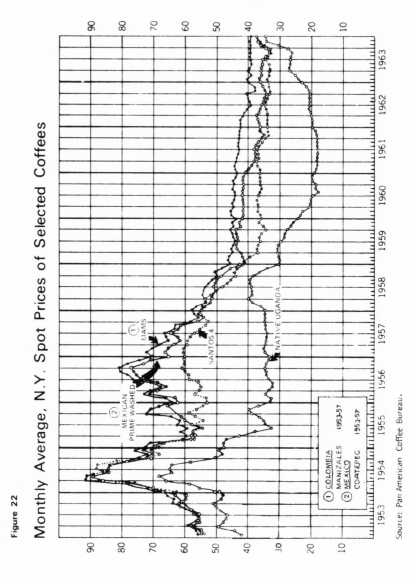

Source: Pan American Coffee Bureau.

**Figure 23**

# Coffee: Shares of Import Volume, by Consuming Areas (percentage)

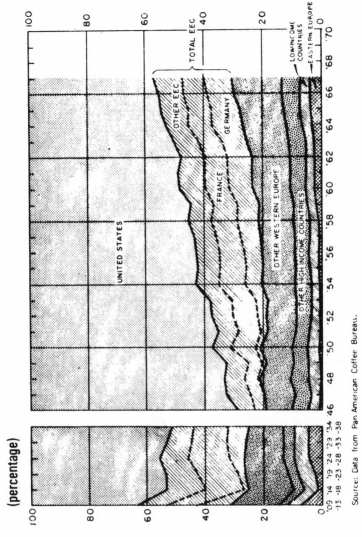

Source: Data from Pan American Coffee Bureau.

127

**Figure 24**

## Price Differentials Between Three Main Types of Coffee
### (New York Sugar and Coffee Exchange—spot)

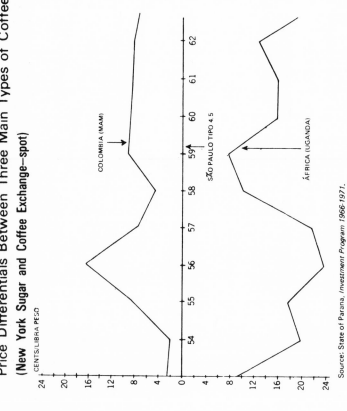

Source: State of Parana, *Investment Program 1966-1971.*

# Spot Price Differentials of Brazils
# in Relation to Robustas

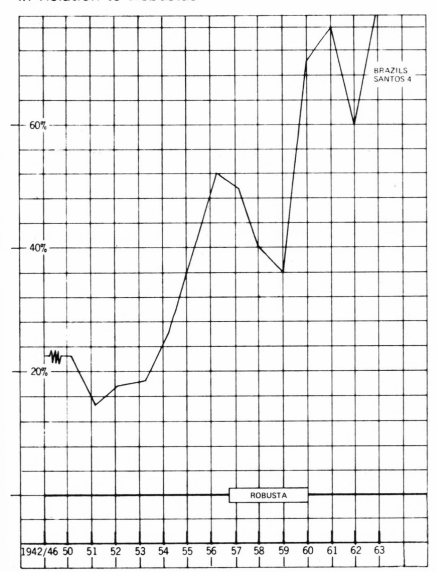

Source: Data from Pan American Coffee Bureau.

Figure 25B

Monthly Spot Price Percentage Differential of Selected Coffees in Relationship to Mams (percent above or below mams price level)

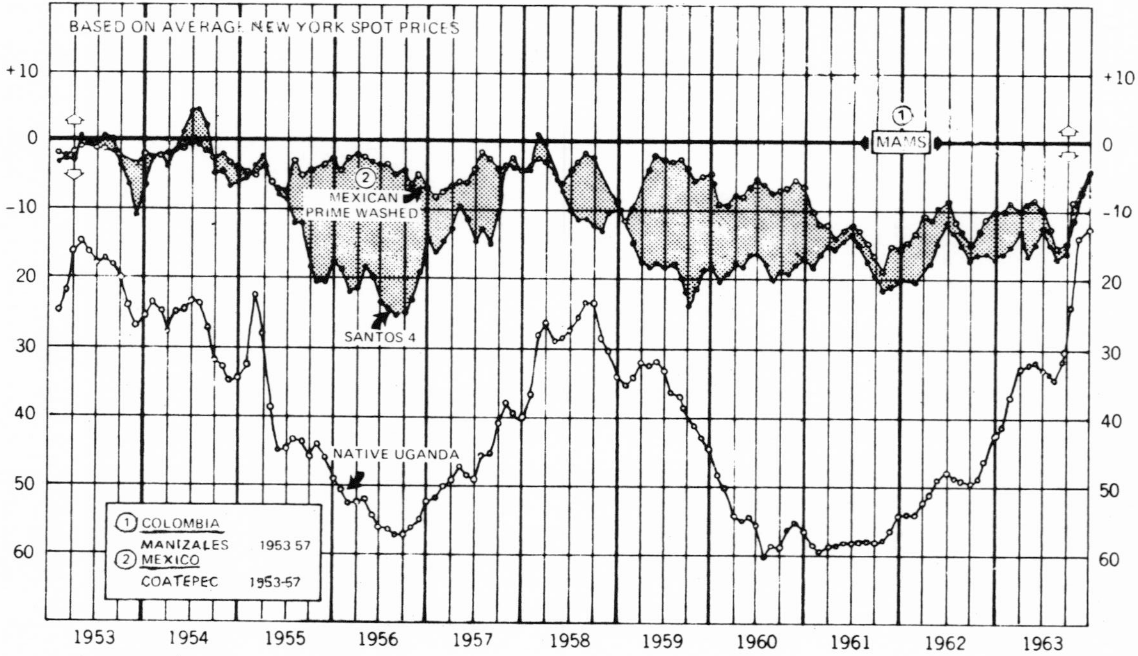

Source: Pan American Coffee Bureau.

130

# otal U.S. Coffee Imports by Types; Total Consumption and
# Consumption per Head and U.S. National Income Index

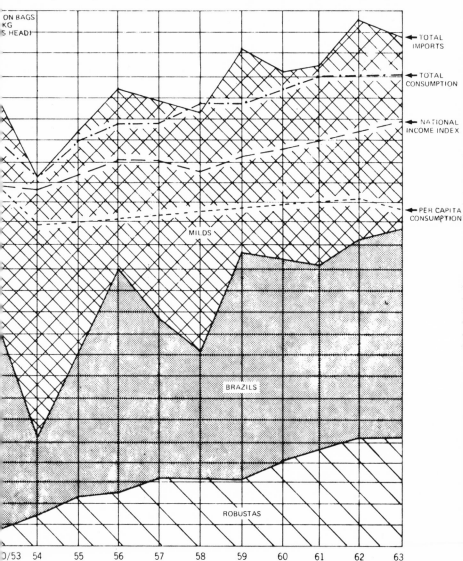

ON BAGS
KG
S HEAD)

← TOTAL IMPORTS

← TOTAL CONSUMPTION

← NATIONAL INCOME INDEX

← PER CAPITA CONSUMPTION

MILDS

BRAZILS

ROBUSTAS

0/53  54  55  56  57  58  59  60  61  62  63

ources: Based on data from FAO, Commodity Bulletin Series, No. 33; Pan American Coffee Bureau; and U.S. epartment of Commerce.

131

(1)　The graphic representations (Figs. 24, 25A, 25B) show that Brazil allowed a consistent widening of the price differential by 10 percent, then 25 percent, or in the case of Robustas by 36 percent and 52 percent, between 1954 and 1956, a deviation from the normal pattern of the preceding years. This was accompanied by a steady increase of Robusta imports into the United States (Fig. 26). This increase stopped temporarily in 1957-58 and decreased in 1959. In the face of the general increase of coffee imports, this decrease seems to have been induced by the more aggressive price policies of Brazil, which reduced the price differential from 50 percent to 38 percent. The new price policy after 1959 led to a further widening in differentials until 1962, which was again accompanied by a steady increase in imports of Robustas, stopping in 1962 and again following 1962. The statistical picture can be evaluated in view of the market structure in the United States. This is evidence that Brazil's policy of ignoring the development of price differentials between her own product and the Robustas, competing with Brazils on the markets for second quality blends and soluble coffee, led first to a decline of the market for second quality blends through soluble coffees, and also to an absolute displacement of Brazil's own types of coffee on the market for solubles in the United States.

This analysis is sometimes confused by some facts that seem to prove the opposite: Several authors[61] state that increases of imports of Robustas are due to the expanding use of soluble coffee, widely used because of its convenience, Robustas being preferred to Brazils in its production because they have certain technical advantages. But contrasting the increase of consumption of soluble coffees with the general development of the average price level for green coffees and the changes of price differentials between Brazils and Robustas, it is evident that the consumption in soluble coffee increased at a very high growth rate, particularly between 1954 and 1958. It made still further inroads, but very much smaller, comparatively, in later years and has remained completely stable since 1962.[62] That is, in times of general high average prices and high price differentials between Brazils and Robustas, soluble consumption developed and remained at the level reached then, when the general average price for coffee fell but the price differential persisted.[63] It seems, thus, that the causal chain can as well be explained the other way round: the existence of a price differential between Brazils and Robustas has been the underlying force in introducing soluble coffee "to market the considerably cheaper African coffees,"[64] thus reducing the market for second quality blends in favor of solubles. Because the price differential has been the result of the policy of the supplying country, it must be assumed that the price policy of Brazil had been decisive in producing this result. Insofar as a consumer preference existed for soluble coffee, because of its more convenient use, it seems that a price reduction of Brazils, especially of hard Brazils, with the aim of abolishing the price differential between Robustas and those Brazils altogether, would have reduced the share of Robustas in the production of solubles or perhaps may have even displaced that supply altogether.

The fact that the price increase – and hence the narrowing of the price differential between both types in 1958 and late 1963, and a spread in 1958 and 1964 – did not change the consumption of soluble coffees is explained by the fact that in both types retail prices of soluble coffee in the United States market did not move parallel to the prices for Robustas, but in the opposite direction.[65]

(2) Reactions in the structure of the United States imports to changes in price differentials between Milds and Brazils are observable. Two narrowings before 1959 led to heavy increases of Milds imports into the United States, two widenings led to similar gains in the Brazils. The elasticity of substitution between the two types seems to be high.

But with the exception of 1954 and 1956, the export volume of the producers of Milds to the United States remained stable at the 1950-54 level, after a fixed price differential and average prices were agreed upon. It thus had no impact on the export volume of Brazil (Fig. 26).

Reactions of demand to changes in price differentials on the remaining markets – more or less the West-European market – were to a certain extent similar. Brazilian exports were stagnant from 1952 to 1956 and lost their market share, due to the very high growth rates of European markets in that period. The trend altered in 1958-60, but it fell back to its old line afterward.[66] Contrary to the development in the United States, inroads were made by Robusta as well as Mild producers.

To evaluate this development as a result of price policies, it is necessary to distinguish between preferential markets (discussed at the end of Chapter 3) and unrestricted markets. Since the proportion of preferential markets shrank from 1955 to 1965 to some 20 percent of the total of European imports, it seems permissible to assume that the development of Brazilian coffee exports in relation to Robustas as well as Milds exports had the same causes[67] as in the United States market.

A conclusion about the excess capacity in the world coffee industry can thus not be solely restricted to the appraisal of the internal domestic policy of one oligopolist – Brazil. The price maintenance policy of Brazil on the world market for coffee obviously gave incentives to outside suppliers on the world sub-markets on which Brazils could be substituted to enlarge their capacity. The export of that output displaced Brazils in sub-markets, which were formerly their own. The evaluation of the displacement cannot rely upon the usual concept of "excess capacity" in an oligopolistic industry insofar as the concept of excess capacity is based on a cost-price relationship. But one cannot say that this one exists on the coffee world market, because there is no reason to assume that a price decline in Robustas, competitive to Brazils, need lead to a shrinking output in Robustas, because the production of the latter was also regulated and subsidized by governmental marketing policy. The use of cost criteria to establish an equilibrium capacity, an overproduction of which could be termed as "excess capacity," is then meaningless here. In regard to the policy of the competing oligopolist in the period under review, we have to restrict the excess capacity approach to the effects of the external price policy in relation to the stocks in hand of the competitors at the end of the period, and to an increase in saleable output, which took place in competing countries in the period under review. The latter is represented by the structure of imports into consuming countries. The Robusta imports from 1952 to 1964 amounted to some 100 million bags,[68] the surplus accumulated in Brazil to about 60 million bags. It thus seems evident that besides "the tendency to create excess capacity − higher than a long-run equilibrium at the given world market price would allow for − on its domestic markets," the Brazilian external price maintenance policy created new and excess capacity in the narrower sense in Africa by encouraging substitution in importing countries against her own stocked coffee types. The excess capacity − represented by the amount of stock retention − can thus be interpreted as the result of another example of an unsuccessful valorization of the world market[69] by the Brazilian government, acting as an oligopolistic seller of its domestic coffee production.[70]

The "Excessive" Price
Fluctuations and Cycles

It has been argued that the existing surplus has not been the result of a cycle, but was mainly created by a mistaken price policy of an oligopolistic seller on his domestic as well as on the external (or export) market. It has furthermore been established that world market prices of various types of coffees reflected the external price policies of primary exporters. That organization of marketing is put down in our assumption of a seller's oligopoly for primary sellers, and certain conduct and performance dimensions of these oligopolists. But if we assume that a coffee cycle did not exist, it is then necessary for a conclusive argument to examine other reasons for the instability of the world coffee market. (See beginning section of Chapter 4.) In our case, the price development must be the result of the conduct of oligopolistic sellers.

**Price Fluctuations as Results of Oligopolistic Price Cutting Between "Primary Sellers"**: A Historical Description. An analysis of this kind can disregard changes in final demand as it has been shown that total consumption of coffee did not, with very slight exceptions, fluctuate (Fig. 26). Research on the causes of price fluctuations thus has only to investigate the variations of supply or the mutual reactions of sellers during the period under review. Because the empirical material has not yet been grouped in order to test the latter hypothesis which argues that the instability on the world coffee market may be the result of its oligopolistic structure on both sides of the market of primary selling and buying for processing, a descriptive summary of price changes and national policies to influence the external price of the domestic coffee exports precedes the analysis.[71] Price movements or fluctuations which need a causal interpretation are: the generally parallel price increases of all types of coffee in 1954, a similar price fall in the post-boom year 1955-56, a short, cyclical price movement of all Milds coffees only in 1956 and 1957, and the general price decrease after 1959.

It seems difficult to describe price formation before the boom year 1954 as a result of a conscious price policy of oligopolistic sellers in regard to their sales in relation to those of other types (or competitors). The increasing demand for coffees of the Milds type and Brazils led — though all countries intervened indirectly into the domestic price formation for their own coffee production — to world market prices exceeding the dollar equivalent of domestic minimum prices and no retention took place. Demand cleared the market. The export price policy of the several oligopolists followed the world market price development. It was in fact a non-aggressive policy though no collusion took place.

As the price increase in 1954 will be analyzed below, the investigation starts with the price decrease in 1955. The price fall of the average of coffee prices for all types cannot be explained solely as a manifestation of a basic imbalance of market supply and demand through competitive forces. For at the end of the boom year export and/or domestic minimum prices times the coffee rate fixed prices for export sales from all oligopolists — for Brazils at about 61 cts/lb. or more than 80 cents for Colombian Milds.[72] Export prices of the residual Central American Milds (FEDECAMA) followed suit, including the Colombian Milds, whereas only the exports from Africa, and particularly from the French territories, were free of governmental price regulations. As can be seen in Figure 26 this price policy led to a very large decline of Brazilian imports into the United States and a significant change of the structure of American imports, which favored the intake of Milds and Robustas. On August 14, 1954, Brazil changed her exchange policy[73] — and established a factual export price of 65 cents November 11, 1954, and February 5, 1955, of 58 and 55 cts/lb.[74] following the world market price at the New York Exchange. Brazilian exports reached a new quarterly maximum in the beginning of 1955. On October 15, 1954, the Colombian Federation changed its factual export minimum price.[75] Obviously, the change of the Brazilian price did not alter the existing price differential between Brazils and Robustas, but between Milds and Brazils. The import demand for

Robustas, for coffee blends of second quality as well as for soluble coffee, increased, but an important substitution took place between Brazils and Milds on the sectoral market for first quality bean blends, principally hampering the exports of lower quality Milds of Central American producers other than Colombia. In spite of a "gentlemen's agreement,"[76] these countries lowered their export prices in February; the impact was at once mirrored in the prices in the New York Exchange. Colombia followed and a price war between all Milds producing countries and Brazil continued for about two months, in which all exporters experienced gains in the volume of exports, but Brazil secured the largest increase. All countries, except Colombia, cleared their harvest; the latter had to build up stocks,[77] and Brazil did not dispose of all stocks retained in 1954.[78] A new producer coffee agreement was initiated by the Milds-producing countries, including Colombia, to defend the price level arrived at, but again Brazil abstained from joining it.

The Milds control scheme was declared ineffective when prices rose in 1956. Price movements on the world market 1956-57 were restricted to coffees of this type, whereas the prices of Brazils were still kept at the level of the preceding year. In the same year Brazil again made larger inroads into the market share of the Milds-producing countries. But in spite of that, the dollar equivalents of the domestic prices for Milds were overbid and stocks of all FEDECAMA countries were cleared at the end of the crop year 1956, stocks being only slightly reduced in Brazil.[79]

In 1957 the "gentlemen's agreement" of the Milds exporters required them to state their minimum export prices openly and thus aimed at stabilizing the price differentials at the level of the previous year. But as early as the first quarter of that year stocks rose in the FEDECAMA countries, and Salvador and Mexico started to reduce their export minimum prices, all other Milds-producing suppliers following suit. Though the export minimum price of Colombia accompanying the price leadership of the residual Milds producer declined and dipped at the jointly agreed minimum price and rested there, the prices of other Milds continued to be fixed at declining levels with the effect that all producers broke the agreement of 1957. At the end of 1957 the harvest of all Milds-producing countries except Colombia were cleared, whereas the latter, as well as Brazil, had again to retain part of her crop. As a result the price differentials between Brazils and Milds narrowed and Brazilian exports fell off. At the same time a new agreement came into force, this time with the participation of Brazil,[80] but, in spite of several approaches, without the signature of a Robusta-producing country. The main feature of the renewed agreement was the provision for export quotas, based on a percentage retention of the crop and not on an estimated demand.

In the first quarter of 1958 prices of Colombian Milds fell near to the Brazils, when the quotas established in the Mexico Agreement showed themselves to be too high for the Milds producers, except Colombia, to maintain prices at the level reached at the end of 1957. The former countries insisted on their export quotas, which led to a reduction in the world market prices of these types, and induced Colombia and Brazil to follow them, although Brazil tried to keep export prices at about the highest level. This resulted in an extreme narrowing of price differentials between Milds and Brazils, accompanied by renewed changes in the structure of United States imports as indicated elsewhere. Huge surpluses accumulated in Brazil and again in Colombia, whereas the whole crop of all other Milds-producing countries was cleared.

In 1959 Brazil started a new price development. She changed her exchange rate policy with the result that the dollar equivalent of the domestic minimum price fell some 35 cts-lb. This decision was promptly reflected in the world market price, but this time the collusion in the agreement proved reliable. Colombia held its supplies at a minimum price, designed to keep its export price at the level reached at the end of 1958, followed by the residual Milds producers keeping their "agreement to maintain minimum sales prices in line with those established by Colombia,"[81] and a widening of the price differentials took place. Against this the price differentials between Brazils and Robustas declined considerably. Furthermore the IBC announced publicly that it had sold a respectable volume of hard Brazils to soluble producers, priced at the going price for Robustas. As can be seen in Figure 26, the price policy led to a reduction of Milds imports into the United States as well as of Robustas for the first time since the end of World War II, both reductions being offset by a steep increase in exports of Brazils into the United States. The stock policy of Colombia and Brazil increased their stockholdings, and it started for the first time in some African countries producing Robustas,[82] but all residual Latin American producers marketed their entire crops. In the same year the first Robusta-producing countries, France, the French Communities, and Portugal, joined the renewed agreement.[83]

1960 displayed a development similar to 1959 in the influence of quotas on prices: again the quotas contributed to the African Robusta producers proved to be too high. Whereas Brazil and Colombia could sell less than the agreement allowed for and maintain their export prices, the Robusta-producing countries exported as much as their quotas with the result that their prices fell again and the price differentials between these coffees and Brazils again widened. Their exports increased, the whole crop being marketed at the end of the year. Exports of Brazils decreased due to a substitution of Brazils by Robustas, whereas this time exports of Milds remained stable, resulting in marketing of the complete harvest of the FEDECAMA countries, and an increase in stocks in Colombia as well as in Brazil.

There was a similar development in 1961 in regard to prices and imports into the United States for Brazils and Robustas, but this led to a new price policy of the FEDECAMA states. They argued that they had merely fulfilled their export quotas and allowed their prices to fall to the prices of Brazils. They gained an increase in the intake of Milds on the costs of Brazils. Again all countries except Brazil and Colombia cleared their annual crop, whereas these two increased their stocks.

The year 1962 proved to be comparable to the development of 1961.

140

**Conduct Dimensions.** The historical review of changes in national export or de facto export prices and in world market prices reveals two different results:

(1) The prices on the New York Exchange must have followed the changes in the domestic price policy of the oligopolistic sellers in general, although the price development sometimes preceded the new set of domestic prices, as discussed earlier, or followed with some time lag. Obviously that part of the price performance cannot be adequately explained by quoting the prices of the primary sellers and will be dealt with below. But as the export prices of coffee producing countries were set by the national marketing boards, and price levels maintained, the changes of prices can be attributed only to changes in the prices of primary sellers (see early pages of Chapter 5). Insofar as the world market prices of different types of coffee mirror the changes in price policy, the latter are the causes of the average year-to-year fluctuations on the world market.

(2) We established earlier the hypothesis that output in Brazil has not been the result of the price movements on the world market. If output is independent, the price fluctuations observed in different types can then be the result of changes in demand or supply of the industry as a whole, or for one type of coffee, or show changes in conduct between competitors, unrelated to the two former causal factors.[84] The last incidence is the possibility of price warfare between the oligopolists, i.e., "periodically price-cuttings war in order to regain their market position."[85] This source of price instability exists, as is generally accepted, especially on markets of differentiated oligopoly,[86] as is the case in coffee. The relative proportion of exports and prices in the world market secured by various sellers will then depend on the establishment of stable price differentials. A change

in the latter, so that lower-priced sellers begin to "take business away" from higher priced sellers, may degenerate into a price cut, and the general level of prices may then be intermittently reduced as a result of price warfare.

As discussed in Chapter 1 of this book, price warfare is the result of differences between competitors, on their first conduct dimension, that is, "the price policies of sellers: these are effectively the principles, methods, and resultant actions that they employ in establishing what prices to charge, what output to produce, etc.," and their second dimension: "the manner in which and devices and mechanism by which the intrinsically rivalrous action of sellers in an industry are co-ordinated, adapted to each other, or made mutually consistent in reacting to demand for products in the common market."

The following discussion will analyze the first conduct principle.

In regard to the price development of all types of coffee, with a general exception for Robustas in 1955, the decrease in 1958 with the exception of the types of Rio 7 and the general decrease in 1959, the hypothesis of a seller's conduct aiming at "defending its own absolute export volume into the United States" seems to be plausible in regard to Brazil.* It would reject the hypothetical conduct of "selling the entire output out of existing capacity," whereby price fluctuations could be interpreted as a result of a cyclical development of production, whether or not influenced by governments. The latter cause would be dismissed as a causative factor if the former applied.

For the first price decline after 1955 the second conduct hypothesis would have required a Brazilian price policy designed to reduce its own "factual" export price after 1955, especially in 1956, to such an extent that all stored supplies, which were kept in government storage out of the harvest in 1954-55, could be

---

* That Brazil's policy was also defensive in not striving to maintain its market share is shown in Figure 27.

142

sold. This — as we have shown — did not take place when the Brazilian Institute of Coffee set the "factual" export price at about 50 cts/lb. in 1955 and in the following year and continued to do so in 1956, despite its stocks from the preceding retention, which Brazil could not sell at that price. By this action she established a price differential and an export to the United States which regained, to a large extent, her old export position, at least in relation to the exports of other Milds producers. Obviously she disregarded the African Robusta competition in her price policy and tried to establish the old market share of the Milds producers which had forced her out of her market in 1954. Since then in all the following years she had never set her "factual" export price in such a way that all her stocks were depleted.

Secondly Brazil accumulated stocks to maintain the going export price without considering the amount of stocked coffee as long as this price maintenance policy did not result in a considerable decline of her actual volume of exports. It seems thus plausible to argue that Brazil followed a policy of price reduction from 1957-59 until she re-established her export volume in 1959 at a level comparable to 1950-54 and 1955-56, due to the price differential she re-established in 1959. Brazil's independent policy of "defending her own absolute export volume" meant thus that the price policy of Brazil was designed to eliminate the output effects of her own domestic policy to reach the world market via increases in her export, which would have meant a decrease in prices for Brazils and by this a decrease of the general price level as well as a disturbing change in the demand curves of her competitors (Mams, and Robustas). By doing so since 1954, Brazil followed an independent conduct of joint industry revenue[87] which would have led to a joint revenue and fixed revenue shares for all producers, dependent only on changes of demand at a collusive price, if they later had adhered to the same policy. As it was connected with the factual export price then fixed, this would have led to a given absolute value of exports earnings for the industry as a whole, changing only in line with changes in the total volume of demand per year. This would have meant a protection of export earnings of Brazil and all others as absolute values. If her competitors had agreed to a collusive policy, a stable absolute value of export earnings for Brazil and every other producing country would have resulted. Since this policy did not turn out to be feasible until the agreement of 1962, Brazil could only gain a stable part in the declining proceeds of coffee earnings. Her policy was thus designed to keep her "share in the total of foreign exchange receipts from coffee proceeds" by fixing the amount exported and adjusting her price, only if its other variable, volume of exports, started to decline as a result of non-collusive policies of her competitors (Fig. 28).

This association makes for difficulties, as normally decreases in factual export prices were accompanied by increases in production. Evaluating this relationship between output and prices, the previous conduct of the IBC and public statements should be kept in mind. The comparison of the conduct of the IBC shows that this organization normally accumulated all surpluses of previous years to maintain the market price. If the IBC had wished to dispose of its entire output or fix its stocks at a given level, a different exchange rate would have been necessary.

In favor of this hypothesis are hints in public statements of interested groups in the Brazilian debate about her coffee policy. It was pleaded for by the Brazilian exporters, who asked for a reduction of factual export prices because their export volume declined,[88] and is found in remarks of the Central Bank of Brazil, that the necessary foreign exchange could not be achieved since prices were upheld and export thus too small.[89] The amount of domestic stocks was never publicly discussed.

In general, the same conduct seems to be a plausible interpretation of the price policy of Colombia, insofar as in 1954 the Colombian policy was already designed to retain stocks in order to maintain the prices of her products. But these obviously were set to follow the prices of her competitive Milds from other Central American countries at a slightly higher premium. The same conduct applied to her price policy in 1956-57 and 1957-58. There was no connection between Brazilian and Colombian price

144

Figure 27

# Coffee: Shares of Export Volume, by Producing Areas (percentage)

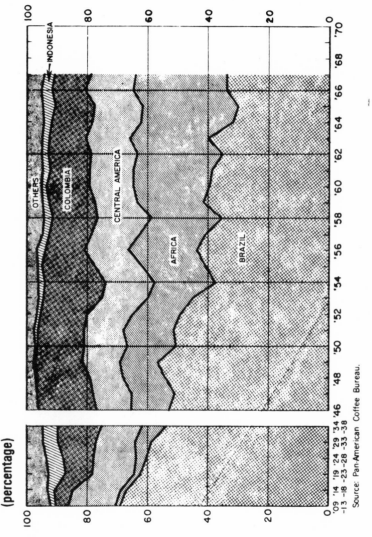

Source: Pan-American Coffee Bureau.

**Figure 28**

## Coffee: World Export Values (millions of U.S. dollars)

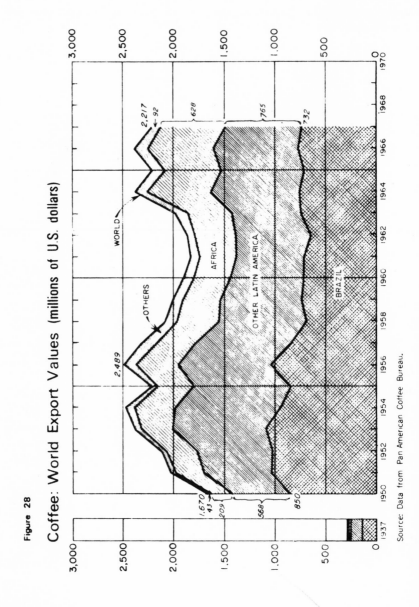

Source: Data from Pan American Coffee Bureau.

and no collusion between the two countries, has been shown. An evaluation of the Colombian price policy is then bound to follow the course of the price policy of the formerly mentioned competing FEDECAMA producers. A change in the price policy of Colombia has taken place since the first Latin American agreement. From that time Colombia maintained de facto export prices in relation to the Brazilian market price (Fig. 22) which led, as indicated above, to a retention policy of her domestic production above the demand and the set level.

Contrary to the price policy of these two oligopolists it can be established that all residual Milds-producing countries followed a conduct of "selling the entire output out of existing capacity" – and the same conduct was used by the African Robustas producers till about 1960, the time of their entrance into the International Coffee Agreement.

It is, secondly, equally important to analyze the second conduct dimension. Combined with the first it allows for a causal interpretation of the price fluctuations as a market performance of competition as follows:

The price increase of Brazils in 1954 can be explained* as a result of speculative forces, not connected with shifts in the industry demand or supply curve. It was in fact accompanied by an increase in the production of Milds.[90] The preference for Milds if no price differential between the former and Brazils exist kept the quotation of Milds at about the level of Brazils. Since we have assumed that there were no shifts in the industry demand curve and the market divided into distinct compartments, then this preference leads to some decrease in total demand, but even more to a substitutional shift in Milds. As shown in Figure 26 this led to a deep decline in Brazil's export to the United States. If we assume that the IBC followed her conduct principle, her principle of conduct would lead her to act first in "defensive" price cutting, but only to such an extent that price differentials were

---

* See under the heading "Price Fluctuations as a Result of Imperfections on the New York Coffee Exchange," later in this section.

re-established to assure her old export volume.[91] The facts do fit: her "factual" export minimum prices fell first to a middle between the top level and the 1953 average. But this decrease was followed by the FEDECAMA Milds producers who, acting along their conduct principle, wanted to dispose of their annual crop. Colombia followed her competitors. A price war to regain price differentials that would assure stable world market shares began between the "defensive" oligopolist Brazil, who started the price cutting only to regain her market shares, and the "aggressive" selling policy of the smaller Milds-producing countries, who wanted to maximize their individual profits by selling out their increased crop. The second aspect of market conduct therefore reveals no collusion between the oligopolists Brazil and the Milds producers, and a competitive pricing between the smaller FEDECAMA Milds producers themselves. Colombia acted as a price-taker and adapted her export price to the prices of the Central American producers. This reaction of Colombia can be seen in that she still kept stocks at the end of the trade year and the "defensive" aspect of Brazil's price cutting in the same fact. Thus the general price level was fixed at the price at which the entire output of the FEDECAMA Milds producers could be marketed. According to our assumption, this should have taken place near the previous year's price, but the price was free to move until the final disposal of the FEDECAMA crop.

The same hypothesis would fit the facts in 1957-59. As explained above, the widening of the price differential in favor of Brazil in 1956-57 led to a decrease in the exports of the FEDECAMA Milds producers at high prices. This time the decision of Brazil to keep her prices stable, thus enforcing a widening of the price differentials, must have been regarded as "aggressive" by the Milds producers as it would certainly aggravate the marketing of the next year's crop, whereas it was regarded as "defensive" by Brazil as it led only to a renewal of the export volume of 1950-54. The individual revenue maximization principle of the FEDECAMA Milds producers led to a competitive pricing between themselves and to a break-up of the open collusion with Colombia. Price differentials between them and Brazil declined again because of this defensive move (from the point of view of Brazil), but led to an aggressive substitution shift in her disfavor. That forced Brazil again to take a defensive action, and again Colombia followed as a price-taker. The price-cutting war went on until the smaller Milds-producing countries were able to dispose of their crop and price differentials between this group and Brazil were set again by Brazil to regain her export volume. Thus again the non-collusive behavior of the two competing producers Brazil and FEDECAMA and the price-taking of Colombia led to a price war before old price differentials were re-established. This behavior was followed instead of the first "Mexico Agreement" being applied.

The new agreement in 1958 assured collusion between the producers of Brazils and FEDECAMA Milds and Colombia. The differential established led to a decline of Colombia's export favoring the entire exportation of the FEDECAMA states, but no retaliation was invoked by Colombia, who acted this time according to the joint profit principle in line with the price for Brazils. The same has happened since 1961 when again the FEDECAMA states lowered their prices and narrowed their differentials to Brazils and followed the prices of Brazils, thus decreasing the export volume of Brazil. But again no new defensive price cutting was applied either by Colombia or by Brazil to re-establish the price differential and her export volume to the United States.

Contrary to this line of explanation goes an evaluation of the price increases in Milds in 1955 and 1956. But again the key lies with development of crops of the FEDECAMA producers, that is, the producers the output of which competes directly with Colombia. Their crop fell in 1954-56 by some 25 percent. This led to increased prices for the FEDECAMA crop since, firstly, Colombia followed again her role as a price-taker for her competitive output – a conduct facilitated by the fact that the output of Colombia declined slightly as well.[92] Secondly, the reduction of retail prices through a tax reduction in the Federal Republic of Germany and the fact that an extended amount of dollars was available for coffee imports in the whole of Western Europe[93] made for a larger share of Western European purchasers in the whole exports of Milds.[94] Thirdly, as explained above, the substitution of Milds for Robustas is restricted, especially in regard to European consumer preferences. All three reasons seem to be involved in the development of a price difference, which actually was much larger than the one established in 1959 and the following years. The residual part will be treated immediately.

An analysis of this kind shows the reason for the price fluctuations between Milds and Brazils. It established as well a dominant role of Brazil as a price leader for both types. But it does not yet explain why the prices of the two groups actually fell in 1958-60 to a level below that of 1953, thus exemplifying the "cyclical development of coffee prices" in its downswing, especially as the absolute volume of exports of both types of coffee did not exceed that one before 1953. Thus this policy should have resulted in an average price at about the level of 1950-55 or steadily increasing. Nor does it illuminate a question of minor importance, why the price differentials between Brazils and Milds of some 15 cts/lb. had to be narrowed to allow for similar comparative exports after 1959.

To analyze this development one has to investigate the conduct of the third competing group, the Robusta producers. Their principle of conduct (first aspect) was stated above and, to deduce from the market structure, their second aspect of conduct was highly competitive and non-collusive in regard to their competitors on the world coffee market. Their cheap sales led to an increase in demand for soluble coffees, which is represented by the fact that the total consumption in the United States increased by about the same amount of green coffee as imported from Africa. But under our assumption in regard to a stable demand for coffee over time, or at least an increasing stable rate, the decreases in prices of Milds and Brazils can then be interpreted as resulting from shifts of the single-product demand curves of the Brazilian coffee type Brazils through substitution by Robustas only, and the same is the sole explanation for a decline of the prices of Milds. It follows that the cheaper exports of African Robustas did not only increase demand for cheaper coffees – that is, the consumption of less expensive green coffee beans – but shifted the demand curve for the more expensive coffees to the less. The price decrease in the general price level for coffees can thus be explained by the "price-cutting" or "aggressive price policy" of the newcomer who established price differentials between his own output and that of Brazil. This led to a substitution of Brazils for Robustas and forced Brazil to "defensive price cutting" to maintain her first conduct principle. The price decline on the world coffee market is then the result of the entry of new competitors.

To evaluate this fact one has to consider the incentives to entry. In relation to a model of a coffee cycle, the price movement should have occurred because of a shift in the industry's demand and a delayed, time-lagged reaction of production (supply). But, as already indicated, the response of world supply to the price change which occurred in 1955-56 was delayed in the same year by Brazil's stock policy, which reduced her exports to the level given in 1950-53, and the same in the following years, which caused the world market price to stay where it was. That is, the price formation was not only influenced by the shift of a demand curve and the supply curve of the coffee industry, but by the amount of retention. It reduced the export of Brazil and therefore stopped the decrease in world market price for that product. It was then the *retention policy of the Brazilian Government* which by keeping stocks of exports since 1954 prevented a reaction of world market supply to an increase in price which should have shown up in following lower world market prices for coffee. And the price on the world market for Brazilian coffee was a price maintained in spite of the effective threat of entry which existed in this open oligopoly and which led to the increase in African capacity.

The idea that the price maintenance of Brazil effected the increase in output in the Robusta producing countries can only be based upon the assumption that the average cost of production for Robustas in those countries was lower than the price these producers could receive along their demand curve for their product under the price maintenance policy of Brazil for Brazils. These absolute cost advantages should then have made profitable the production of Robusta coffee. A number of statements exist to the effect that the production of Robusta is cheaper than that of Brazils.[95] If we assume this to be the case, then the coffee price development of the world market does not reflect a delayed short-run reaction of supply to an initial change of demand as reflected in a cyclical "cobweb" price gyration. Instead it represents a shift in the supply curve to the right due to the technical progress in the coffee industry achieved by large-scale innovation in the form of cheaper growing Robusta types. The low price since 1959 represents then a new lower cost price, achieved through still workable competition in the world coffee industry. Whereas the relationship between costs and world market price could have been the most important causative factor for the development of the Robusta coffee production in Africa until 1956-57, it certainly does not apply to the data later than that, as then the leading countries in African Robusta production paid subsidies to maintain domestic production or to raise it.[96]

No attempt is made to assess the quantitative influence of these subsidies on production and prices, since subsidies were normally, as observers on the spot indicated,[97] directed to open up new areas suitable to coffee production, to supply subsidized inputs and technical help in coffee production. No statistics are available to show this impact. It was stated as well in one of these reports[98] that during the time of subsidization production increased because of an increase in capacity. Since effectively the whole output of Robusta was exported[99] till the African states entered the International Coffee Agreement of 1962, the world market price was determined as well by the amount of subsidies available, that is, by oligopolistic conducts unrelated to cost relationships.

**Price Fluctuations as a Result of Imperfections on the New York Coffee Exchange.** Besides the results of a direct policy of the oligopolistic sellers, further influences of different conducts can be named as additional causes for price fluctuations, especially for those excessive short-term movements mentioned in Chapter 2. These are the effects of the organization of the principal market, respectively of marketing practices of primary sellers and buyers for processing (manufacturers) on the New York Exchange.

Whereas it must be admitted that there is still a coffee exchange in New York despite the changes in the market structure of the coffee market, there is clear evidence that the latter influenced the volume of turnover on the exchange in the period under review.[100] Three distinct types of imperfection can be distinguished:

(1) The influence of producing countries via their national marketing policies on the export price of their national crop and therefore on the world market price quotations in New York for different types of coffee brought forward new price forming influences, which were not connected with an experienced assessment of changes in production or consumption. But only these and their influences on the price formation can be appraised by the trade, whereas influence of the pricing policies of exporting countries cannot be precisely assessed. The trade reacted to the risk of price manipulation by reducing its stocks and operating on a hand-to-mouth basis. The small stockholding of importers and processors reduced the supply of warrants on the futures market, where those volumes were normally hedged. The same increased risk induced speculators to abstain from buying stocks over a time period by selling long on the futures market. Thus again the risk for the stockholder increased and forced the price for a distant future below near ones, causing a backward trend. This implied that each stockholder, hedging on his own market, had to pay a large carrying charge, meaning prohibitive hedging costs, and this was thus another disincentive to using the market as a

hedging medium. Furthermore in an assessment of the differences between spreads of different futures the hedger was drawn into the role of a price forecaster. This impaired the use of the futures market as a hedging medium for traders and manufacturers alike.

(2) L.L. Johnson has put forward a different reason for large processing buyers being unwilling to hedge their stocks. He argues that large roasters are not faced with the same "price risk" as dealers and therefore do not need to hedge. "The latter sell the identical product they purchase so that any change in the price of that directly affects their profit position. The former sell a different product — roasted coffee and, provided that the retail price does not move directly with green spot prices, the roaster may be able to insulate himself from the effects of green spot movements. If, when green prices fall, the retail price falls with a sufficent lag, the roaster may suffer no capital loss on inventory. Conversely, if there is a sufficient lag between spot price rises and retail roasted price rises capital gains also may not arise."[101] Johnson's findings in connection with those of the FTC concerning the price formation on the retail coffee market in the United States showed that the oligopolistic roasters on the United States market were able to pursue such a price policy on the retail market, followed in their leadership by all small roasters "making for lags in both directions extending over many weeks between Santos 4 price movements and retail roasted [Santos] blend."[102] Johnson's findings were confirmed by discussions with roasters, who stated that they generally attempt to price on the basis of average inventory costs so that regular merchandising and roasting profits are assured regardless of the movements of green spot prices.[103]

All these features reduced the amount of turnover on the New

154

York Coffee Exchange and made the New York terminal market a thin futures market.

(3) It is obvious that under these conditions of "increasing risks" only firms with sufficient financial resources of their own or others to fall back upon can survive. This has resulted in an increasing tendency to change the character of the coffee dealing firm, which has tended to become an exporter's or importer's agent. This evolution has been matched by moves of the large exporting firms as well as the producers' organizations to build up marketing positions in the exchange itself. It has changed the structure of principal markets in such a way that now three layers exist: besides the independent dealer described above, a large number of brokerage firms act as manufacturer's or exporter's agents. They purchase on the orders of a particular buyer or seller, taking a commission; "and a purchase or sale through a broker is then virtually a direct one between the manufacturer and the exporter or vice versa,"[104] leaving the broker with no independent risk of his own. This new group of exporter- or manufacturer-owned broker firms, as well as the latter group of dependent brokers, trade on the actual markets as well as on the futures market as a member of the "ring."

The result of the thin futures market for coffee on the New York Coffee Exchange has been investigated by the U.S. Federal Trade Commission. In its analysis the FTC concluded that the "thinness of the futures market" was the reason for excessive[105] price reactions to small-scale changes in supply and demand, respectively small speculative purchases or sales.

The upward price spiral in the boom period of autumn, 1953, to the middle of May, 1954, was initiated by the sudden heavy buying activity of a group of traders connected with exporters' interests. Their increase in demand led to a first price increase. The Brazilian Government followed this rise by raising the domestic minimum price, making for a de facto export-minimum price near the top reached on the futures market. This again led to a further increase in demand for inventories, reflected in long positions being taken by trading, manufacturing, and speculative interests, and to a new upward movement of prices. Part of this long interest demanded delivery against future contracts, which was unusual. As the physical import of Brazilian coffees, which serve as a contract base, was comparatively small, a squeeze of physical Brazilian coffee developed. This led to an excessive increase in spot prices on the actual market as well. The FTC mentioned that a stronger demand for inventories by traders increased demand at the actual market, which led to an increase in prices for spot coffee as well. But it stated that the increase in demand on the thin futures market, which created a squeeze in physical coffee, was the initial causal factor that produced the upward spiral in physical coffee on the actual market.[106]

It seems that the squeeze hypothesis has not proved satisfactory, if one contrasts the delivery quote of 203,700 bags,[107] the delivery against future contracts in the period under review, with the storage of about 1.6 million bags in the hands of trading activities in New York. To prove the "squeeze" hypothesis, a model has to be developed, showing why other trading interests did not sell in order to satisfy demand for actual coffees at the going price.

To construct this model one must go back to the effects of a thin futures market. Such a state of business was firstly an indicator: it showed that coffee trading was restricted mainly to such interests, which were able to carry the storage risks caused by price fluctuation and pass it on. It is secondly the reason why trading interests not connected or endowed with such financial strength will only be able to do business on such a market if they speculate.[108] Market partners, whom one can assume to trade under those financial conditions with physical coffees, are firstly primary sellers, who can hedge the risks of their inventories with the marketing scheme of their country, and secondly large buyers for processing, directly or via their integrated export or import agents. Independent traders do not have such a second form of risk insurance of their physical inventories. Thus if there is still hedging on the futures market, hedging done under these auspices can only be done by those traders who can use no other methods of passing on their inventory risks. Futures supplied under such circumstances then represent the stocks of physical coffees of independent traders, or the "free" market. These supplies are the only alternative opportunity of obtaining supplies that are not yet under the control of primary exporters or manufacturers. If this market is small, it is a residual market for physical supplies not held by either the exporters or the manufacturers. If therefore an increase in demand seems to arise, as for instance through the Brazilian interests in 1954, making for an increase in price, exporters' agents as well as manufacturers are interested in controlling these supplies: manufacturers, in order to obtain the supplies available outside the price setting of the exporter oligopolists,[109] exporters in order to prevent an underselling of their own price supplies. Also, if such a situation develops, independent traders who are bound to be speculators on a lopsided futures market will speculate according to the tendency of the market. And outside speculators, who are not normally in the market, will also enter. This again increases demand on a thin market in futures, confronting the small supply of "independent" stocks available. Speculation is then destabilizing and must be so as a stabilizing speculation would assume quite different conditions of entry.

This model of behavior fits the empirical facts in 1953-54 stated in the FTC report, that "after a period of unusually heavy speculative buying by Brazilian interests, which led to a first price increase, thereafter continued demand for long contracts by domestic coffee trade interests, accompanied by moderate increases in buying by ... speculative interests, in a market rendered thin by the withdrawal of selling interests, produced price increases late in January, while in February, with the total volume of trading further reduced, comparatively small buying by domestic speculators and trade interests started the market on the second upswing."[110]

Our model of the New York Coffee Exchange price formation is then one of an exchange at which, by reason of the third aspect of conduct of an oligopolistic seller or buyer (his marketing practices), both sellers and buyers form a small and interrelated group. The main market form is that of a bilateral oligopoly. Between these, a group of small traders exists (teilmonopol) whose supply is kept solely for speculation on future developments of the price quotations of the large sellers.[111] The group of small traders faces increased demand from both their competitors, as they are a source of independent "free" supply, if the price of the primary sellers increases. If the prices of the primary sellers are falling, they will certainly be forced to undercut the price quotations of their competitors on the supply side to a considerable extent in order to attract business, because then, as there are no other means of reducing risk, losses can be minimized only by selling out when the price decreases. Secondly, independent of initial change in the price of primary sellers, price-disturbing influences can occur if integrated traders suddenly enter the thin market in order to raise the price, thus cornering the market in favor of the exporting oligopolist and inducing by the very fact of a price rise the price-raising forces, indicated under the first heading. Contrary, excessive price decreases could occur if manufacturing buyers disposed of considerable amounts of their stocks, as small amounts quite capable of upsetting the supply situation on the free market could always be purchased by integrated traders, thus neutralizing the effect of a sale of coffee from manufacturer's stocks.[112]

This feature of the market structure, combined with the fact that the free market for physical supplies is a very small one, explains the fact that the quotations on the New York Coffee Exchange follow the year-to-year average price trend of the primary sellers, but sometimes considerably exceed or fall short of the prices of the former, and/or that a "squeeze effect" may arise. If such random price fluctuations can have the magnitude of the 1953-54 boom in coffee prices, it seems possible to conclude that the excessive price fluctuations that could not be explained above by an analysis of the conduct of primary sellers between each other are attributable to the imperfections of the terminal market in New York, the prices of which are quoted as world market prices.[113]

## NOTES

1. J.S. Bain, "The Theory of Monopolistic Competition after Thirty Years: The Impact on Industrial Organization," AER, *Papers and Proceedings,* LIV (1964).

2. This concept of market differentiation is called *Bedarfmarkt Konzept.* See L. Abbot, *Quality and Competition,* (New York: Columbia University Press, 1955), p. 94; H. Arndt, *Anpassung und Gleichgenicht am Markt,* in J.N.St. 170 (1958), p. 224.

3. *Conjunctura Economica,* Vol. IX, No. 12, 6.

4. S. Weintraub, *Price Theory* (New York-London: Pitman, 1949), p. 168.

5. *Ibid.,* pp. 168, 172.

6. H.S. Houthakker, "The Scope and Limits of Futures Trading," ed. T. Scitovsky, *The Allocation of Economic Resources* (Stanford University Press, 1959), pp. 144-147.

7. I. Baer and O.G. Saxon, *Commodity Exchanges and Futures Trading* (New York: Harper and Brothers, 1949), p. 56.

8. C.P. Kindleberger, *Flexible Exchange Rates,* eds. Tamagna *et al., Monetary Management* (Englewood Cliffs, N.J.: Prentice Hall, 1963), p. 410.

9. FAO, *CBS-33,* p. 31.

10. *Ibid.,* p. 30.

11. UN, *Economic Survey of Latin America 1955,* p. 85.

12. UN, *Economic Bulletin for Latin America 1964,* Vol. IX, No. 2, p. 138.

13. *Conjunctura Economica,* Vol. 10, No. 5, Appendix: Monthly Index of Wholesale Prices; UN, *Economic Survey 1957,* p. 117; O. van Teutem, "Coffee in Latin America: The Producers' Problem," UN, *Economic Bulletin for Latin America 1959,* p. 37.

14. UN, *Economic Survey of Latin America 1957,* p. 134.

15. FAO, *Commodity Review 1963; Conjunctura Economica,* Vol. 10. No. 10. All quotations in this magazine after that date refer to exportable grades only. Cf. Consello Nacional de Estatica, *Anuario Estatico do Brazil,* 1962, p. 91; JCO: ICC-7-4.

16. ICO-ICC-7-4. Vol. I, p. 34.

17. J.W. Rowe, *The World's Coffee* (H.M.S.D., 1963), p. 48.

18. ICO-ICC-7-4, Vol. I, p. 33.

19. FAO, *CBS-33*, p. 46. (This increase is not reflected in IBC-1-2, p. 1)

20. The harvest in 1960-61 stood at 29,000 bags, in 1961-62 at 35,000, in 1962-63 and 1963-64 at 27,000. The 1961-62 crop is a very big one, owing to very favorable weather. Cf. Rowe, *op. cit.,* p. 38.

21. Teutem, *op. cit.;* FAO: *Coffee in Latin America,* Vol. II; Brazil, State of São Paolo, pp. 27-29; FAO, *CBS-33,* p. 28.

22. FAO, *CBS-33,* p. 28.

23. *Ibid.,* p. 28.

24. ICO-ICC-7-4, p. 5.

25. *Ibid.*

26. O.T. Ettori, Fisica du Agricultura Em São Paulo, *Agricultura Em São Paulo,* Ans. XI, No. 7 (July 1964), p. 31.

27. *Ibid.,* pp. 32-40.

28. Ettori, *op. cit., passim.*

29. The figures of ICO-ICC-7-4, p. 10, and of the Anuario do Eatistico do Brasil do not quite compare, the latter being one year later in showing changes indicated in the former.

30. Grupa Executivo de Racionalizacao da Cafei Cultura, an organization of JBC to handle the problem of diversification.

31. JBC-GERCA: Relatorio 1964, Rio de Janeiro, p. 15 (cited from ICO-ICC-7-4, Vol. I, p. 19).

32. FAO, *Coffee in Latin America,* Vol. II, p. 28.

33. V.D. Wickizer, *Coffee, Tea, and Cocoa, An Economic and Political Analysis,* Food Research Institute (Stanford University Press, 1951), p. 342; Rowe, *op. cit.,* pp. 14-15.

34. JBC, *Cafeicultura No Paraná,* No. 2 (1964) p. 110.

35. PPA, *Investment Program,* pp. 60-62.

36. Teutem, *op. cit.,* p. 34.

37. FAO, *CBS-33,* p. 29.

38. *Ibid.,* p. 34.

39. A.E. Haarer, *Modern Coffee Production* (London: Leonard Hill, 1962), pp. 35-50.

40. Rowe, *op. cit.,* p. 34.

41. FAO, *CBS-33,* p. 29.

42. This argument would fit with the development of output in Africa up to 1957-58. It is not refuted by the increasing output of those regions since

1957-58, because with the beginning of that crop year in those countries production was also subsidized and producer prices did not follow the declining trend of world market prices. Cf. FAO-UN, *Commodity Stabilization Funds in the French Area,* p. 31. It is in line with Teutem's statement *(op. cit.,* pp. 41-43) that the possibilities of increasing production of alternative crops (crop diversification) have been underestimated in the past. They have been realized by farmers in the postwar years.

43. Rowe, *op. cit.,* p. 37; FAO, *Commodity Review 1962,* pp. II-55.

44. FAO, *Commodity Review 1962,* pp. II-54; ICO-ICC-7-4, p. 23.

45. UN, *Economic Survey 1957,* p. 134.

46. UN, *Economic Bulletin for Latin America,* Vol. IX, No. 2 (November 1964), p. 103: "The Government tried to keep the bonuses paid to coffee producers at the same level for as long as possible. However, coffee growers and exporters, operating as an organized pressure group, not only succeeded in obtaining frequent adjustments, but also enjoyed the assurance that their total coffee production would be purchased. This policy did nothing to discourage production, since the percentage payable was calculated to maintain their rate of return."

47. *Ibid.,* pp. 87-112; UN, *Economic Survey,* 1958, p. 123.

48. A Brazilian commission stated before a GATT committee that the policy of the Brazilian Government aimed at a support for the domestic producers "not with the object of obtaining higher prices, but in order to avoid difficult social situations." It is accepted that this policy to support the coffee prices was rather in conflict with the government's policy of restricting coffee production. Cf. GATT, Document L 1317, Geneva, 21.10.60, "Report of Committee II on Consultation with Brazil on Agricultural Support Measures," p. 5.

49. ICO-ICC-7-4, Vol. I, p. 15.

50. Rowe, *op. cit.,* p. 38.

51. *Ibid.,* p. 39.

52. *Ibid.,* p. 37.

53. *Ibid.;* FAO, Commodity Review 1962, pp. II-56; JCO-JCC-7-4, Vol. I, p. 33.

54. JCO-JCC-7-4, p. 33, footnote 1.

55. JCO-JCC-7-4, p. 33.

56. Rowe, *op. cit.,* p. 190.

57. J.S. Bain, *Price Theory* (New York: Holt, Rinehart and Winston, 1963), p. 87.

58. *Ibid.,* p. 233. The qualification arises since the market organization of the world coffee industry has a third layer between the primary seller and buyer for processing, the impact of which will be analyzed below.

59. Federal Trade Commission, *Economic Report of the Investigation of Coffee Prices* (Washington, D.C.: Government Printing Office, July 30, 1954), p. 53.

60. *Ibid.,* p. 59.

61. FAO, *CBS-33,* p. 25; Teutem, *op. cit.,* p. 35: "A special factor favoring the use of African coffees has been the recent shift in the consumption pattern of the United States and some other countries toward an increased use of soluble coffees"; Rowe, *op. cit.,* p. 34.

62. PACB, *Annual Coffee Statistics 1964,* p. 35.

63. *Ibid.,* p. 34.

64. See also the discussion on the first Coffee Conference in Curitiba, Paraná, January 18-21, 1954, *World First Coffee Congress,* 5th Pan-American Coffee Congress, *Observator Economico e Finansiero,* No. 215 (March 1954), English reprint, p. 24; FAO, *Monthly Bulletin, op. cit.,* Vol. 5. No. 2. p. 37.

65. PACB, *op. cit.,* p. 104, Table CP-15.

66. FAO, *Commodity Review 1963,* p. 96.

67. GATT, *Trade in Tropical Products* (Geneva, 1963), p. 48.

68. ICO, *An Analysis of Coffee Prices 1953-1963/64,* EB42 Table 3, Appendix 4.

69. Historical evidence of those schemes starts in 1898. Cf. H. Roth, *Die Uebererzeugung in der Welthandelsware Kaffee im Zeitraum von 1790-1929;* I. Rowe, *Brazilian Coffee,* Royal Economic Society's Memorandum No. 34; GATT, Trade in Tropical, *op. cit.,* p. 36.

70. The Brazilian defense for that policy, "that if Brazil had not supported coffee by controlling supplies, she would probably still be a colonial economy with colonial methods, planting and supplying the whole world with coffee at 20 cts/lb." (cf. *Survey of the Brazilian Economy 1960,* Brazilian Embassy, [Washington, D.C., 1960] , p. 29), is perfectly nonsensical, as Brazil followed a domestic policy designed to achieve the first part of her allegation, and an external policy designed to prevent the beneficial outcome.

71. Source of information, if not quoted otherwise: *Conjunctura Economica,* monthly eds., Vols. II-XI, the monthly editorial on the development of the world coffee industry.

72. As a result of a "gentlemen's agreement" between all Milds producers, to keep certain price differentials. ICO, *An Analysis, op. cit.,* p. 3.

73. As well as the director of its IBC. *Op. cit.,* Appendix I, p. 4.

74. FTC, *Economic Report of the Investigation of Coffee Prices,* p. 119; ICO, *op. cit.,* Appendix I, pp. 3-4.

75. ICO, *op. cit.,* p. 71.

76. "However from 1955 to 1957 countries producing Milds entered into 'gentlemen's agreements' to maintain prices," Survey of the Brazilian Embassy, *op. cit.,* p. 20.

77. UN, *Economic Survey of Latin America 1956,* p. 43. This information supplies no precise figure since the federation denies information on the stock figures.

78. *UN Economic Survey of Latin America 1957,* Table 127: Brasil: Supplies and Disposal of Exportable Crop 1953-54/57-58, p. 124.

79. *Ibid.,* p. 124.

80. The Mexico Agreement. Cf. ICO, *Convention and Basic Documents* (Rio de Janeiro, 1958), p. 32.

81. PACB, *op. cit.,* p. 146.

82. FAO, *CBS-33,* Table 13, p. 15.

83. PACB, *op. cit.,* p. 17.

84. J.S. Bain, "Theory of Monopolistic Competition after Thirty Years: The Impact on Industrial Organization," AER, *Papers and Proceedings,* p. 432.

85. Bain, *Price Theory, op. cit.,* p. 306.

86. *Ibid.,* p. 273.

87. It was a maximization policy as well but not a policy which aimed at an independent revenue maximization, the antinomy to the joint maximum approach. Whether it was maximum or not cannot be established as the second maximum condition, the shape of individual cost curves, is not known. See W.J. Baumol, *Business Behavior, Value and Growth* (New York: Macmillan, 1959), p. 45.

88. *Conjunctura Economica,* Vol. VIII, No. 11 (November 1961), 1-12.

89. *Ibid.,* Vol. VI, No. 10 (October 1959), 4-6.

90. UN, *Economic Bulletin for Latin America 1957,* p. 133.

91. W. Krelle, *Preistheorie* (Tuebingen-Zuerich, 1961), p. 237, refers to an action designed to regain a market share as a "defensive," an action to gain new increases of market shares out of a given situation as "aggressive" price cutting war. In Anglo-Saxon literature, see Weintraub, *op. cit.,* p. 180.

92. Which because of stocks in hand did not reduce her exportable supply relatively to the preceding year. See UN, *Economic Survey 1956, op. cit.,* p. 43.

93. The FEDECAMA states sold only against U.S. dollars. Cf. Coffee Congress, *Observatore Economica,* pp. 13-19; U.S. Senate, 83rd Congress, Special Subcommittee of the Committee on Banking and Currency, *Study of Coffee Prices: Hearing,* Part I (Washington, D.C.: Government Printing Office, 1954), p. 143.

94. Including re-exports from the United States, and the total volume of imports into the United States increased by 4 million bags.

95. Rowe, *op. cit.,* p. 181; FAO, *CBS-33,* p. 9; UN, *Economic Survey 1963, op. cit.,* p. 200; FAO, *Commodity Review 1961,* p. 16.

96. FAO-UN, *Commodity Stabilization Funds in the French Area,* p. 32; FAO-UN, *The Role of Marketing Boards for Export Crops in Developing Countries,* No. E/CN 13/50. Also, IBRD, *The Economic Development of Uganda,* p. 37; ICO-ICC, Mission to OMCAF Countries (London, 1963), *passim.*

97. A.E. Haarer, *Modern Coffee Production* (London: Leonard Hill, 1962). pp. 35-50; GATT, *Development Plan Study* (March 16, 1965), pp. 60-93; FAO-Coffee: *Recent Developments,* pp. 13-17.

98. GATT, *Development, op. cit.,* p. 86. "However, statistics show that in the period 1954-62 the acreage under Robusta coffee increased from 262,000 to 561,000."

99. ICO-ICC-7-4, p. 59.

100. FTC, *Report, op. cit., passim;* R.W. Gray, "The Characteristics of Bias in Some Thin Future Markets," *Food Research Studies,* Vol. 1, No. 3 (1960), pp. 296-314; L.L. Johnson, "Price Instability, Hedging and Trade Volume in the Coffee Futures Market," *Journal of Political Economy,* Vol. 65, No. 4 (1957), pp. 306-321; U.S. Senate, 83rd Congress, *A Study, op. cit., passim.*

101. Johnson, *op. cit.,* p. 321.

102. *Ibid.*

103. *Ibid.*

104. FTC, *op. cit.,* p. 135.

105. FTC, *op. cit.,* Summary, p. XV: "However, the price rise was far in excess of what might be expected under the competitive laws of supply and demand."

106. FTC, *op. cit.,* p. 137.

107. *Ibid.,* p. 140.

108. Gray, *op. cit.,* p. 311.

109. FTC., *op. cit.,* p. 446: "Both Nestle Co. and General Foods reported using the exchange as a source of supply. The reason given was that the coffee was of good quality and was the *cheapest coffee available."*

110. *Ibid.,* p. 18.

111. This form of bilateral oligopoly "represents roughly the sort of actual bilateral oligopoly which is usually encountered." Cf. Bain, *Industrial, op. cit.,* pp. 336-337.

112. Sales of Nestlé and General Foods, resold on the exchange, were

purchased by Leon Israel, a firm oriented to producers' interests in Brazil. Cf. FTC, *op. cit.,* p. 446.

113. For the influence of these forces in the 1955-57 price cycle, see *Conjunctura Economica,* Vol. VIII, No. 4, pp. 3-7.

# 5

# An Evaluation of the Competitive Aspects of the International Coffee Agreement

## The World Coffee Market as an "Exception"

An evaluation of the coffee agreement as an "exemption" must be carried out on two lines. One is based on whether the coffee market is an "exception" to be regulated through a control of outputs and prices. Secondly, an evaluation of the ICA is needed to determine whether it forms an "exemption" by providing for a competitive performance – that is, for relative price stability and long-run equilibrium tendencies as defined under pricing in pure competition.

Contrary to the traditional model, our analysis (see Chapter 4) revealed the bilateral oligopolistic structure of the world coffee market. It revealed as well the fact that the product "green coffee" is differentiated. The market structure of the world coffee market is a differentiated bilateral oligopoly. The third structure dimension was demonstrated by the fact that in the period under review all oligopolists introduced a production policy that led to an output independent of the development of the world market price for their product. The amount of coffee grown was not primarily influenced by the changes in demand for the three different coffee types, but principally by certain policies of the government of one or all producing countries toward their coffee producers.

These policies materialized in regulations of domestic as well as export prices to produce and sell the product. The ability of governments to carry out such a comprehensive domestic and external marketing scheme lies in the financial strength[1] to stock or to dispose of the output through subsidies in competition with other producing countries. Such conduct depends on the country's ability to shift parts of its national income for such a purpose. In terms of oligopoly analysis these policies are the result of strategies or oligopolistic conduct. The structural feature of different production costs of various exporting oligopolists may influence but do not determine these strategies. The selling policy of one country is thus only secondly a question of production-cost relationships between the various coffee-producing countries.

If there is no collusion, the model of differentiated oligopoly leaves room for two "market performances":

(1)   "One general possibility for oligopoly behavior is that the forces of antagonism and distrust among rivals are so strong that no collusive agreement among sellers is possible and that no regular pattern of reaction to rival's price changes becomes established. If such a situation of uncertainty prevails the individual seller obviously has no determinate demand curve for his output; rather he has a series of alternative conjectures as to the possible reactions of his rivals to any price changes which he may make. Under these circumstances no certain pattern of price output determination can be attributed to oligopolistic markets, both are in general logically indeterminate within a considerable range. A stable price at some indeterminate level and chaotic price instability are both clear possibilities.[2]

(2)   No competitive "long-run equilibrium" can be reached.[3]

Our analysis has secondly established that the price instability on the coffee market, short-term as well as cobweb cyclical, has been the result of the non-collusive strategies of the different market participants.

It seems thus that the world coffee market under its presently existing market structure and conduct is "a situation in which active competition does not produce one or more competitive results." The world coffee market, therefore, produces neither price stability nor a long-run equilibrium, if there is no collusive action between all producers and manufacturers. The further dimension added as a result of the oligopolistic structure is the uncertainty in regard to the competitors' strategies. Collusion must therefore be a restriction of the freedom of all oligopolists to use independent market strategies. These may take several forms, but such a collusion has to regulate either the price or the amount of the product going to the market. A collusion on an oligopoly market has thus the typical "per se restrictive" features. This need for collusion between producers to achieve the avoidance of indeterminate instability is then the reason why the world coffee economy as it exists now must be regarded as an exception to be regulated through a control of output and/or prices as a first step to achieve competitive results. But, as we have established in the analysis, this is not because of the particular agroeconomic features of the coffee tree, which would create an "unconditional genuine exception." The set of structures and conducts that we think are now prevailing on the world coffee market is one where market structures were erected by national governments and concentration of private enterprises on the side of manufacturing which created a "conditional genuine exception" in the international trade of coffee. This means that the exception is a result of the policies taken by governments and private entrepreneurs, and it cannot be established whether competition on the world coffee market would not be able to produce competitive results if the "conditional" imperfections were abolished.

## The International Coffee Agreement as an "Exception"

Two features of the coffee agreement as an exemption arise from the foregoing analysis:

(1) The coffee market is one in which oligopolistic warfare could be brought about by non-collusive behavior of one producing member, the exchange acting as one competing group of by an oligopsonist on the side of manufacturing.[4] A collusion therefore must exist between all these three competing groups. Since the oligopolists are national marketing organizations of various independent states, and the traders and the oligopsonistic manufacturers are nationals of either importing or exporting countries, it follows that the collusion must have the form of an international comprehensive policy regulation.

(2) Furthermore it must be an agreement on a common policy of price determination on the world market. The reason for that lies firstly in the afore mentioned conduct feature that the output policy of every oligopolist is not determined by the relation of production cost and world market price, but obviously by certain socioeconomic policies — that is, it is determined by the financial strength an oligopolist is willing to use to achieve these policies. And secondly the collusion must agree on a common policy of price differentials between the different types of coffee in order that the industry as a whole may be able to establish an industry demand curve and every oligopolist a definite "ceteris paribus" demand curve for his own output,[5] which is a part of the industry demand curve.[6]

The necessity of dealing with these two problems prevents the use of a non-restrictive (market-conforming) measure such as a buffer stock. A buffer stock cannot be designed to prevent price instability as a result of oligopolistic market strategies; it can only damp the price effects of one causative factor, i.e., production cycles under a price formation of pure competition.[7]

The same considerations apply to the multilateral long-term agreement type, the main aim and advantage of which is to maintain an unregulated "free market" in addition to the regulated market.[8] The free market should serve as a place where a long-run equilibrium price should emerge, which in turn should be used as a guide for the agreement price. This combination of a regulated and free market thus serves as a mechanism to foster the efficient allocation of resources. However, this would not be the case on the world coffee market, where bilateral oligopolistic price formation exists.

The negative statement on these two forms of price stabilization schemes does not yet prove whether a fresh device will not result in a better performance nor does it follow that the "restrictive quota agreement type" is the best form of an exemption. But as we are interested only in evaluating the present International Coffee Agreement, we do not concern ourselves with the question whether an entirely new agreement scheme would be better, but whether the existing agreement is suitable to serve as an exemption for the world coffee market.

## The Main Effects[9] of the Agreement

Besides considering the principal structures and conducts as a possible source of instability one has to fall back on the actual forms of monopolistic imperfections in the world coffee market in displayed form of rivalrous conduct and the results as stated in our analysis. Secondly, all relevant regulations of the international agreement have to be analyzed in the light of the particular forms of imperfections. This information is needed since the agreement should not only be able to solve the questions of principle but deal as well with the ad hoc problems – that is, the particular performance in the industry which arose in 1959 and led to the institution of the agreement.

As the result of the investigation into the conduct of the oligopolists we established certain assumptions about the behavior of the competing market participants. It showed that the conduct of the different market partners did not directly increase price instability. This was firstly due to the non-aggressive, or passive, price conduct of the dominant selling oligopolist, Brazil, before 1958 and the increase in explicit collusion in form of a cartel agreement of all producers since 1960-62. But indirectly Brazil's policy increased potential instability by allowing for a development of a huge surplus and creation of industries in other countries which would not have existed if it had not been for Brazil's policy of maintenance of the world coffee price for Brazils. It secondly influenced the development of the price policies on the world market in that the ownership of her surplus forced competing countries to follow Brazil's price policy as Brazil was able to supply coffee out of stocks if she decided to wage price warfare against other producers. In theoretical terms Brazil's capacity was able to expand for a considerable time at indefinite limits and made thus her supply elasticity indefinite. Under the market structure conditions as stated on the world coffee market this could have led to a total displacement of her competitors.[10] An impact of an "aggressive" influence making for instability of one of the dominant buyers could only be traced in relation to the efficiency of the futures market and will be dealt with below.

A second oligopolistic conduct making for increased instability was the "thinness" of the futures market, which was a result of the conduct of the primary sellers and buyers for processing alike. It established the exchange as sometimes a third group fo competitors between the two dominant sides, able to induce conduct of one of the two large groups in the market, led to a price instability. The influence of the exchange trading can be explained in terms of a market analysis to have created a "teilologopol,"[11] which as established in economic theory makes for "higher instability" and *"Verstaerkereffekte."*[12]

The world coffee market faced then two problems in price formation:

(1) One was the problem of excess capacity. This has to be seen in two aspects: Firstly, unilateral action or collusive action of a group of oligopolists created new entry, that is new capacity reflecting at least in part low production

costs relative to the maintained price in the world market. Secondly, excess capacity is a weapon in oligopolistic price warfare between these Robusta-producing countries and Brazil. This is relevant, since a price war could be started by Brazil not because of her superior financial strength, which would have made Brazil a "dominant oligopolist *ex definitione.*" Quite contrary to this, the financial strength of both competing groups could be evaluated as equal, both being still poor economies.[13] The dominance of Brazil lay therefore in the fact that she had accumulated surpluses of coffee. A policy of setting the price of Brazils in such a way that it equaled that for Robustas would then have resulted in the disappearance of Robustas from the market. Such a move would have led — assuming that the scale of stocks represents a comparatively unlimited supply at the quoted price — to an absolute shift of demand from Brazils to Robustas because of the low price elasticity of demand for the industry and the fact that both products were near-substitutes on the market for second quality blends as well as on the market for solubles.[14] That Brazil was obviously willing to go into a price war can be inferred from the fact that she started discriminatory pricing, selling directly in large purchase contracts to soluble coffee manufacturers.

(2)   The second problem was the assurance of cooperation from all marketing channels if collusion was to be considered. As we described above the exchange was in its structure considerably integrated. But still independent trading firms existed and an exchange was open by definition to any outside supplier and speculative entry. A collusion to determine prices by collusive undertaking of the trade not quoting prices outside a fixed range cannot be reconciled with the function of trading there and will not be accepted by

trading interests. Secondly, the open entry makes the exchange still potentially atomistic in its structure. Both features make collusion of both primary market sides with the exchange and the independent trade impossible. Furthermore the institution of a terminal market allows for a loophole for those primary sellers and buyers for processing in that it permits these market partners to sell surpluses outside the collusive agreement: as international traders are anonymous in their supplies, small sales would not be traceable back to the primary supplier, who broke an existing collusion on price maintenance. Under this structure of a "thin" terminal market for coffee, comparatively small changes in the supply and demand situation would create relatively large swings in prices. Prices quoted in the exchange could then be considerably below and/or higher than those prices quoted by primary sellers. Lower prices quoted by independent traders could induce manufacturers to switch their supply base away from primary suppliers to independent traders or could induce manufacturers to request lower prices from their primary suppliers on the base of exchange quotations. Exchange trading and exchange prices can therefore be a tempting opener for non-collusive behavior by manufacturers, if these are oligopsonists. If exchange trading should be maintained, an exemption must be designed to prevent conduct that could lead to a renewal of non-collusive action.

The regulations of the agreement must be seen against these dimensions of exceptional structure and conduct in order to establish whether it is a suitable exemption — that is, whether it solves the two problems of oligopolistic price instability and disequilibrium.

**The Achievement of Long-run Equilibrium.** The latter point has been looked after through the provision in the agreement to establish export quotas in such a way that the general level of coffee prices does not fall below the level attained in 1962. This price fixation and the distribution of quotas has been the result of a "bargaining" process between importing countries and exporters.

These "per se restrictive" regulations influence the two problems of price formation as follows:

(1) It separates the price formation on the world market from the independent production policies of the oligopolistic primary producers. By this device all problems of the surplus being used as a strategical parameter of action in an oligopolistic price war become obsolete from the point of view of the price formation on the world market.

(2) Secondly, it prevented the world market price from being driven down to an indeterminate, uneconomic level through oligopolistic price war between the competing primary producers, a price which would not serve as an indicator for an efficient allocation of resources. The "bargaining" interpretation of the price level to be attained in the International Coffee Agreement as a form of collusive action between bilateral oligopolists seems thus to be defensible even on the line of an argument based on the classical model of non-restricted international trade, as represented in the relict GATT agreement.

The third question is whether the allocation of quotas and the price set represent the point where the minimized industry marginal costs of production equal the demand curve of the industry, or at least would be set at that point where every producer's own marginal production cost would equal his "ceteris paribus" demand curve for his own product. Such a price determination raises two points. It firstly requires the International Coffee Organization (ICO) to obtain "minimized marginal cost curves." This seems to be theoretically impossible and leaves only the search for historically given cost curves, which cannot form the basis of price determination as defined as "long-run equilibrum price" in a dynamic world. Secondly, it is obvious that a selling price policy determined by the marginal cost of production as a possible conduct for the oligopolists would require a change in their selling conduct, that is, in their national policy. At the moment it is not the costs of production, but the costs of different aims that determine the domestic as well as the export price policy of the oligopolists. These different costs include opportunity costs of retention in relation to social changes in the farm population, foreign exchange earnings, and others. If such a change of conduct could be brought about by an international commodity agreement, it could well lead to a tendency toward a long-run equilibrium. There are two obstacles to that aim; firstly, the history of international commodity agreements has shown that agreements have not resulted in such a change, and, secondly, the theory of industrial organization has not been able to advise measures or conduct that would achieve such a result.

If such a change in the national policy of a producer country cannot yet be attained through an international commodity agreement, it follows that no long-run equilibrium price, as defined under pure competition, can be arrived at. This, then, leaves room only for bargaining between both sides of the market determined through an identity of interests. The bargaining solution prevents the two results stated above (surplus as a weapon in price war and oligopolistic indeterminate prices). Given the structure of the world coffee industry, the ICA seems thus to be the only possible second-best solution that could be aimed at. The further regulation of production and production goals is thus not relevant, if we analyze the International Coffee Agreement as a form of exemption, since the production policy does not influence the price determination on the world market so long as the agreement stays in operation. If the consumer countries agree to regard foreign exchange earnings of producing countries as a point of common interest in the bargaining solution, however, then our approach connects itself with the macroeconomic development approach to the coffee agreement as stated in the Chapter 1. This has in fact been the case in the International Coffee Agreement and policy recommendations like production goals for each producing country and financial assistance to diversification under the agreement are thus compatible effects with microeconomic policy recommendations of the Agreement. It shall be noted here that such recommendations impose of course a great task for applied economics. Yet these problems do not come under the microeconomic headings of our study. This leads to the fourth point. Since the international coffee market has the structure of a bilateral oligopoly, neither a long-run equilibrium nor a tendency to create such a price can be reached without collusion, and no effort to create a free market would bring about the wanted result. It follows from this market analysis that an agreement cannot be temporary, but must be designed to last as long as the oligopolistic price formation exists on the world coffee market. The analysis reveals to our mind that the regulation of the coffee market is comparable to that envisaged for trade in primary products originating from economically developed countries.[15]

The price formation in the world coffee market has been one of differentiated oligopoly. To insure a second-best solution the agreement must go further and establish fixed price differentials between goods if price instability is to be avoided. Changes in the price differentials influence the single product demand curve of each competitor. A collusion is thus based on a stable single demand curve for the product of one competitor. A price change of the export price of one oligopolist changes the demand curve facing all other oligopolists. It destroys the precondition of a collusive policy of all competitors, which is based on a stable, single demand for each olipolist. The instrument with which the International Coffee Agreement was able to influence the export policy was the export quotas, and a *pro rata* adoption of all export quotas related to short-term fluctuations in the average indicator price range. Article 42 (2-3), which provides for establishing a scale of price differentials for various grades and qualities of coffee and appropriate measures of the council to correct a change in the differentials, has not yet been applied by the council.

As a collusion based on fixed price differential is the only method of determining an industry demand curve, the non-application of Rule 42 (2-3) seems to be the first criticism that must be applied against the ICA as a means to "regulate" the "exception" coffee market. An "exemption" for this problem must provide for a policy of fixed price differentials between the different products.

**The Achievement of Price Stability.** The second problem is that of price instability in the sense defined above. We distinguished two types of causative factors, one the "aggressive" price policies of different primary sellers; the other the result of a "thin" futures market on the coffee exchange. There was a third possible source, the buying policy of oligopsonistic buyers.

The first type of price instability has been dealt with by the same toolbox of measures in the ICA, which assures the "second-best solution" for the problem of a "long-run equilibrium." Export quotas and average indicator price range assure that the competing oligopolists must only follow a collusive policy. This rule is in fact a powerful one by the provision of Article 61, which provides that a member who has failed to fulfill his obligation under the agreement may be required to withdraw from the membership of the ICA, and that the importing countries limit their imports from non-members to a given average of preceding years. Its application against a non-collusive policy of one oligopolist is twofold: if an oligopolist country tries to raise its price, this can only be done by setting its price higher or not fulfilling its quota obligation. A rise in price would lead to a reduction of its exports – that is, the country would not be fulfilling its quota obligation. The council must then regard such an export policy as a breach of the agreement and therefore apply the import restriction clause, which would raise the price of that type of coffee in markets of importers to at least that price level

178

which was established in the agreement. Substitution would thus not take place. Vice versa, the "import restriction clause" of the agreement would have to be applied against an oligopolist underselling its output below the established price by an increase of its export higher than its quota. From the point of view of the first aspect of price instability, the obligation of the importing members of the agreement to restrict the imports from non-member exporters is then the most important regulation in the agreement, for it provides a means of securing the collusive behavior of the producing oligopolists.

But again the regulation of the international agreement fails to contribute to the aim of price stability in that the application of the price differential clause has been avoided. A seller country will be able to use mistakes in the estimated export quotas to widen or narrow its price differential, in order to export its allotted quota. This would make for shifts in the demand curve of all other coffee producing countries and lead to disturbances in the scale of price differentials, the basis of collusion. The pro-rata adjustment of all coffees may eventually fit just the changes in the demand curve of the individual producers. But such a result would be the outcome of pure coincidence, whereas an export-quota policy against one producer or a group of producing countries, exporting one type of coffee, would assure the price differential and thus increase the price stability.

The second and third types of price instability can be treated together. The third factor, the purchase policy of manufacturers, is not related to governmental agencies and would be mirrored only in dealings of traders at the exchange, integrated or supplied by large manufacturers. Serious price disturbances can only occur, as described above, if the independent price policies of traders are backed by a primary seller or a large buyer for processing, using their stocks to bring forward supplies at the traders' price quotations. If the price movement is not backed by one of these sides of the market, the movement of prices is bound to be short-term and random. Two questions have to be asked: whether the tools of the agreement are suitable to avoid the backing of price developments by primary sellers and buyers for processing, which started off as random, and secondly whether the agreement deals with the question of random fluctuations at all.

The first part of the first question has been dealt with already in the analysis related to the first type of price instability: efforts of one or more primary sellers to back random market price changes would lead to a change in its exports, and action of the council to change export quotas would follow because of a change in the indicator price range. But, as already explained, this would not only lead to a change of the quotas of the primary seller who backed the move of its particular type of coffee, but would also influence the export quotas of all other producers. Price changes of minor importance could then occur for all coffees, a result which could be avoided if export quotas were adjustable to influence the price of one product only – that is, to stabilize not the price range, bu the actual price differential. The tools of the agreement in regard to this first aspect of price instability under investigation are then able to avoid a more pronounced backing of one primary seller, but allows for a certain amount of price instability, which is unnecessary.

The second aspect of the first question is the backing of a price development by an oligopsonistic buyer for processing. Direct measures of the agreement, treating this cause of price instability, are not evident. The agreement does not prescribe that re-exporters must price their sales in accordance with the established indicator price range of primary exporters, nor does it provide for limitations on stock holdings in the hands of importers – the oligopsonists. As these may be principal causative factors that would create random fluctuations on the exchange as well, it can be concluded that the agreement is not equipped with direct means to protect the market against price fluctuations of the second part of the first aspect nor against the general second aspect, leaving thus the exemption as not sufficiently equipped for reaching its aim to avoid price instability of that kind. It can only fall back on indirect measures against it, which are again provided for by the export quota restrictions. The change in export quotas due to a change in the indicator price range would certainly influence the supply side of the coffee market. Because we assumed that the price instability was not caused by a change in the demand of the industry, the change in supply would over time lead to an absorption of stocks through consumption. This would re-establish the long-run stability between supply and demand at the given indicator price range. As not only the long-run stability is looked for, it seems fair to conclude that though the indirect measures would avoid oligopolistic warfare, the ICA has not yet managed to remove unnecessary random fluctuations which may arise out of speculative behavior of stocks in the hands of an oligopsonistic buyer for processing or through the price destabilizing influences of a thin futures market.

Another indirect influence on price stability may lie in the fact that the agreement provides, for the foreseeable future, an indicative price range and assures a constant supply through its policy on stocks in producing countries, and elimination of shortfalls. This could influence the attitude of oligopsonists to avoid stock-holding[16] and reduce the number of independent trade interests holding stocks for speculation.*

The Secondary Effects of the Agreement

Besides its effects in the direction of the two objects analyzed on the preceding pages, which we may call the main effects of the ICA, it creates secondary effects.[17] They can be contrary to further aims of the school of non-restrictive trade in the international coffee market and are therefore additional and disadvantageous and must be evaluated to analyze the appropriateness of the ICA as an exemption. One of these is the aim of establishing free entry into trading activities, that is, avoiding a restraint of trade in the countries concerned. This may not be the aim of all countries in the world coffee market. The

---

* This was partly discussed in the second section of Chapter 4. That this seems to be the case has been mentioned to the author by trading firms as well as by officials of the ICO.

analysis of market structure in domestic and export trade in the majority of producing countries makes it clear that this has not been a policy objective in the major producing countries. But it is certainly of importance to member countries like the United States, Germany, and other Western European importing countries. The agreement does not contain any restrictive implements in regard to trade interests. It allows for a free price policy of all traders concerned, unlimited stock holdings of all so interested in the importing countries and especially for free re-exports of coffee. In a direct sense it does not interfere with trading interests. And as analyzed above, by not restricting these activities of trade, it does not fulfill all the demands of a proper exception to avoid unnecessary random price instability on the coffee market.

Obviously, to evaluate the ICA the price instability factors must be balanced against the free entry into trade that is still available. As indicated above, the agreement provides for instruments to avoid price instability, which would lead to price warfare between oligopolists. As this possibility was the strongest case against price instability on the world coffee market and that is for the agreement, it may be concluded that the still inherent factors making for price instability are compensated by the fact that the agreement does not hamper entry and free execution of business by traders.

Such a comparison hides one fact: the ICA allows still for some degree of price fluctuation in the world coffee market and thus, as indicated earlier, the price risks of independent traders still exist. The agreement does nothing to increase the strength of forces that make for a better developed futures market, which is the only means for independent traders to hedge their risk. It does nothing to prevent the displacement of independent trade and will lead to a further process of integration of independent traders into the sales organization of both oligopolistic primary seller and buyer for manufacturing. It does not hamper the increase in concentration on the coffee market nor diminish the conditions of entry into coffee trade. Leaving the situation as it is, it does not provide for more competitive or less restrictive conditions in the coffee trade of those countries that want their economy guided by a policy of workable competition.

## The Coffee Agreement – A Case of Successful Economics?

The decision to publish this manuscript has provided an occasion to compare actual problems during the life span of the first and second agreements with those foreseen on the basis of the theoretical considerations in the preceding chapter.

The first impression is that the International Coffee Agreements of 1962 and 1968 have been successful in establishing a policy of "collusion" among primary suppliers that prevents price instability resulting from oligopolistic price warfare. Prices between 1962 and 1969-70 have remained remarkably stable in face of the huge surpluses that were threatening the market at the time when the first agreement went into force. Compared to the non-agreement period, when prices fluctuated by 12.4 percent per annum, fluctuation between 1964 and 1967-69 declined to 6.9 percent per annum. The agreement also presents good results in respect to matching the goals of a long-run equilibrium as a microeconomic goal and insuring sufficient foreign exchange earnings as a macroeconomic goal, as discussed previously.

A study of the First International Coffee Agreement[18] leads to the conclusion that while the agreement raised exchange earnings of producing countries from approximately $500 million in 1962 to $2.18 billion (in U.S. dollars) in 1963-67, it did not tend to maximize earnings by way of a producer cartel (Fig. 29). In fact foreign exchange earnings remained slightly below the maximum earning of $2.35 billion that coffee earned in 1953-57 when the "coffee cycle" peaked. Thus bargaining between consumers and producers proved effective in achieving economic results acceptable to both parties of the market.

However, this goal was achieved only after the agreement was amended to take care of some criticisms which in fact are closely related to the theoretical issues raised in the preceding section. Moveover, the agreement has recently experienced difficulties when prices soared above the agreement ceiling price. It will be argued that our analysis has pointed to some of the problems that the agreement is now facing. We shall deal with the problems and their solutions in the same order as the issues have been raised in this chapter.

The need for executing Article 42 of the first agreement, i.e., to establish prices by grade and price differential between grades, has been mentioned at various points. As one of the pre-essentials for a proper collusive policy among major producers offering non-homogeneous products. In 1963-64, when the council could not agree on the need, and, therefore, did not yet establish price differential, quotas were readjusted frequently, and a system that proved awkward, time-consuming, and impractical and at times tended to destabilize prices.[19]

In 1966, finally the council adopted a selectivity price system for the crop years 1966-67 and thereafter under which four price ranges, or price differential, between the four major types of coffee were established. This system required adjustment of part of the export quotas for one type of coffee when the daily average price of any type, taken for a period of fifteen days, remained below the floor or above the ceiling of a price range that was agreed upon for a particular type of coffee. This system has remained, essentially, in force until today. The same procedure, of course, has also prevented a modificiation of the strict principle of pro-rata market-sharing and has tended to reflect changes in consumer taste.

Under the heading "The Achievement of Price Stability," the discussion "pointed to possible loopholes in the quota provision of the agreement in such cases where primary suppliers, i.e., producing countries, did not fulfill their allocated export quota" with the aim of raising prices. It was argued then, however, that such cases should be regarded as conflicting with the duties accepted by signatories of the agreement and penalties, in particular import restrictions, should be invoked by member importing countries, provided that this action could be limited to

Figure 29

## Exports of Coffee from the Developing Countries

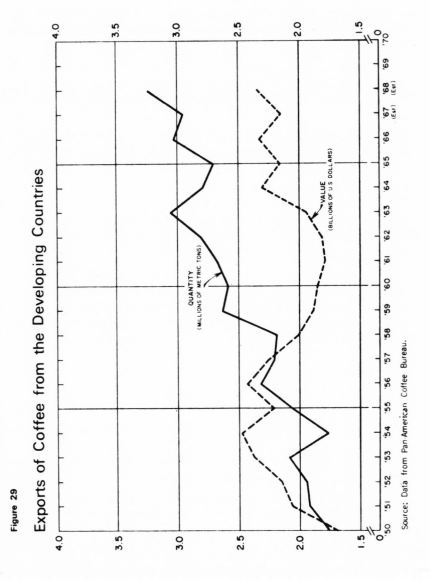

Source: Data from Pan American Coffee Bureau.

aim against one exporting country or a group of countries exporting one type of coffee.

The history of the 1964 price increase is a case in point. At that time Brazil did not fulfill its quota obligation in order to raise the average indicator price. Since no price differential policy was established at that date, the policy of Brazil could not be counteracted in a regular way and governments of importing countries were faced with serious problems. The provision of waivers,* i.e., selective increases in export quotas of other producing countries, in the end, provided a means to counteract the Brazilian policy. However, this policy of "stop-valving" with an instrument originally not designed for this purpose was resented in the council and led, *inter alia,* to the adoption of the "selectivity" price system.

In 1970, when prices rose to an unprecedented high despite continuous increases in the export quota to meet more than any possible increase in construction (export quotas for the marketing year 1969-70 were raised from 46 million bags to 51.8 million bags versus an estimated consumption of 46 million bags), a third loophole mentioned before became evident. As argued earlier, price instability could also occur as a result of inventory policy of large buyers for processing – a case against which measures of the agreement were not evident.

The price rise in 1970, seen against the available supply, can be explained only by inventory accumulation of large buyers for processing and traders, in anticipation of a further shortage of supplies in 1972.[20] Demand for inventories at that time was, and is, raising market's demand above consumption. Faced with available export supplies calculated on the basis of projected consumption, prices will remain high. In the last meeting of the International Coffee Organization producers and consumers were unable to reach agreement among themselves on this issue.

*Article 60 of the first agreement provided that the council might grant a "waiver," i.e., allow an increase in the export quota, to member countries which on account of exceptional or emergency circumstances, *force majeure,* constitutional obligations, *et al,* were likely to suffer serious hardships.

186

Producers did not accept any further increase in export quotas, as requested by consumers, claiming that an increase could only lead to further inventory accumulation. There is no evidence that the disagreement might lead to a breakdown of the agreement. The close of the council meeting without result, however, points vividly to the practical relevance of our criticism, which was pointed out previously on the basis of purely theoretical reasoning.

Finally, and hand in hand with a third loophole, the policy of the agreement "of not strengthening a futures market in coffee" is proving its relevance in the present situation. It is argued elsewhere that a thin futures market in coffee is, *on principle,* as well as a matter of fact in 1954, destabilizing the price and increasing price fluctuations. The reasons for this phenomenon should not be repeated here. However, the inability of traders to hedge and thus, to carry stocks with greatly reduced financial risks, has led to a decline in stocks that could now be released to dampen the increase in coffee prices,[21] which is now presenting such problems in the management of the agreement which, overall, has shown to be justified in economic terms and which has also been successful for nearly eight years.

**NOTES**

1.  FAO, "The International Effects of National Grain Policies," Commodity Policy Series No. 8 (Rome, 1955), pp. 8-10.

2.  J.S. Bain, *Price Theory,* rev. ed. (New York: Holt, Rinehart & Winston, 1963), p. 207.

3.  This is the reason for the present author to argue against Rowe's solution. See J.W. Rowe, *The World's Coffee* (London: Her Majesty's Stationery Office, 1963), pp. 193, 198), who has not taken account of this "exceptional" feature when he argued a "restoration of a proper equilibrum between supply and demand to be the aim of the World Coffee Agreement."

4.  This is the result of our assumption that the coffee market is a bilateral "teiloligopol." Cf. W. Krelle, *Preistheorie* (Tubingen-Zurich, 1961), p. 417.

5.  Bain, *op. cit.,* pp. 275, 284, 336: "The character of responses to changed prices of one oligopolist is intrinsically uncertain, so that seller's demand curve will be potentially indeterminate unless the uncertainty has been

removed by collusive agreement or by tacit collusion established by long experience by rivals with each other's action or policy."

6.  J.S. Bain, "Theory of Monopolistic Competition after Thirty Years, the Impact on Industrial Organization," AER, *Papers and Proceedings,* Vol. LIV (1964), p. 336.

7.  R.S. Porter, "Buffer Stocks and Economic Stability," *Oxford Economic Papers,* New Series, Vol. II (1950), pp. 95-118.

8.  H. Tyszinski, "Economics of the Wheat Agreement," *Economica 1949,* pp. 27-39, and "Commodity Agreements and Price Fluctuations," *The Economic Journal,* Vol. LXI (1951), pp. 655-658.

9.  V.W. Joehr and H.H. Singer, *The Role of the Economist to Official Advisors* (London: Allen and Unwin, 1955), p. 52.

10. It is obvious that the "defensive" price move of Brazil in 1958-59 increased the willingness of the Robusta producers to join the agreement because of the large stocks Brazil had in hand to compete with African Robusta producers. This fits with a theoretical reasoning in oligopolist price-cutting "that if firms are of the same size [in financial strength, market shares, etc.] it appears a new motive for inventories holdings, to ward off a rival's price-cutting propensities with the retaliatory weapon of sizeable inventories. The cost of an excessive inventory carryover may be less than the costs of acquiescence to downward price revisions." Cf. S. Weintraub, *Price Theory* (New York-London: Pitman, 1949), p. 172.

11. Krelle, *op. cit.,* p. 455; Bain, *op. cit.,* p. 334.

12. Krelle, *op. cit.,* p. 457.

13. FAO, "The International Effects of National Grain Policies," Commodity Policy Studies No. 8 (Rome, 1955).

14. E.H. Chamberlin, *The Theory of Monopolistic Competition,* 8th ed. (Cambridge, Mass., 1962), p. 90.

15. G. Blau, "International Commodity Agreements," paper presented at the IER Congress on Economic Development (Vienna, Austria, 1962).

16. Patton & Co., *Coffee Intelligence* (February 4, 1963, and October 5, 1965).

17. Joehr and Singer, *op. cit.,* p. 52.

18. Singh, "The International Coffee Agreement, 1968 – Background and Analysis," IBRD Report No. Ec-165 (August 1, 1968), pp. 18-19.

19. Singh, *op. cit.,* p. 12.

20. Robin Reves, "Coffee–A Survey: Supply Moves into Shortage," *Financial Times* (February 27, 1970).

21. *Ibid.,* p. 30.

# Appendixes

# INTERNATIONAL COFFEE AGREEMENT OF 1962

## Preamble

The Governments Parties to this Agreement,

Recognizing the exceptional importance of coffee to the economies of many countries which are largely dependent upon this commodity for their export earnings and thus for the the continuation of their development programmes in the social and economic fields;

Considering that close international co-operation on coffee marketing will stimulate the economic diversification and development of coffee-producing countries and thus contribute to a strengthening of the political and economic bonds between producers and consumers;

Finding reason to expect a tendency toward persistent disequilibrium between production and consumption, accumulation of burdensome stocks, and pronounced fluctuations in prices, which can be harmful both to producers and to consumers; and

Believing that, in the absence of international measures, this situation cannot be corrected by normal market forces,

Have agreed as follows:

## CHAPTER I – OBJECTIVES

## ARTICLE 1

### Objectives

The objectives of the Agreement are:

(1) to achieve a reasonable balance between supply and demand on a basis which will assure adequate supplies of coffee to consumers and markets for coffee to rpoducers at equitable prices, and which will bring about long-term equilibrium between production and consumption;

(2) to alleviate the serious hardship caused by burdensome surpluses and excessive fluctuations in the prices of coffee to the detriment of the interests of both producers and consumers;

(3) to contribute to the development of productive resources and to the promotion and maintenance of employment and income in the Member countries, thereby helping to bring about fair wages, higher living standards, and better working conditions;

(4) to assist in increasing the purchasing power of coffee-exporting countries by keeping prices at equitable levels and by increasing consumption;

(5) to encourage the consumption of coffee by every possible means; and

(6) in general, in recognition of the relationship of the trade in coffee to the economic stability of markets for industrial products, to further international co-operation in connexion with world coffee problems.

# CHAPTER II – DEFINITIONS

## ARTICLE 2

### Definitions

For the purposes of the Agreement:

(1) "Coffee" means the beans and berries of the coffee tree, whether parchment, green or roasted, and includes ground, decaffeinated, liquid and soluble coffee. These terms shall have the following meaning:

(a) "green coffee" means all coffee in the naked bean form before roasting:

(b) "coffee berries" means the complete fruit of the coffee tree; to find the equivalent of coffee berries to green coffee, multiply the net weight of the dried coffee berries by $0 \cdot 50$;

(c) "parchment coffee" means the green coffee bean contained in the parchment skin; to find the equivalent of parchment coffee to green coffee, multiply the net weight of the parchment coffee by $0 \cdot 80$;

(d) "roasted coffee" means green coffee roasted to any degree and includes ground coffee; to find the equivalent of roasted coffee to green coffee, multiply the net weight of roasted coffee by $1 \cdot 19$;

(e) "decaffeinated coffee" means green, roasted or soluble coffee from which caffein has been extracted; to find the equivalent of decaffeinated coffee to green coffee in green, roasted or soluble form by $1 \cdot 00$, $1 \cdot 19$ or $3 \cdot 00$, respectively;

(f) "liquid coffee" means the water-soluble solids derived from roasted coffee and put into liquid form; to find the equivalent of liquid to green coffee, multiply the net weight of the dried coffee solids contained in the liquid coffee by $3 \cdot 00$;

(g) "soluble coffee" means the dried water-soluble solids

derived from roasted coffee; to find the equivalent of soluble coffee to green coffee, multiply the net weight of the soluble coffee by 3·00.

(2) "Bag" means 60 kilogrammes or 132·276 pounds of green coffee; "ton" means a metric ton of 1,000 kilogrammes or 2,204·6 pounds; and "pound" means 453·597 grammes.

(3) "Coffee year" means the period of one year, from 1 October through 30 September; and "first coffee year" means the coffee year beginning 1 October, 1962.

(4) "Export of Coffee" means, except as otherwise provided in Article 38, any shipment of coffee which leaves the territory of the country where the coffee was grown.

(5) "Organization", "Council" and "Board" mean, respectively, the International Coffee Organization, the International Coffee Council, and the Executive Board established under Article 7 of the Agreement.

(6) "Member" means a Contracting Party; a dependent territory or territories in respect of which separate Membership has been declared under Article 4; or two or more Contracting Parties or dependent territories, or both, which participate in the Organization as a Member group under Article 5 or 6.

(7) "Exporting Member" or "exporting country" means a Member or country, respectively, which is a net exporter of coffee; that is, whose exports exceed its imports.

(8) "Importing Member" or "importing country" means a Member or country, respectively, which is a net importer of coffee; that is, whose imports exceed its exports.

(9) "Producing Member" or "producing country" means a Member or country, respectively, which grows coffee in commercially significant quantities.

(10) "Distributed simple majority vote" means a majority of the votes cast by exporting Members present and voting, and a

majority of the votes cast by importing Members present and voting, counted separately.

(11) "Distributed two-thirds majority vote" means a two-thirds majority of the votes cast by exporting Members present and voting and a two-thirds majority of the votes cast by importing Members present and voting, counted separately.

(12) "Entry into force" means, except where the context otherwise requires, the date on which the Agreement first enters into force, whether provisionally or definitively.

## CHAPTER III – MEMBERSHIP

### ARTICLE 3

### Membership in the Organization

Each Contracting Party, together with those of its dependent territories to which the Agreement is extended under paragraph (1) of Article 67, shall constitute a single Member of the Organization, except as otherwise provided under Article 4, 5 or 6.

### ARTICLE 4

### Separate Membership in Respect of Dependent Territories

Any Contracting Party which is a net importer of coffee may, at any time, by appropriate notification in accordance with paragraph (2) of Article 67, declare that it is participating in the Organization separately with respect to any of its dependent territories which are net exporters of coffee and which it designates. In such case, the metropolitan territory and its non-designated dependent territories will have a single Membership, and its designated dependent territories, either individually or collectively as the notification indicates, will have separate Membership.

# ARTICLE 5

## Group Membership upon Joining the Organization

(1) Two or more Contracting Parties which are net exporters of coffee may, by appropriate notification to the Secretary-General of the United Nations at the time of deposit of their respective instruments of ratification or accessing, and to the Council at its first session, declare that they are joining the Organization as a Member group. A dependent territory to which the Agreement has been extended under paragraph (1) of Article 67 may constitute part of such a Member group if the Government of the State responsible for its international relations has given appropriate notification thereof under paragraph (2) of Article 67. Such Contracting Parties and dependent territories must satisfy the following conditions:

- (a) they shall declare their willingness to accept responsibility for group obligations in an individual as well as a group capacity;
- (b) they shall subsequently provide sufficient evidence to the Council that the group has the organization necessary to implement a common coffee policy, and that they have the means of complying, together with the other parties to the group, with their obligations under the Agreement; and
- (c) they shall subsequently provide evidence to the Council either:
  - (i) that they have been recognized as a group in a previous international coffee agreement; or
  - (ii) that they have:
    - (a) a common or co-ordinated commercial and economic policy in relation to coffee, and
    - (b) a co-ordinated monetary and financial policy, as well as the organs necessary for implementing such a policy, so that the Council is satisfied that the Member group can comply with the spirit of group membership and the group obligations involved.

(2) The Member group shall constitute a single Member of the Organization, except that each party to the group shall be treated as if it were a single Member as regards all matters arising under the following provisions:

(a) Chapters XI and XII;
(b) Articles 10, 11 and 19 of Chapter IV; and
(c) Article 70 of Chapter XIX.

(3) The Contracting Parties and dependent territories joining as a Member group shall specify the Government or organization which will represent them in the Council as regards all matters arising under the Agreement other than those specified in paragraph (2) of this Article.

(4) The Member group's voting rights shall be as follows:

(a) the member group shall have the same number of basic votes as a single Member country joining the Organization in an individual capacity. These basic votes shall be attributed to and exercised by the Government or organization representing the group;

(b) in the event of a vote on any matters arising under provisions specified in paragraph (2) of this Article, the parties to the Member group may exercise separately the votes attributed to them by the provisions of paragraph (3) of Article 12 as if each were an individual Member of the Organization, except for the basic votes, which shall remain attributable only to the Government or organization representing the group.

(5) Any Contracting Party or dependent territory which is a party to a Member group may, by notification to the Council, withdraw from that group and become a separate Member. Such withdrawal shall take effect upon receipt of the notification by the Council. In case of such withdrawal from a group, or in case a party to a group ceases, by withdrawal from the Organization or otherwise, to be such a party, the remaining parties to the group may apply to the Council to maintain the group, and the group shall continue to exist unless the Council disapproves the

application. If the Member group is dissolved, each former party to the group will become a separate Member. A Member which has ceased to be a party to a group may not, as long as the Agreement remains in force, again become a party to a group.

## ARTICLE 6

### Subsequent Group Membership

Two or more exporting Members may, at any time after the Agreement has entered into force with respect to them, apply to the Council to form a Member group. The Council shall approve the application if it finds that the Members have made a declaration, and have provided evidence, satisfying the requirements of paragraph (1) of Article 5. Upon such approval, the Member group shall be subject to the provisions of paragraphs (2), (3), (4) and (5) of that Article.

## CHAPTER IV – ORGANIZATION AND ADMINISTRATION

## ARTICLE 7

### Establishment, Seat and Structure of the International Coffee Organization

(1) The International Coffee Organization is hereby established to administer the provisions of the Agreement and to supervise its operation.

(2) The seat of the Organization shall be in London.

(3) The Organization shall function through the International Coffee Council, its Executive Board, its Executive Director, and its staff.

# ARTICLE 8

## Composition of the International Coffee Council

(1) The highest authority of the Organization shall be the International Coffee Council, which shall consist of all the Members of the Organization.

(2) Each Member shall be represented on the Council by a representative and one or more alternates. A Member may also designate one or more advisers to accompany its representative or alternates.

# ARTICLE 9

## Powers and Functions of the Council

(1) All powers specifically conferred by the Agreement shall be vested in the Council, which shall have the powers and perform the functions necessary to carry out the provisions of the Agreement.

(2) The Council shall, by a distributed two-thirds majority vote, establish such rules and regulations, including its own rules of procedure and the financial and staff regulations of the Organization, as are necessary to carry out the provisions of the Agreement and are consistent therewith. The Council may, in its rules of procedure, provide a procedure whereby it may, without meeting, decide specific questions.

(3) The Council shall also keep such records as are required to perform its functions under the Agreement and such other records as it considers desirable, and shall publish an annual report.

# ARTICLE 10

## Election of the Chairman and Vice-Chairmen of the Council

(1) The Council shall elect, for each coffee year, a Chairman and a first, a second and a third Vice-Chairman.

(2) As a general rule, the Chairman and the first Vice-Chairman shall both be elected either from among the representatives of exporting Members, or from among the representatives of importing Members, and the second and the third Vice-Chairman shall be elected from representatives of the other category of Members; these offices shall alternate each coffee year between the two categories of Members.

(3) Neither the Chairman nor any Vice-Chairman acting as Chairman shall have the right to vote. His alternate will in such case exercise the Member's voting rights.

## ARTICLE 11

### Sessions of the Council

As a general rule, the Council shall hold regular sessions twice a year. It may hold special sessions if it so decides. Special sessions shall also be held when either the Executive Board, or any five Members, or a Member or Members having at least 200 votes so request. Notice of sessions shall be given at least thirty days in advance, except in cases of emergency. Sessions shall be held at the seat of the Organization, unless the Council decides otherwise.

## ARTICLE 12

### Votes

(1) The exporting Members shall together hold 1,000 votes and the importing Members shall together hold 1,000 votes, distributed within each category of Members—that is, exporting and importing Members, respectively—as provided in the following paragraphs of this Article.

(2) Each Member shall have five basic votes, provided that the total number of basic votes within each category of Members does not exceed 150. Should there be more than thirty exporting Members or more than thirty importing Members, the number of

basic votes for each Member within that category of Members shall be adjusted so as to keep the number of basic votes for each category of Members within the maximum of 150.

(3) The remaining votes of exporting Members shall be divided among those Members in proportion to their respective basic quotas, except that in the event of a vote on any matter arising under the provisions specified in paragraph (2) of Article 5, the remaining votes of a Member group shall be divided among the parties to that group in proportion to their respective participation in the basic export quota of the Member group.

(4) The remaining votes of importing Members shall be divided among those Members in proportion to the average volume of their respective coffee imports in the preceding three-year period.

(5) The distribution of votes shall be determined by the Council at the beginning of each coffee year, and shall remain in effect during that year, except as provided in paragraph (6) of this Article.

(6) The Council shall provide for the redistribution of votes in accordance with this Article whenever there is a change in the Membership of the Organization, or if the voting rights of a Member are suspended or regained under the provisions of Article 25, 45 or 61.

(7) No Member shall hold more than 400 votes.

(8) There shall be no fractional votes.

## ARTICLE 13

### Voting Procedure of the Council

(1) Each representative shall be entitled to cast the number of votes held by the Member represented by him, and cannot divide its votes. He may, however, cast differently from such votes any votes which he exercises pursuant to paragraph (2) of this Article.

(2) Any exporting Member may authorize any other exporting Member, and any importing Member may authorize any other importing Member, to represent its interest and to exercise its right to vote at any meeting or meetings of the Council. The limitation provided for in paragraph (7) of Article 12 shall not apply in this case.

## ARTICLE 14

### Decisions of the Council

(1) All decisions of the Council shall be taken, and all recommendations shall be made, by a distributed simple majority vote unless otherwise provided in the Agreement.

(2) The following procedure shall apply with respect to any action by the Council which under the Agreement requires a distributed two-thirds majority vote:

- (a) if a distributed two-thirds majority vote is not obtained because of the negative vote of three or less exporting or three or less importing Members, the proposal shall, if the Council so decides by a majority of the Members present and by a distributed simple majority vote, be put to a vote again within 48 hours:
- (b) If a distributed two-thirds majority vote is again not obtained because of the negative vote of two or less importing or two or less exporting Members, the proposal shall, if the Council so decides by the majority of the Members present and by a distributed simple majority vote, be put to a vote again within 24 hours:
- (c) if a distributed two-thirds majority vote is not obtained in the third vote because of the negative vote of one exporting Member or one importing Member, the proposal shall be considered adopted;
- (d) if the Council fails to put a proposal to a further vote, it shall be considered rejected.

(3) The Members undertake to accept as binding all decisions of the Council under the provisions of the Agreement.

## ARTICLE 15

### Composition of the Board

(1) The Executive Board shall consist of seven exporting Members and seven importing Members, elected for each coffee year in accordance with Article 16. Members may be re-elected.

(2) Each Member of the Board shall appoint one representative and one or more alternates.

(3) The Chairman of the Board shall be appointed by the Council for each coffee year and may be re-appointed. He shall not have the right to vote. If a representative is appointed Chairman, his alternate will have the right to vote in his place.

(4) The Board shall normally meet at the seat of the Organization, but may meet elsewhere.

## ARTICLE 16

### Election of the Board

(1) The exporting and the importing Members on the Board shall be elected in the Council by the exporting and the importing Members of the Organization respectively. The election within each category shall be held in accordance with the following paragraphs of this Article.

(2) Each Member shall cast all the votes to which it is entitled under Article 12 for a single candidate. A Member may cast for another candidate any votes which it exercises pursuant to paragraph (2) of Article 13.

(3) The seven candidates receiving the largest number of votes shall be elected; however, no candidate shall be elected on the first ballot unless it receives at least 75 votes.

(4) If under the provisions of paragraph (3) of this Article less than seven candidates are elected on the first ballot, further ballots shall be held in which only Members who did not vote for any of the candidates elected shall have the right to vote. In each further ballot, the minimum number of votes required for election shall be successively diminished by five until seven candidates are elected.

(5) Any Member who did not vote for any of the Members elected shall assign its votes to one of them, subject to paragraphs (6) and (7) of this Article.

(6) A Member shall be deemed to have received the number of votes originally cast for it when it was elected and, in addition, the number of votes assigned to it, provided that the total number of votes shall not exceed 499 for any Member elected.

(7) If the votes deemed received by an elected Member would otherwise exceed 499, Members which voted for or assigned their votes to such elected Member shall arrange among themselves for one or more of them to withdraw their votes from that Member and assign or reassign them to another elected Member so that the votes received by each elected Member shall not exceed the limit of 499.

## ARTICLE 17

### Competence of the Board

(1) The Board shall be responsible to and work under the general direction of the Council.

(2) The Council may, by a distributed simple majority vote, delegate to the Board the exercise of any or all of its powers, other than the following:

- *(a)* annual distribution of votes under paragraph (5) of Article 12;
- *(b)* approval of the administrative budget and assessment of contributions under Article 24;
- *(c)* determination of quotas under the Agreement;

*(d)* imposition of enforcement measures other than those whose application is automatic;

*(e)* suspension of the voting rights of a Member under Article 45 or 61;

*(f)* determination of individual country and world production goals under Article 48;

*(g)* establishment of a policy relative to stocks under Article 51;

*(h)* waiver of the obligations of a Member under Article 60;

*(i)* decision of disputes under Article 61;

*(j)* establishment of conditions for accession under Article 65;

*(k)* a decision to require the withdrawal of a Member under Article 69;

*(l)* extension or termination of the Agreement under Article 71; and

*(m)* recommendation of amendments to Members under Article 73.

(3) The Council may at any time, by a distributed simple majority vote, revoke any delegation of powers to the Board.

## ARTICLE 18

### Voting Procedure of the Board

(1) Each member of the Board shall be entitled to cast the number of votes received by it under the provisions of paragraphs (6) and (7) of Article 16. Voting by proxy shall not be allowed. A member may not split its votes.

(2) Any action taken by the Board shall require the same majority as such action would require if taken by the Council.

## ARTICLE 19

### Quorum for the Council and the Board

(1) The quorum for any meeting of the Council shall be the

presence of a majority of the Members representing a distributed two-thirds majority of the total votes. If there is no quorum on the day appointed for the opening of any Council session, or if in the course of any Council session there is no quorum at three successive meetings, the Council shall be convened seven days later; at that time and throughout the remainder of that session the quorum shall be the presence of a majority of the Members representing a distributed simple majority of the votes. Representation in accordance with paragraph (2) of Article 13 shall be considered as presence.

(2) The quorum for any meeting of the Board shall be the presence of a majority of the members representing a distributed two-thirds majority of the total votes.

## ARTICLE 20

### The Executive Director and the Staff

(1) The Council shall appoint the Executive Director on the recommendation of the Board. The terms of appointment of the Executive Director shall be established by the Council and shall be comparable to those applying to corresponding officials of similar inter-governmental organizations.

(2) The Executive Director shall be the chief administrative officer of the Organization and shall be responsible for the performance of any duties devolving upon him in the administration of the Agreement.

(3) The Executive Director shall appoint the staff in accordance with regulations established by the Council.

(4) Neither the Executive Director nor any member of the staff shall have any financial interest in the coffee industry, coffee trade, or coffee transportation.

(5) In the performance of their duties, the Executive Director and the staff shall not seek or receive instructions from any

Member or from any other authority external to the Organization. They shall refrain from any action which might reflect on their position as international officials responsible only to the Organization. Each Member undertakes to respect the exclusively international character of the responsibilities of the Executive Director and the staff and not to seek to influence them in the discharge of their responsibilities.

## ARTICLE 21

### Co-operation with other Organizations

The Council may make whatever arrangements are desirable for consultation and co-operation with the United Nations and its specialized agencies and with other appropriate inter-governmental organizations. The Council may invite these organizations and any organizations concerned with coffee to send observers to its meetings.

## CHAPTER V—PRIVILEGES AND IMMUNITIES

## ARTICLE 22

### Privileges and Immunities

(1) The Organization shall have in the territory of each Member, to the extent consistent with its laws, such legal capacity as may be necessary for the exercise of its functions under the Agreement.

(2) The Government of the United Kingdom of Great Britain and Northern Ireland shall grant exemption from taxation on the salaries paid by the Organization to its employees, except that such exemption need not apply to nationals of that country. It shall also grant exemption from taxation on the assets, income and other property of the Organization.

# CHAPTER VI—FINANCE

## ARTICLE 23

### Finance

(1) The expenses of delegations to the Council, representatives on the Board, and representatives on any of the committees of the Council or the Board shall be met by their respective Governments.

(2) The other expenses necessary for the administration of the Agreement shall be met by annual contributions from the Members assessed in accordance with Article 24.

(3) The financial year of the Organization shall be the same as the coffee year.

## ARTICLE 24

### Determination of the Budget and Assessment of Contributions

(1) During the second half of each financial year, the Council shall approve the administrative budget of the Organization for the following financial year, and shall assess the contribution of each Member to that budget.

(2) The contribution of each Member to the budget for each financial year shall be in the proportion which the number of its votes at the time the budget for that financial year is approved bears to the total votes of all the Members. However, if there is any change in the distribution of votes among Members in accordance with the provisions of paragraph (5) of Article 12 at the beginning of the financial year for which contributions are assessed, such contributions shall be correspondingly adjusted for that year. In determining contributions, the votes of each Member shall be calculated without regard to the suspension of any Member's voting rights or any redistribution of votes resulting therefrom.

(3) The initial contribution of any Member joining the Organization after the entry into force of the Agreement shall be assessed by the Council on the basis of the number of votes to be held by it and the period remaining in the current financial year, but the assessments made upon other Members for the current financial year shall not be altered.

(4) If the Agreement comes into force more than eight months before the beginning of the first full financial year of the Organization, the Council shall at its first session approve an administrative budget covering only the period up to the commencement of the first full financial year. Otherwise the first administrative budget shall cover both the initial period and the first full financial year.

## ARTICLE 25

### Payment of Contributions

(1) Contributions to the administrative budget for each financial year shall be payable in freely convertible currency, and shall become due on the first day of that financial year.

(2) If any Member fails to pay its full contribution to the administrative budget within six months of the date on which the contribution is due, both its voting rights in the Council and its right to have its votes cast in the Board shall be suspended until such contribution has been paid. However, unless the Council so decides by a distributed two-thirds majority vote, such Member shall not be deprived of any of its other rights nor relieved of any of its obligations under the Agreement.

(3) Any Member whose voting rights have been suspended, either under paragraph (2) of this Article or under Article 45 or 61, shall nevertheless remain responsible for the payment of its contribution.

# ARTICLE 26

## Audit and Publication of Accounts

As soon as possible after the close of each financial year, an independently audited statement of the Organization's receipts and expenditures during that financial year shall be presented to the Council for approval and publication.

# CHAPTER VII—REGULATION OF EXPORTS

# ARTICLE 27

## General Undertakings by Members

(1) The Members undertake to conduct their trade policy so that the objectives set forth in Article 1 and, in particular, paragraph (4) of that Article, may be achieved. They agree on the desirability of operating the Agreement in a manner such that the real income derived from the export of coffee could be progressively increase so as to make it consonant with their needs for foreign exchange to support their programmes for social and economic progress.

(2) To attain these purposes through the fixing of quotas as provided for in this Chapter and in other ways carrying out the provisions of the Agreement, the Members agree on the necessity of assuring that the general level of coffee prices does not decline below the general level of such prices in 1962.

(3) The Members further agree on the desirability of assuring to consumers prices which are equitable and which will not hamper a desirable increase in consumption.

# ARTICLE 28

## Basic Export Quotas

(1) For the first three coffee years, beginning on 1 October

1962, the exporting countries listed in Annex A shall have the basic export quotas specified in that Annex.

(2) During the last six months of the coffee year ending 30 September 1965, the Council shall review the basic export quotas specified in Annex A in order to adjust them to general market conditions. The Council may then revise such quotas by a distributed two-thirds majority vote; if not revised, the basic export quotas specified in Annex A shall remain in effect.

## ARTICLE 29

### Quota of a Member Group

Where two or more countries listed in Annex A form a Member group in Accordance with Article 5, the basic export quotas specified for those countries in Annex A shall be added together and the combined total treated as a single quota for the purposes of this Chapter.

## ARTICLE 30

### Fixing of Annual Export Quotas

(1) At least 30 days before the beginning of each coffee year the Council shall adopt by a two-thirds majority vote an estimate of total world imports for the following coffee year and an estimate of probable exports from non-member countries.

(2) In the light of these estimates the Council shall forthwith fix annual export quotas which shall be the same percentage for all exporting Members of the basic export quotas specified in Annex A. For the first coffee year this percentage is fixed at 99, subject to the provisions of Article 32.

## ARTICLE 31

### Fixing of Quarterly Export Quotas

(1) Immediately following the fixing of the annual export

quotas the Council shall fix quarterly export quotas for each exporting Member for the purpose of keeping supply in reasonable balance with estimated demand throughout the coffee year.

(2) These quotas shall be, as nearly as possible, 25 per cent of the annual export quota of each Member during the coffee year. No Member shall be allowed to export more than 30 per cent in the first quarter, 60 per cent in the first two quarters, and 80 per cent in the first three quarters of the coffee year. If exports from any Member in one quarter are less than its quota for that quarter, the outstanding balance shall be added to its quota for the following quarter of that coffee year.

## ARTICLE 32

### Adjustment of Annual Export Quotas

If market conditions so require, the Council may review the quota situation and may vary the percentage of basic export quotas fixed under paragraph (2) of Article 30. In so doing, the Council shall have regard to any likely shortfalls by Members.

## ARTICLE 33

### Notification of Shortfalls

(1) Exporting Members undertake to notify the Council at the end of the eighth month of the coffee year, and at such later dates as the Council may request, whether they have sufficient coffee available to export the full amount of their quota for that year.

(2) The Council shall take into account these notifications in determining whether or not to adjust the level of export quotas in accordance with Article 32.

## ARTICLE 34

### Adjustment of Quarterly Export Quotas

(1) The Council shall in the circumstances set out in this

212

Article vary the quarterly export quotas fixed for each Member under paragraph (1) of Article 31.

(2) If the Council varies the annual export quotas as provided in Article 32, then the change in that annual quota shall be reflected in the quotas for the current and remaining quarters, or the remaining quarters, of the coffee year.

(3) Apart from the adjustment provided for in the preceding paragraph, the Council may, if it finds the market situation so requires, make adjustments among the current and remaining quarterly export quotas for the same coffee year, without, however, altering the annual export quotas.

(4) If on account of exceptional circumstances an exporting Member considers that the limitations provided in paragraph (2) of Article 31 would be likely to cause serious harm to its economy, the Council may, at the request of that Member, take appropriate action under Article 60. The Member concerned must furnish evidence of harm and provide adequate guarantees concerning the maintenance of price stability. The Council shall not, however, in any event, authorize a Member to export more than 35 per cent of its annual export quota in the first quarter, 65 per cent in the first two quarters, and 85 per cent in the first three quarters of the coffee year.

(5) All Members recognize that marked price rises or falls occurring within brief periods may unduly distort underlying trends in price, cause grave concern to both producers and consumers, and jeopardize the attainment of the objectives of the Agreement. Accordingly, if such movements in general price levels occur within brief periods, Members may request a meeting of the Council which, by distributed simple majority vote, may revise the total level of the quarterly export quotas in effect.

(6) If the Council finds that a sharp and unusual increase or decrease in the general level of prices is due to artificial manipulation of the coffee market through agreements among importers or exporters or both, it shall then decide by a simple

majority vote on what corrective measures should be applied to readjust the total level of the quarterly export quotas in effect.

## ARTICLE 35

### Procedure for Adjusting Export Quotas

(1) Annual export quotas shall be fixed and adjusted by altering the basic export quota of each Member by the same percentage.

(2) General changes in all quarterly export quotas, made pursuant to paragraphs (2), (3), (5) and (6) of Article 34, shall be applied *pro rata* to individual quarterly export quotas in accordance with appropriate rules established by the Council. Such rules shall take account of the different percentages of annual export quotas which the different Members have exported or are entitled to export in each quarter of the coffee year.

(3) All decisions by the Council on the fixing and adjustment of annual and quarterly export quotas under Articles 30, 31, 32 and 34 shall be taken, unless otherwise provided, by a distributed two-thirds majority vote.

## ARTICLE 36

### Compliance with Export Quotas

(1) Exporting Members subject to quotas shall adopt the measures required to ensure full compliance with all provisions of the Agreement relating to quotas. The Council may request such Members to adopt additional measures for the effective implementation of the quota system provided for in the Agreement.

(2) Exporting Members shall not exceed the annual and quarterly export quotas allocated to them.

(3) If an exporting Member exceeds its quota for any quarter, the Council shall deduct from one or more of its future quotas a total amount equal to that excess.

(4) If an exporting Member for the second time while the agreement remains in force exceeds its quarterly quota, the Council shall deduct from one or more of its future quotas a total amount equal to twice that excess.

(5) If an exporting Member for a third or subsequent time while the Agreement remains in force exceeds its quarterly quota, the Council shall make the same deduction as provided in paragraph (4) of this Article, and in addition the Council may take action in accordance with Article 69 to require the withdrawal of such a Member from the Organization.

(6) The deductions in quotas provided in paragraphs (3), (4) and (5) of this Article shall be made by the Council as soon as it receives the necessary information.

## ARTICLE 37

### Transitional Quota Provisions

(1) Exports of coffee after 1 October 1962 shall be charged against the annual export quota of the exporting country concerned at such time as the Agreement enters into force in respect of that country.

(2) If the Agreement enters into force after 1 October 1962, the Council shall, during its first session, make such modifications as may be necessary in the procedure for the fixing of annual and quarterly export quotas in respect of the coffee year in which the Agreement enters into force.

## ARTICLE 38

### Shipments of Coffee from Dependent Territories

(1) Subject to paragraph (2) of this Article, the shipment of coffee from any of the dependent territories of a Member to its metropolitan territory or to another of its dependent territories for domestic consumption therein or in any other of its dependent

territories shall not be considered as the export of coffee, and shall not be subject to any export quota limitations, provided that the Member concerned enters into arrangements satisfactory to the Council with respect to the control of re-exports and such other matters as the Council may determine to be related to the operation of the Agreement and which arise out of the special relationship between the metropolitan territory of the Member and its dependent territories.

(2) The trade in coffee between a Member and any of its dependent territories which, in accordance with Article 4 or 5, is a separate Member of the Organization or a party to a Member group, shall however be treated, for the purposes of the Agreement, as the export of coffee.

## ARTICLE 39

### Exporting Members not Subject to Quotas

(1) Any exporting Member whose average annual exports of coffee for the preceding three-year period were less than 25,000 bags shall not be subject to the quota provisions of the Agreement, so long as its exports remain less than that quantity.

(2) Any Trust Territory administered under a trusteeship agreement with the United Nations whose annual exports to countries other than the Administering Authority do not exceed 100,000 bags shall not be subject to the quota provisions of the Agreement, so long as its exports do not exceed that quantity.

## ARTICLE 40

### Exports not Charged to Quotas

(1) In order to facilitate the increase of coffee consumption in certain areas of the world having a low *per capita* consumption and considerable potential for expansion, exports to countries listed in Annex B shall not, subject to the provisions of sub-paragraph *(f)* of this paragraph, be charged to quotas. The

**216**

Council, at the beginning of the second full coffee year after the Agreement enters into force, and annually thereafter, shall review the list with a view to determining whether any country or countries should be deleted from it, and may, if it so decides, delete any such country or countries.

In connection with exports to the countries listed in Annex B, the provisions of the following sub-paragraphs shall be applicable:

*(a)* At its first session, and thereafter whenever it deems necessary, the Council shall prepare an estimate of imports for internal consumption by the countries listed in Annex B, after reviewing the results obtained in the previous year with regard to the increase of coffee consumption in those countries and taking into account the probable effect of promotion campaigns and trade arrangements. Exporting Members shall not in the aggregate export to the countries listed in Annex B more than the quantity set by the Council, and for that purpose the Council shall keep those Members informed of current exports to such countries. Exporting Members shall inform the Council not later than thirty days after the end of each month of all exports made to each of the countries listed in Annex B during that month.

*(b)* Members shall apply such statistics and other information as the Council may require to assist it in controlling the flow of coffee to countries listed in Annex B and its consumption therein.

*(c)* Exporting Members shall endeavour to renegotiate existing trade agreements as soon as possible in order to include in them provisions preventing re-exports of coffee from the countries listed in Annex B to other markets. Exporting Members shall also include such provisions in all new trade agreements and in all new sales contracts not covered by trade agreements, whether such contracts are negotiated with private traders or with government organizations.

*(d)* In order to maintain control at all times of exports to countries listed in Annex B, the Council may decide upon further precautionary steps, such as requiring coffee bags destined to those countries to be specially marked and requiring that the exporting Members receive from such countries banking and contractual guarantees to prevent re-exportation to countries not listed in Annex B. The Council may, whenever it deems necessary, engage the services of an internationally recognized world-wide organization to investigate irregularities in, or to verify exports to, countries listed in Annex B. The Council shall call any possible irregularity to the attention of the Members.

*(e)* The Council shall annually prepare a comprehensive report on the results obtained in the development of coffee markets in the countries listed in Annex B.

*(f)* If coffee exported by a Member to a country listed in Annex B is re-exported to any country not listed in Annex B, the Council shall charge the corresponding amount to the quota of that exporting Member. Should there again be a re-exportation from the same country listed in Annex B, the Council shall investigate the case, and unless it finds extenuating circumstances, may at any time delete that country from Annex B.

(2) Exports of coffee beans as raw material for industrial processing for any purposes other than human consumption as a beverage or foodstuff shall not be charged to quotas, provided that the Council is satisfied from information supplied by the exporting Member that the coffee beans are in fact used for such other purposes.

(3) The Council may, upon application by an exporting Member, decide that coffee exports made by that Member for humanitarian or other non-commercial purposes shall not be charged to its quota.

# ARTICLE 41

## Assurance of Supplies

In addition to ensuring that the total supplies of coffee are in accordance with estimated world imports, the Council shall seek to ensure that supplies of the types of coffee that consumers require are available to them. To achieve this objective, the Council may, by a distributed two-thirds majority vote, decide to use whatever methods it considers practicable.

# ARTICLE 42

## Regional and Inter-regional Price Arrangements

(1) Regional and inter-regional price arrangements among exporting Members shall be consistent with the general objectives of the Agreement, and shall be registered with the Council. Such arrangements shall take into account the interests of both producers and consumers and the objectives of the Agreement. Any Member of the Organization which considers that any of these arrangements are likely to lead to results not in accordance with the objectives of the Agreement may request that the Council discuss them with the Members concerned at its next session.

(2) In consultation with Members and with any regional organization to which they belong, the Council may recommend a scale of price differentials for various grades and qualities of coffee which Members should strive to achieve through their pricing policies.

(3) Should sharp price fluctuations occur within brief periods in respect of those grades and qualities of coffee for which a scale of price differentials has been adopted as the result of recommendations made under paragraph (2) of this Article, the Council may recommend appropriate measures to correct the situation.

## ARTICLE 43

### Survey of Market Trends

The Council shall keep under constant survey the trends of the coffee market with a view to recommending price policies, taking into consideration the results achieved through the quota mechanism of the Agreement.

# CHAPTER VIII–CERTIFICATES OF ORIGIN AND RE-EXPORT

## ARTICLE 44

### Certificates of Origin and Re-export

(1) Every export of coffee from any Member in whose territory that coffee has been grown shall be accompanied by a certificate of origin modelled on the form set forth in Annex C, issued by a qualified agency chosen by that Member. Each such Member shall determine the number of copies of the certificate it will require and each copy shall bear a serial number. The original of the certificate shall accompany the documents of export, and a copy shall be furnished to the Organization by that Member. The Council shall, either directly or through an internationally recognized world-wide organization, verify the certificates of origin, so that at any time it will be able to ascertain the quantities of coffee which have been exported by each Member.

(2) Every re-exporter of coffee from a Member shall be accompanied by a certificate of re-export issued by a qualified agency chosen by that Member, in such form as the Council may determine, certifying that the coffee in question was imported in accordance with the provisions of the Agreement, and, if appropriate, containing a reference to the certificate or certificates of origin under which that coffee was imported. The original of

the certificate of re-export shall accompany the documents of re-export, and a copy shall be furnished to the Organization by the re-exporting Member.

(3) Each Member shall notify the Organization of the agency or agencies designated by it to perform the functions specified in paragraphs (1) and (2) of this Article. The Council may at any time, for cause, declare certification by a particular agency unacceptable to it.

(4) Members shall render periodic reports to the Organization concerning imports of coffee, in such form and at such intervals as the Council shall determine.

(5) The provisions of paragraph (1) of this Article shall be put into effect not later than three months after the entry into force of the Agreement. The provisions of paragraph (2) shall be put into effect at such time as the Council shall decide.

(6) After the respective dates provided for under paragraph (5) of this Article, each Member shall prohibit the entry of any shipment of coffee from any other Member which is not accompanied by a certificate of origin or a certificate of re-export.

# CHAPTER IX—REGULATION OF IMPORTS

## ARTICLE 45

### Regulation of Imports

(1) In order to prevent non-member exporting countries from increasing their exports at the expense of Members, the following provisions shall apply with respect to imports of coffee by Members from non-member countries.

(2) If three months after the Agreement enters into force, or at any time thereafter, the Members of the Organization represent less than 95 per cent of world exports in the calendar year 1961, each Member shall, subject to paragraphs (4) and (5) of this Article, limit its total annual imports from non-member countries as a group to a quantity not in excess of its average annual imports from those countries as a group during the last three years prior to the entry into force of the Agreement for which statistics are available. However, if the Council so decides, the application of such limitations may be deferred

(3) If at any time the Council, on the basis of information received, finds that exports from non-member countries as a group are distributing exports of Members, it may, notwithstanding the fact that the Members of the Organization represent 95 per cent or more of world exports in the calendar year 1961, decide that the limitations of paragraph (2) shall be applied.

(4) If the Council's estimate of world imports adopted under Article 30 for any coffee year is less than its estimate of world imports for the first full coffee year after the Agreement enters into force, the quantity which each Member may import from non-member countries as a group under the provisions of paragraph (2) shall be reduced by the same proportion.

(5) The Council may annually recommend additional limitations on imports from non-member countries if it finds such limitations necessary in order to further the purposes of the Agreement.

(6) Within one month from the date on which limitations are applied under this Article, each Member shall inform the Council of the quantity of its permissible annual imports from non-member countries as a group.

(7) The obligations of the preceding paragraphs of this Article shall not derogate from any conflicting bilateral or multilateral obligations which importing Members have entered into with non-member countries before 1 August 1962; provided that any

importing Member which has such conflicting obligations shall carry them out in such a way as to minimize the conflict with the obligations of the preceding paragraphs, take steps as soon as possible to bring its obligations into harmony with those paragraphs, and inform the Council of the details of the conflicting obligations and of the steps taken to minimize or eliminate the conflict.

(8) If an importing Member fails to comply with the provisions of this Article, the Council may, by a distributed two-thirds majority vote, suspend both its voting rights in the Council and its right to have its votes cast in the Board.

## CHAPTER X–INCREASE OF CONSUMPTION

### ARTICLE 46

#### Promotion

(1) The Council shall sponsor a continuing programme for promoting the consumption of coffee. The size and cost of this programme shall be subject to periodic review and approval by the Council. The importing Members will have no obligation as respects the financing of this programme.

(2) If the Council after study of the question so decides, it shall establish within the framework of the Board a separate committee of the Organization, to be known as the World Coffee Promotion Committee.

(3) If the World Coffee Promotion Committee is established, the following provisions shall apply:

(a) The Committee's rules, in particular those regarding membership, organization, and financial affairs, shall be determined by the Council. Membership in the Committee shall be limited to Members which contribute to the promotional programme established in paragraph (1) of this Article.

*(b)* In carrying out its work, the Committee shall establish a technical committee within each country in which a promotional campaign will be conducted. Before a promotional campaign is inaugurated in any Member country, the Committee shall advise the representative of that Member in the Council of the Committee's intention to conduct such a campaign and shall obtain that Member's consent.

*(c)* The ordinary administrative expenses relating to the permanent staff of the Committee, other than the costs of their travel for promotion purposes, shall be charged to the administrative budget of the Organization, and shall not be charged to the promotion funds of the Committee.

## ARTICLE 47

### Removal of Obstacles to Consumption

(1) The Members recognize the utmost importance of achieving the greatest possible increase of coffee consumption as rapidly as possible, in particular through the progressive removal of any obstacles which may hinder such increase.

(2) The Members affirm their intention to promote full international co-operation between all coffee exporting and importing countries.

(3) The Members recognize that there are presently in effect measures which may to a greater or lesser extent hinder the increase in consumption of coffee, in particular:

*(a)* import arrangements applicable to coffee, including preferential and other tariffs, quotas, operations of

Government import monopolies and official purchasing agencies, and other administrative rules and commercial practices;

*(b)* export arrangements as regards direct or indirect subsidies and other administrative rules and commercial practices; and

*(c)* internal trade conditions and domestic legal and administrative provisions which may affect consumption.

(4) The Members recognize that certain Members have shown their concurrence with the objectives stated above by announcing their intention to reduce tariffs on coffee or by taking other action to remove obstacles to increased consumption.

(5) The Members undertake, in the light of studies already carried out and those to be carried out under the auspices of the Council or by other competent international organizations, and of the Declaration adopted at the Ministerial Meeting in Geneva on 30 November, 1961:

*(a)* to investigate ways and means by which the obstacles to increased trade and consumption referred to in paragraph (3) of this Article could be progressively reduced and eventually, whenever possible, eliminated, or by which their effects could be substantially diminished;

*(b)* to inform the Council of the results of their investigation, so that the Council can review, within the first eighteen months after the Agreement enters into force, the information provided by Members concerning the effect of these obstacles and, if appropriate, the measures planned to reduce the obstacles or diminish their effects:

*(c)* to take into account the results of this review by the Council in the adoption of domestic measures and in proposals for international action; and

*(d)* to review at the session provided for in Article 72 the results achieved by the Agreement and to examine the adoption of further measures for the removal of such obstacles as may still stand in the way of expansion of trade and consumption, taking into account the success of the Agreement in increasing income of exporting Members and in developing consumption.

(6) The Members undertake to study in the Council and in other appropriate organizations any requests presented by Members whose economies may be affected by the measures taken in accordance with this Article.

# CHAPTER XI—PRODUCTION CONTROLS

## ARTICLE 48

### Production Goals

(1) The producing Members undertake to adjust the production of coffee while the Agreement remains in force to the amount needed for domestic consumption, exports, and stocks as specified in Chapter XII.

(2) Not later than one year after the Agreement enters into force, the Council shall, in consultation with the producing Members, by a distributed two-thirds majority vote, recommend production goals for each of such Members and for the world as a whole.

(3) Each producing Member shall be entirely responsible for the policies and procedures it applies to achieve these objectives.

# ARTICLE 49

## Implementation of Production-Control Programmes

(1) Each producing Member shall periodically submit written reports to the Council on the measures it has taken or is taking to achieve the objectives of Article 48, as well as on the concrete results obtained. At its first session the Council shall, by a distributed two-thirds majority vote, establish a time-table and procedures for the presentation and discussion of such reports. Before making any observations or recommendations the Council will consult with the Members concerned.

(2) If the Council determines by a distributed two-thirds majority vote either that any producing Member has not, within a period of two years from the entry into force of the Agreement, adopted a programme to adjust its production to the goals recommended by the Council in accordance with Article 48, or that any producing Member's programme is not effective, it may by the same majority decide that such Member shall not enjoy any quota increases which may result from the application of the Agreement. The Council may by the same majority establish whatever procedures it considers appropriate for the purpose of verifying that the provisions of Article 48 have been complied with.

(3) At such time as it considers appropriate, but in any event not later than the review session provided for in Article 72, the Council may, by a distributed two-thirds majority vote, in the light of the reports submitted for its consideration by the producing Members in accordance with paragraph (1) of this Article, revise the production goals recommended in accordance with paragraph (2) of Article 48.

(4) In applying the provisions of this Article, the Council shall maintain close contact with international, national and private organizations which have an interest in or are responsible for financing or, in general, assisting the development plans of the primary producing countries.

## ARTICLE 50

### Co-operation of Importing Members

Recognizing the paramount importance of bringing the production of coffee into reasonable balance with world demand, the importing Members undertake, consistently with their general policies regarding international assistance, to co-operate with the producing Members in their plans for limiting the production of coffee. Their assistance may be provided on a technical, financial or other basis, and under bilateral, multilateral or regional arrangements, to producing Members implementing the provisions of this Chapter.

## CHAPTER XII—REGULATION OF STOCKS

## ARTICLE 51

### Policy Relative to Coffee Stocks

(1) At its first session the Council shall take measures to ascertain world coffee stocks, pursuant to systems which it shall establish, and taking into account the following points: quantity, countries of origin, location, quality, and condition. The Members shall facilitate this survey.

(2) Not later than one year after the Agreement enters into force, the Council shall, on the basis of the data thus obtained and in consultation with the Members concerned, establish a policy relative to such stocks in order to complement the recommendations provided for in Article 48 and thereby to promote the attainment of the objectives of the Agreement.

(3) The producing Members shall endeavour by all means

within their power to implement the policy established by the Council.

(4) Each producing Member shall be entirely responsible for the measures it applies to carry out the policy thus established by the Council.

## ARTICLE 52

### Implementation of Programmes for Regulation of Stocks

Each producing Member shall periodically submit written reports to the Council on the measures it has taken or is taking to achieve the objectives of Article 51, as well as on the concrete results obtained. At its first session, the Council shall establish a time-table and procedures for the presentation and discussion of such reports. Before making any observations or recommendations, the Council shall consult with the Members concerned.

## CHAPTER XIII—MISCELLANEOUS OBLIGATIONS OF MEMBERS

## ARTICLE 53

### Consultation and Co-operation with the Trade

(1) The Council shall encourage Members to seek the views of experts in coffee matters.

(2) Members shall conduct their activities within the framework of the Agreement in a manner consonant with the established channels of trade.

## ARTICLE 54

### Barter

In order to avoid jeopardizing the general price structure, Members shall refrain from engaging in direct and individually linked barter transactions involving the sale of coffee in the traditional markets.

## ARTICLE 55

### Mixtures and Substitutes

Members shall not maintain any regulations requiring the mixing, processing or using of other products with coffee for commercial resale as coffee. Members shall endeavour to prohibit the sale and advertisement of products under the name of coffee if such products contain less than the equivalent of 90 per cent green coffee as the basic raw material.

# CHAPTER XIV—SEASONAL FINANCING

## ARTICLE 56

### Seasonal Financing

(1) The Council shall, upon the request of any Member who is also a party to any bilateral, multilateral, regional or inter-regional agreement in the field of seasonal financing, examine such agreement with a view to verifying its compatibility with the obligations of the Agreement.

(2) The Council may make recommendations to Members with a view to resolving any conflict of obligations which might arise.

(3) The Council may, on the basis of information obtained from the Members concerned, and if it deems appropriate and suitable, make general recommendations with a view to assisting Members which are in need of seasonal financing.

# CHAPTER XV–INTERNATIONAL COFFEE FUND

## ARTICLE 57

### International Coffee Fund

(1) The Council may establish an International Coffee Fund. The Fund shall be used to further the objective of limiting the production of coffee in order to bring it into reasonable balance with demand for coffee, and to assist in the achievement of the other objectives of the Agreement.

(2) Contributions to the Fund shall be voluntary.

(3) The decision by the Council to establish the Fund and the adoption of guiding principles to govern its administration shall be taken by a distributed two-thirds majority vote.

# CHAPTER XVI–INFORMATION AND STUDIES

## ARTICLE 58

### Information

(1) The Organization shall act as a centre for the collection, exchange and publication of:

(a) statistical information on world production, prices, exports and imports, distribution and consumption of coffee; and

(b) in so far as is considered appropriate, technical information on the cultivation, processing and utilization of coffee.

(2) The Council may require Members to furnish such information as it considers necessary for its operations, including regular statistical reports on coffee production, exports and imports, distribution, consumption, stocks and taxation, but no information shall be published which might serve to identify the operations of persons or companies producing, processing or marketing coffee. The Members shall furnish information requested in as detailed and accurate a manner as is practicable.

(3) If a Member fails to supply, or finds difficulty in supplying, within a reasonable time, statistical and other information required by the Council for the proper functioning of the Organization, the Council may require the Member concerned to explain the reasons for non-compliance. If it is found that technical assistance is needed in the matter, the Council may take any necessary measures.

## ARTICLE 59

### Studies

(1) The Council may promote studies in the fields of the economics of coffee production and distribution, the impact of governmental measures in producing and consuming countries on the production and consumption of coffee, the opportunities for expansion of coffee operation of the Agreement on producers and consumers of coffee, including their terms of trade.

(2) The Organization shall continue, to the extent it considers

necessary, the studies and research previously undertaken by the Coffee Study Group, and shall periodically carry out studies on trends and projections on coffee production and consumption.

(3) The Organization may study the practicability of prescribing minimum standards for exports from Members who produce coffee. Recommendations in this regard may be discussed by the Council.

# CHAPTER XVII—WAIVER

## ARTICLE 60

### Waiver

(1) The Council may, by a two-thirds distributed majority vote, relieve a Member of an obligation which, on account of exceptional or emergency circumstances, *force majeure,* constitutional obligations, or international obligations under the United Nations Charter([1]) for territories administered inder the trusteeship system, either:

*(a)* constitutes a serious hardship;

*(b)* imposes an inequitable burden on such Member; or

*(c)* gives other Members an unfair or unreasonable advantage.

(2) The Council, in granting a waiver to a Member, shall state explicitly the terms and conditions on which and the period for which the Member is relieved of such obligation.

---

([1])"Treaty Series No. 67 (1946)", Cmd. 7015

# CHAPTER XVIII–DISPUTES AND COMPLAINTS

## ARTICLE 61

### Disputes and Complaints

(1) Any dispute concerning the interpretation or application of the Agreement which is not settled by negotiation, shall, at the request of any Member party to the dispute, be referred to the Council for decision.

(2) In any case where a dispute has been referred to the Council under paragraph (1) of this Article, a majority of Members, or Members holding not less than one-third of the total votes, may require the Council, after discussion, to seek the opinion of the advisory panel referred to in paragraph (3) of this Article on the issues in dispute before giving its decision.

(3) *(a)* Unless the Council unanimously agrees otherwise, the panel shall consist of:

- (i) two persons, one having wide experience in matters of the kind in disputes and the other having legal standing and experience, nominated by the exporting Members;
- (ii) two such persons nominated by the importing Members; and
- (iii) a chairman selected unanimously by the four persons nominated under (i) and (ii), or, if they fail to agree, by the Chairman of the Council.

- *(b)* Persons from countries whose Governments are Contracting Parties to this Agreement shall be eligible to serve on the advisory panel.
- *(c)* Persons appointed to the advisory panel shall act in their personal capacities and without instructions from any Government.

*(d)* The expenses of the advisory panel shall be paid by Council.

(4) The opinion of the advisory panel and the reasons therefor shall be submitted to the Council which, after considering all the relevant information, shall decide the dispute.

(5) Any complaint that any Member has failed to fulfil its obligations under the Agreement shall, at the request of the Member making the complaint, be referred to the Council, which shall make a decision on the matter.

(6) No Member shall be found to have committed a breach of its obligations under the Agreement except by a distributed simple majority vote. Any finding that a Member is in breach of the Agreement shall specify the nature of the breach.

(7) If the Council finds that a Member has committed a breach of the Agreement, it may, without prejudice to other enforcement measures provided for in other articles of the Agreement, by a distributed two-thirds majority vote, suspend that Member's voting right in the Council and its right to have its votes cast in the Board until it fulfils its obligations, or the Council may take action requiring compulsory withdrawal under Article 69.

# CHAPTER XIX—FINAL PROVISIONS

## ARTICLE 62

### Signature

The Agreement shall be open for signature at United Nations Headquarters until and including 30 November 1962 by any Government invited to the United Nations Coffee Conference, 1962, and by the Government of any State represented before independence as a dependent territory at that Conference.

## ARTICLE 63

### Ratification

The Agreement shall be subject to ratification or acceptance by the signatory Governments in accordance with their respective constitutional procedures. Instruments of ratification or acceptance shall be deposited with the Secretary-General of the United Nations not later than 31 December 1963. Each Government depositing an instrument of ratification or acceptance shall, at the time of such deposit, indicate whether it is joining the Organization as an exporting Member or an importing Member, as defined in paragraphs (7) and (8) of Article 2.

## ARTICLE 64

### Entry into Force

(1) The Agreement shall enter into force between those Governments which have deposited instruments of ratification or acceptance when Governments representing at least twenty exporting countries having at least 80 per cent of total exports in the year 1961, as specified in Annex D, and Governments representing at least ten importing countries having at least 80 per cent of world imports in the same year, as specified in the same Annex, have deposited such instruments. The Agreement shall enter into force for any Government which subsequently deposits an instrument of ratification, acceptance or accession on the date of such deposit.

(2) The Agreement may enter into force provisionally. For this purpose, a notification by a signatory Government containing an undertaking to seek ratification or acceptance in accordance with its constitutional procedures as rapidly as possible, which is received by the Secretary-General of the United Nations not later than 30 December 1963, shall be regarded as equal in effect to an

instrument of ratification or acceptance. It is understood that a Government which gives such a notification will provisionally apply the Agreement and be provisionally regarded as a party thereto until either it deposits its instrument of ratification or acceptance or until 31 December 1963, whichever is earlier.

(3) The Secretary-General of the United Nations shall convene the first session of the Council, to be held in London within 30 days after the Agreement enters into force.

(4) Whether or not the Agreement has provisionally entered into force in accordance with paragraph (2) of this Article, if by 31 December 1963 it has not definitively entered into force in accordance with paragraph (1), those Governments which have by that date deposited instruments of ratification or acceptance may consult together to consider what action the situation requires, and may, by mutual consent, decide that it shall enter into force among themselves.


## ARTICLE 65

### Accession

The Government of any State Member of the United Nations or of any of its specialized agencies and any Government invited to the United Nations Coffee Conference, 1962, may accede to this Agreement upon conditions that shall be established by the Council. In establishing such conditions the Council shall, if such country is not listed in Annex A, establish a basic export quota for it. If such country is listed in Annex A, the respective basic export quota specified therein shall be the basic export quota for that country unless the Council decides otherwise by a distributed two-thirds majority vote. Each Government depositing an instrument of accession shall, at the time of such deposit, indicate whether it is joining the Organization as an exporting Member or an importing Member, as defined in paragraphs (7) and (8) of Article 2.

## ARTICLE 66

### Reservations

Reservations may not be made with respect to any of the provisions of the Agreement.

## ARTICLE 67

### Notifications in respect of Dependent Territories

(1) Any Government may, at the time of signature or deposit of an instrument of acceptance, ratification or accession, or at any time thereafter, by notification the the Secretary-General of the United Nations, declare that the Agreement shall extend to any of the territories for whose international relations it is responsible, and the Agreement shall extend to the territories named therein from the date of such notification.

(2) Any Contracting Party which desires to exercise its rights under Article 4 in respect of any of its dependent territories, or which desires to authorize one of its dependent territories to become part of a Member group formed under Article 5 or 6, may do so by making a notification to that effect to the Secretary-General of the United Nations, either at the time of the deposit of its instrument of ratification, acceptance or accession, or at any later time.

(3) Any Contracting Party which has made a declaration under paragraph (1) of this Article may at any time thereafter, by notification to the Secretary-General of the United Nations, declare that the Agreement shall cease to extend to the territory named in the notification, and the Agreement shall cease to extend to such territory from the date of such notification.

(4) The Government of a territory to which the Agreement has been extended under paragraph (1) of this Article and which has subsequently become independent may, within 90 days after the attainment of independence, declare by notification to the Secretary-General of the United Nations that it has assumed the

rights and obligations of a Contracting Party to the Agreement. It shall, as from the date of such notification, become a party to the Agreement.

## ARTICLE 68

### Voluntary Withdrawal

No Contracting Party may give notice of voluntary withdrawal from the Agreement before 30 September 1963. Therafter, any Contracting Party may withdraw from the Agreement at any time by giving a written notice of withdrawal to the Secretary-General of the United Nations. Withdrawal shall become effective 90 days after the notice is received.

## ARTICLE 69

### Compulsory Withdrawal

If the Council determines that any Member has failed to carry out its obligations under the Agreement and that such failure significantly impairs the operations of the Agreement, it may, by a distributed two-thirds majority vote, require the withdrawal of such Member from the Organization. The Council shall immediately notify the Secretary-General of the United Nations of any such decision. Ninety days after the date of the Council's decision, that Member shall cease to be a Member of the Organization, and, if such Member is a Contracting Party, a party to the Agreement.

## ARTICLE 70

### Settlement of Accounts with Withdrawing Members

(1) The Council shall determine any settlement of accounts with a withdrawing Member. The Organization shall retain any amounts already paid by a withdrawing Member, and such Member shall remain bound to pay any amounts due from it to

the Organization at the time the withdrawal becomes effective; provided, however, that in the case of a Contracting Party which is unable to accept an amendment and consequently either withdraws or ceases to participate in the Agreement under the provisions of paragraph (2) of Article 73, the Council may determine any settlement of accounts which it finds equitable.

(2) A Member which has withdrawn or which has ceased to participate in the Agreement shall not be entitled to any share of the proceeds of liquidation or the other assets of the Organization upon termination of the Agreement under Article 71.

## ARTICLE 71

### Duration and Termination

(1) The Agreement shall remain in force until the completion of the fifth full coffee year after its entry into force, unless extended under paragraph (2) of this Article, or earlier terminated under paragraph (3).

(2) The Council, during the fifth full coffee year after the Agreement enters into force, may, by vote of a majority of the Members having not less than a distributed two-thirds majority of the total votes, either decide to renegotiate the Agreement, or to extend it for such period as the Council shall determine.

(3) The Council may at any time, by vote of a majority of the Members having not less than a distributed two-thirds majority of the total votes, decide to terminate the Agreement. Such termination shall take effect on such date as the Council shall decide.

(4) Notwithstanding termination of the Agreement, the Council shall remain in being for as long as necessary to carry out the liquidation of the Organization, settlement of its accounts, and disposal of its assets, and shall have during that period such powers and functions as may be necessary for those purposes.

240

## ARTICLE 72

### Review

In order to review the Agreement, the Council shall hold a special session during the last six months of the coffee year ending 30 September 1965.


## ARTICLE 73

### Amendment

(1) The Council may, by a distributed two-thirds majority vote, recommend an amendment of the Agreement to the Contracting Parties. The amendment shall become effective 100 days after the Secretary-General of the United Nations has received notifications of acceptance from Contracting Parties representing at least 75 per cent of the exporting countries holding at least 85 per cent of the votes of the exporting Members, and from Contracting Parties representing at least 75 per cent of the importing countries holding at least 80 per cent of the votes of the importing Members. The Council may fix a time within which each Contracting Party shall notify the Secretary-General of the United Nations of its acceptance of the amendment, and, if the amendment has not become effective by such time, it shall be considered withdrawn. The Council shall provide the Secretary-General with the information necessary to determine whether the amendment has become effective.

(2) Any Contracting Party, or any dependent territory which is either a Member or a party to a Member group, on behalf of which notification of acceptance of an amendment has not been made by the date on which such amendment becomes effective, shall as of that date cease to participate in the Agreement.

# ARTICLE 74

## Notifications by the Secretary-General

The Secretary-General of the United Nations shall notify all Governments represented by delegates or observers at the United Nations Coffee Conference, 1962, and all other Governments of States Members of the United Nations or of any of its specialized agencies, of each deposit of an instrument of ratification, acceptance or accession, and of the dates on which the Agreement comes provisionally and definitively into force. The Secretary-General of the United Nations shall also notify all Contracting Parties of each notification under Article 5, 67, 68 or 69; of the date to which the Agreement is extended or on which it is terminated under Article 71; and of the date on which an amendment becomes effective under Article 73.

IN WITNESS WHEREOF the undersigned, having been duly authorized to this effect by their respective Governments, have signed this Agreement on the dates appearing opposite their signatures.

The texts of this Agreement in the English, French, Russian, Spanish and Portuguese languages shall all be equally authentic. The originals shall be deposited in the archives of the United Nations, and the Secretary-General of the United Nations shall transmit certified copies thereof to each signatory and acceding Government.

[Here follow the signatures]

**Basic Export Quotas**

(60-kilogramme bags)

| | |
|---|---:|
| Brazil | 18,000,000 |
| Colombia | 6,011,280 |
| Costa Rica | 950,000 |
| Cuba | 200,000 |
| Dominican Republic *(a)* | 425,000 |
| Ecuador | 552,000 |
| El Salvador | 1,429,500 |
| Guatemala | 1,344,500 |
| Haiti *(a)* | 420,000 |
| Honduras | 285,000 |
| Mexico | 1,509,000 |
| Nicaragua | 419,100 |
| Panama | 26,000 |
| Venezuela | 475,000 |
| Cameroun | 762,795 |
| Central African Republic | 150,000 |
| Congo (Brazzaville) | 11,000 |
| Dahomey | 37,224 |
| Gabon | 18,000 |
| Ivory Coast | 2,324,278 |
| Malagasy Republic | 828,828 |
| Togo | 170,000 |
| Kenya | 516,835 |
| Uganda | 1,887,737 |
| Tanganyika | 435,458 |
| Portugal | 2,188,648 |
| Congo (Leopoldville) *(b)* | 700,000 |
| Ethiopia | 850,000 |
| India | 360,000 |
| Indonesia | 1,176,000 |
| Nigeria | 18,000 |
| Rwanda and Burundi *(b)* | 340,000 |
| Sierra Leone | 65,000 |
| Trinidad | 44,000 |
| Yemen | 77,000 |
| **Grand Total** | **45,587,183** |

*(a)* The Republic of Haiti and the Dominican Republic shall be permitted to export 20 per cent more their respective adjusted basic quotas in the

coffee year 1963-64. In no event, however, shall such increases be taken into account for the purpose of calculating the distribution of votes. In the review of the Agreement, provided for in Article 72, the two-year production cycle in those countries shall be given special consideration.

*(b)* In the first coffee year, the Republic of the Congo (Leopoldville), after presentation to the Council of acceptable evidence of an exportable production larger than 700,000 bags, shall be authorized by the Council to export up to 900,000 bags. In the second and third coffee years it is permitted to increase its coffee exports by an amount not to exceed 20 per cent over those for the previous year. After presentation to the Council of acceptable evidence of an exportable production larger than 340,000 bags, Rwanda and Burundi may be authorized by the Council to export a combined total of up to 450,000 bags in the first coffee year, 500,000 bags in the second coffee year and 565,000 bags in the third coffee year. In no event, however, shall the increases allowed those countries in the first three years be taken into account for the purpose of calculating the distribution of votes.

# ANNEX B

## Non-quota Countries of Destination, referred to in Article 40, Chapter VII

The geographical areas below are non-quota countries for purposes of this Agreement:

Bahrein
Basutoland
Bechuanaland
Ceylon
China (Taiwan)
China (mainland)
Federation of Rhodesia and Nyasaland
Hungary
Iran
Iraq
Japan
Jordan
Kuwait
Muscat and Oman
Oman
Philippines
Poland
Qatar
Republic of Korea
North Korea
Republic of Viet-Nam
North Viet-Nam
Romania
Saudi Arabia
Somalia
South-West Africa
Sudan
Swaziland
Thailand
Republic of South Africa
Union of Soviet Socialist Republics

# ANNEX C

## Certificate of Origin

This certificate is made pursuant to the International Coffee Agreement. A copy of this certificate must be submitted with export documents and will be required for export (and import) clearance.

No. ................................  Member ................................
     *(to be cited in any*       *(producing country)*
     *future correspondence)*

I hereby certify that the green, soluble, roasted, semi-roasted or other coffee described below has been produced in ........................ *(producing country)*.

per S.S.:  or other carrier
from:  *(name of port or other point of embarkation)*
to:  *(name of port or country of final destination)*
via:
on or about:  (date)

| Shipping Marks or other identification | Quantity (number of units) | Total Weight | | Observations |
|---|---|---|---|---|
| | | Kg. | lbs. | |
| **Green** | | Gross<br><br>Net | Gross<br><br>Net | |
| **Roasted or Soluble** | | Gross<br><br>Net | Gross<br><br>Net | |

**Other** (specify)

. . . . . . . . . . . . . . . . . . . . . . . . . . . . . . . . . . . . . . . . . . . . . . . . . . . . . . . . . . . . . . . . .

Date . . . . . . . . . . . .  Signature . . . . . . . . . . . . . . . . . . . . .
     *(Certifying Officer)*

     . . . . . . . . . . . . . . . . . . . . .
     *(Certifying Agency)*

# ANNEX D

## List of Exports and Imports in 1961

### I.–EXPORTS

### (thousands of 60-kilogramme bags)

| Country | Bags | Per cent |
|---------|------|----------|
| Bolivia | *(a)* | 0·0 |
| Brazil | 16,971 | 39·2 |
| Burundi and Rwanda | 397 | 0·9 |
| Cameroun | 591 | 1·4 |
| Central African Republic | 121 | 0·3 |
| Colombia | 5,651 | 13·1 |
| Congo (Brazzaville) | *(a)* | 0·0 |
| Congo (Leopoldville) | 499 | 1·2 |
| Costa Rica | 835 | 1·9 |
| Cuba | 85 | 0·2 |
| Dahomey | 40 | 0·2 |
| Dominican Republic | 327 | 0·8 |
| Ecuador | 381 | 0·9 |
| El Salvador | 1,430 | 3·3 |
| Ethiopia | 950 | 2·2 |
| Gabon | *(a)* | 0·0 |
| Ghana | 28 | 0·1 |
| Guatemala | 1,255 | 2·9 |
| Guinea | 200 | 0·5 |
| Haiti | 348 | 0·8 |
| Honduras | 210 | 0·5 |
| India | 539 | 1·2 |
| Indonesia | 1,091 | 2·5 |
| Ivory Coast | 2,618 | 6·0 |
| Jamaica | *(a)* | 0·0 |
| Liberia | 41 | 0·1 |
| Madagascar | 651 | 1·5 |
| Mauritania | *(a)* | 0·0 |
| Mexico | 1,483 | 3·5 |
| Nicaragua | 349 | 0·8 |
| Nigeria | *(a)* | 0·0 |
| Panama | *(a)* | 0·0 |
| Paraguay | 25 | 0·1 |
| Peru | 567 | 1·3 |
| Portugal | 1,976 | 4·5 |
| Rwanda (*see* Burundi) | | |
| Sierra Leone | 85 | 0·2 |
| Tanganyika | 438 | 1·0 |
| Togo | 171 | 0·4 |
| Trinidad and Tobago | 38 | 0·1 |
| United Kingdom (Kenya) | 536 | 1·2 |
| United Kingdom (Uganda) | 1,806 | 4·2 |
| Upper Volta | *(a)* | 0·0 |
| Venezuela | 406 | 0·9 |
| Yemen | 80 | 0·2 |
| **Total** | **43,219** | **100·0** |

*(a)* Less than 22,000 bags.

## II.—IMPORTS

### (thousands of 60-kilogramme bags)

| Country | Bags | Per cent | Country | Bags | Per |
|---|---|---|---|---|---|
| Afghanistan | (a) | 0·0 | Luxembourg (included | | |
| Albania | (a) | 0·0 | in Belgium) | | |
| Argentina | 574 | 1·3 | Mali | (a) | 0 |
| Australia | 156 | 0·4 | Mongolia | (a) | 0 |
| Austria | 218 | 0·5 | Morocco | 129 | 0 |
| Belgium | 1,036 | 2·4 | Nepal | (a) | 0 |
| Bulgaria | 60 | 0·1 | Netherlands | 1,147 | 2 |
| Burma | 60 | 0·1 | New Zealand | 35 | 0 |
| Byelorussian SSR | | | Niger | (a) | 0 |
| (included in USSR) | | | Norway | 450 | 1 |
| Cambodia | (a) | 0·0 | Pakistan | (a) | 0 |
| Canada | 1,119 | 2·6 | Philippines | (a) | 0 |
| Ceylon | (a) | 0·0 | Poland | 89 | 0 |
| Chad | (a) | 0·0 | Republic of Korea | (a) | 0 |
| Chile | 113 | 0·3 | Republic of Viet-Nam | (a) | 0 |
| China | (a) | 0·0 | Romania | (a) | 0 |
| Cyprus | (a) | 0·0 | Saudi Arabia | (a) | 0 |
| Czechoslovakia | 175 | 0·4 | Senegal | (a) | 0 |
| Denmark | 727 | 1·7 | Somalia | (a) | 0 |
| Federal Republic of | | | South Africa | 185 | 0 |
| Germany | 3,540 | 8,540 | Spain | 300 | 0 |
| Federation of Malaya | 109 | 0·2 | Sudan | 154 | 0 |
| Federation of Rhodesia | | | Sweden | 1,295 | 3 |
| and Nyasaland | (a) | 0·0 | Switzerland | 541 | 1 |
| Finland | 638 | 1·5 | Syria | 31 | 0 |
| France | 3,882 | 8·9 | Thailand | 83 | 0 |
| Greece | 132 | 0·3 | Tunisia | 48 | 0 |
| Hungary | 39 | 0·1 | Turkey | 36 | 0 |
| Iceland | 29 | 0·1 | Ukrainian SSR (included | | |
| Iran | (a) | 0·0 | in USSR) | | |
| Iraq | (a) | 0·0 | Union of Soviet Socialist | | |
| Ireland | (a) | 0·0 | Republics | 371 | 0 |
| Israel | 74 | 0·2 | United Arab Republic | 70 | 0 |
| Italy | 1,753 | 4·0 | United Kingdom | 978 | 2 |
| Japan | 244 | 0·6 | United States | 22,464 | 51 |
| Jordan | 23 | 0·0 | Uruguay | 45 | 0 |
| Kuwait | (a) | 0·0 | Yogoslavia | 143 | 0 |
| Laos | (a) | 0·0 | | | |
| Lebanon | 158 | 0·4 | **Total** | **43,393** | **100** |
| Libya | (a) | 0·0 | | | |

(a) Less than 22,000 bags.

# INTERNATIONAL COFFEE AGREEMENT OF 1968

## Preamble

The Governments Parties to this Agreement,

Recognizing the exceptional importance of coffee to the economies of many countries which are largely dependent upon this commodity for their export earnings and thus for the continuation of their development programmes in the social and economic fields;

Considering that close international co-operation on coffee marketing will stimulate the economic diversification and development of coffee-producing countries and thus contribute to a strengthening of the political and economic bonds between producers and consumers;

Finding reason to expect a tendency toward persistent disequilibrium between production and consumption, accumulation of burdensome stocks, and pronounced fluctuations in prices, which can be harmful both to producers and to consumers;

Believing that, in the absence of international measures, this situation cannot be corrected by normal market forces; and

Noting the renegotiation by the International Coffee Council of the International Coffee Agreement, 1962,

Have agreed as follows:

## CHAPTER I – OBJECTIVES

### ARTICLE 1

#### Objectives

The objectives of the Agreement are:

(1) to achieve a reasonable balance between supply and

demand on a basis which will assure adequate supplies of coffee to consumers and markets for coffee to producers at equitable prices and which will bring about long-term equilibrium between production and consumption;

(2) to alleviate the serious hardship caused by burdensome surpluses and excessive fluctuations in the prices of coffee which are harmful both to producers and to consumers;

(3) to contribute to the development of productive resources and to the promotion and maintenance of employment and income in the Member countries, thereby helping to bring about fair wages, higher living standards, and better working conditions;

(4) to assist in increasing the purchasing power of coffee-exporting countries by keeping prices at equitable levels and by increasing consumption;

(5) to encourage the consumption of coffee by every possible means; and

(6) in general, in recognition of the relationship of the trade in coffee to the economic stability of markets for industrial products, to further international co-operation in connection with world coffee problems.

## CHAPTER II – DEFINITIONS

### ARTICLE 2

### Definitions

For the purposes of the Agreement:

(1) "Coffee" means the beans and berries of the coffee tree, whether parchment, green or roasted, and includes ground, decaffeinated, liquid and soluble coffee. These terms shall have the following meaning:

(a) "green coffee" means all coffee in the naked bean form before roasting:

(b) "coffee berries" means the complete fruit of the coffee tree; to find the equivalent of coffee berries to green coffee, multiply the net weight of the dried coffee berries by 0.50;

(c) "parchment coffee" means the green coffee bean contained in the parchment skin; to find the equivalent of parchment coffee to green coffee, multiply the net weight of the parchment coffee by 0.80;

(d) "roasted coffee" means green coffee roasted to any degree and includes ground coffee; to find the equivalent of roasted coffee to green coffee, multiply the net weight of roasted coffee by 1.19;

(e) "decaffeinated coffee" means green, roasted or soluble coffee from which caffein has been extracted; to find the equivalent of decaffeinated coffee to green coffee, multiply the net weight of the decaffeinated coffee in green, roasted or soluble form by 1.00, 1.19 or 3.00 respectively;

(f) "liquid coffee" means the water-soluble solids derived from roasted coffee and put into liquid form; to find the equivalent of liquid to green coffee, multiply the net weight of the dried coffee solids contained in the liquid coffee by 3.00;

(g) "soluble coffee" means the dried water-soluble solids derived from roasted coffee; to find the equivalent of soluble coffee to green coffee, multiply the net weight of the soluble coffee by 3.00.

(2) "Bag" means 60 kilogrammes or 132.276 pounds of green coffee; "ton" means a metric ton of 1,000 kilogrammes or 2,204.6 pounds; and "pound" means 453.597 grammes.

(3) "Coffee year" means the period of one year, from 1 October through 30 September.

251

(4) "Export of Coffee" means, except as otherwise provided in Article 39, any shipment of coffee which leaves the territory of the country where the coffee was grown.

(5) "Organization", "Council" and "Board" mean, respectively, the International Coffee Council, and the Executive Board referred to in Article 7 of the Agreement.

(6) "Member" means a Contracting Party; a dependent territory or territories in respect of which separate Membership has been declared under Article 4; or two or more Contracting Parties or dependent territories, or both, which participate in the Organization as a Member group under Article 5 or 6.

(7) "Exporting Member" or "exporting country" means a Member or country, respectively, which is a net exporter of coffee; that is, whose exports exceed its imports.

(8) "Importing Member" or "importing country" means a Member or country, respectively, which is a net importer of coffee; that is, whose imports exceed its exports.

(9) "Producing Member" or "producing country" means a Member or country, respectively, which grows coffee in commercially significant quantities.

(10) "Distributed simple majority vote" means a majority of the votes cast by exporting Members present and voting, and a majority of the votes cast by importing Members present and voting, counted separately.

(11) "Distributed two-thirds majority vote" means a two-thirds majority of the votes cast by exporting Members present and voting and a two-thirds majority of the votes cast by importing Members present and voting, counted separately.

(12) "Entry into force" means, except as otherwise provided, the date on which the Agreement enters into force, whether provisionally or definitively.

(13) "Exportable production" means the total production of coffee of an exporting country in a given coffee year less the amount destined for domestic consumption in the same year.

(14) "Availability for export" means the exportable production of an exporting country in a given coffee year plus accumulated stocks from previous years.

(15) "Export entitlement" means the total quantity of coffee which a Member is authorized to export under the various provisions of the Agreement, but excluding exports which under the provisions of Article 40 are not charged to quotas.

(16) "Authorized exports" means actual exports covered by the export entitlement.

(17) "Permitted exports" means the sum of authorized exports and exports which under the provisions of Article 40 are not charged to quotas.

## CHAPTER III—MEMBERSHIP

### ARTICLE 3

### Membership in the Organization

(1) Each Contracting Party, together with those of its dependent territories to which the Agreement is extended under paragraph (1) of Article 65, shall constitute a single Member of the Organization, except as otherwise provided under Articles 4, 5 and 6.

(2) A Member may change its category of Membership, previously declared on approval, ratification, acceptance or accession to the Agreement, on such conditions as the Council may agree.

(3) On application by two or more importing Members for a change in the form of their participation in the Agreement and/or their representation in the Organization, and notwithstanding other provisions of the Agreement, the Council may, after

consultation with the Members concerned, determine the conditions which shall be applicable to such changed participation and/or representation.

## ARTICLE 4

### Separate Membership in Respect of Dependent Territories

Any Contracting which is a net importer of coffee may, at any time, by appropriate notification in accordance with paragraph (2) of Article 65, declare that it is participating in the Organization separately with respect to any of its dependent territories which are net exporters of coffee and which it designates. In such case, the metropolitan territory and its non-designated dependent territories will have a single Membership, and its designated dependent territories, either individually or collectively as the notification indicates, will have separate Membership.

## ARTICLE 5

### Group Membership upon Joining the Organization

(1) Two or more Contracting Parties which are net exporters of coffee may, by appropriate notification to the Secretary-General of the United Nations at the time of deposit of their respective instruments of approval, ratification, acceptance or accession and to the Council, declare that they are joining the Organization as a Member group. A dependent territory to which the Agreement has been extended under paragraph (1) of Article 65 may constitute part of such a Member group if the Government of the State responsible for its international relations has given appropriate notification thereof under paragraph (2) of Article 65. Such Contracting Parties and dependent territories must satisfy the following conditions:

  (a) they shall declare their willingness to accept responsibility for group obligations in an individual as well as a group capacity;

(b) they shall subsequently provide sufficient evidence to the Council that the group has the organization necessary to implement a common coffee policy, and that they have the means of complying, together with the other parties to the group, with their obligations under the Agreement; and

(c) they shall subsequently provide evidence to the Council either:

(i) that they have been recognized as a group in a previous international coffee agreement; or

(ii) that they have:

(a) a common or co-ordinated commercial and economic policy in relation to coffee; and

(b) a co-ordinated monetary and financial policy, as well as the organs necessary for implementing such a policy, so that the Council is satisfied that the Member group can comply with the spirit of group membership and the group obligations involved.

(2) The Member group shall constitute a single Member of the Organization, except that each party to the group shall be treated as if it were a single Member as regards all matters arising under the following provisions:

(a) Chapters XII, XIII and XVI;

(b) Articles 10, 11 and 19 of Chapter IV; and

(c) Article 68 of Chapter XX.

(3) The Contracting Parties and dependent territories joining as a Member group shall specify the Government or organization which will represent them in the Council as regards all matters arising under the Agreement other than those specified in paragraph (2) of this Article.

(4) The member group's voting rights shall be as follows:

(a) the Member group shall have the same number of basic votes as a single Member country joining the Organization in an individual capacity. These basic votes shall be attributed to and exercised by the Government or organization representing the group;

(b) in the event of a vote on any matters arising under provisions specified in paragraph (2) of this Article, the parties to the Member group may exercise separately the votes attributed to them by the provisions of paragraph (3) of Article 12 as if each were an individual Member of the Organization, except for the basic votes, which shall remain attributable only to the Government or organization representing the group.

(5) Any contracting Party or dependent territory which is a party to a Member group may, by notification to the Council, withdraw from that group and become a separate Member. Such withdrawal shall take effect upon receipt of the notification by the Council. In case of such withdrawal from a group, or in case a party to a group ceases, by withdrawal from the Organization or otherwise, to be such a party, the remaining parties to the group may apply to the Council to maintain the group, and the group shall continue to exist unless the Council disapproves the application. If the Member group is dissolved, each former party to the group will become a separate Member. A Member which has ceased to be a party to a group may not, as long as the Agreement remains in force, again become a party to a group.

## ARTICLE 6

### Subsequent Group Membership

Two or more exporting Members may, at any time after the Agreement has entered into force with respect to them, apply to the Council to form a Member group. The Council shall approve the application if it finds that the Members have made a declaration, and have provided evidence, satisfying the requirements of paragraph (1) of Article 5. Upon such approval, the Member group shall be subject to the provisions of paragraph (2), (3), (4) and (5) of that Article.

# CHAPTER IV—ORGANIZATION AND ADMINISTRATION

## ARTICLE 7

### Seat and Structure of the International Coffee Organization

(1) The International Coffee Organization established under the 1962 Agreement shall continue in being to administer the provisions and supervise the operation of the Agreement.

(2) The seat of the Organization shall be in London unless the Council by a distributed two-thirds majority vote decides otherwise.

(3) The Organization shall function through the International Coffee Council, its Executive Board, its Executive Director and its staff.

## ARTICLE 8

### Composition of the International Coffee Council

(1) The highest authority of the Organization shall be the International Coffee Council, which shall consist of all the Members of the Organization.

(2) Each Member shall be represented on the Council by a representative and one or more alternates. A Member may also designate one or more advisors to accompany its representative or alternates.

# ARTICLE 9

## Powers and Functions of the Council

(1) All powers specifically conferred by the Agreement shall be vested in the Council, which shall have the powers and perform the functions necessary to carry out the provisions of the Agreement.

(2) The Council shall, by a distributed two-thirds majority vote, establish such rules and regulations, including its own rules of procedure and the financial and staff regulations of the Organization, as are necessary to carry out the provisions of the Agreement and are consistent therewith. The Council may, in its rules of procedure, provide a procedure whereby it may, without meeting, decide specific questions.

(3) The Council shall also keep such records as are required to perform its functions under the Agreement and such other records as it considers desirable. The Council shall publish an annual report.

# ARTICLE 10

## Election of the Chairman and Vice-Chairmen of the Council

(1) The Council shall elect, for each coffee year, a Chairman and a first, a second and a third Vice-Chairman.

(2) As a general rule, the Chairman and the first Vice-Chairman shall both be elected either from among the representatives of exporting Members, or from among the representatives of importing members, and the second and the third Vice-Chairmen, shall be elected from representatives of the other category of Members. These offices shall alternate each coffee year between the two categories of Members.

(3) Neither the Chairman nor any Vice-Chairman acting as Chairman shall have the right to vote. His alternate will in such case exercise the Member's voting rights.

# ARTICLE 11

## Sessions of the Council

As a general rule, the Council shall hold regular sessions twice a year. It may hold special sessions if it so decides. Special sessions shall also be held when either the Executive Board, or any five Members, or a Member or Members having at least 200 votes so request. Notice of sessions shall be given at least thirty days in advance, except in cases of emergency. Sessions shall be held at the seat of the Organization, unless the Council decides otherwise.

# ARTICLE 12

## Votes

(1) The exporting Members shall together hold 1,000 votes and the importing Members shall together hold 1,000 votes, distributed within each category of Members—that is, exporting and importing Members, respectively—as provided in the following paragraphs of this Article.

(2) Each Member shall have five basic votes, provided that the total number of basic votes within each category of Members does not exceed 150. Should there be more than thirty exporting Members or more than thirty importing Members, the number of basic votes for each Member within that category of Members shall be adjusted so as to keep the number of basic votes for each category of Members within the maximum of 150.

(3) The remaining votes of exporting Members shall be divided among those Members in proportion to their respective basic export quotas, except that in the event of a vote on any matter arising under the provisions specified in paragraph (2) of Article 5, the remaining votes of a Member group shall be divided among the parties to that group in proportion to their respective participation in the basic export quota of the Member group. Any exporting Member to which a basic quota has not been allotted shall receive no share of these remaining votes.

(4)   The remaining votes of importing Members shall be divided among those Members in proportion to the average volume of their respective coffee imports in the preceding three-year period.

(5) The distribution of votes shall be determined by the Council at the beginning of each coffee year and shall remain in effect during that year, except as provided in paragraph (6) of this Article.

(6) The Council shall provide for the redistribution of votes in accordance with this Article whenever there is a change in the Membership of the Organization, or if the voting rights of a Member are suspended or regained under the provisions of Articles 25, 38, 45, 48, 54 or 59.

(7)   No Member shall hold more than 400 votes.

(8)   There shall be no fractional votes.

## ARTICLE 13

### Voting Procedure of the Council

(1)   Each representative shall be entitled to cast the number of votes held by the Member represented by him, and cannot divide its votes. He may, however, cast differently any votes which he exercises pursuant to paragraph (2) of this Article.

(2)   Any exporting Member may authorize any other exporting Member, and any importing Member may authorize any other importing Member, to represent its interests and to exercise its right to vote at any meeting or meetings of the Council. The limitation provided for in paragraph (7) of Article 12 shall not apply in this case.

## ARTICLE 14

### Decisions of the Council

(1) All decisions of the Council shall be taken, and all recommendations shall be made, by a distributed simple majority

vote unless otherwise provided in the Agreement.

(2) The following procedures shall apply with respect to any action by the Council which under the Agreement requires a distributed two-thirds majority vote:

(a) if a distributed two-thirds majority vote is not obtained because of the negative vote of three or less exporting or three or less importing Members, the proposal shall, if the Council so decides by a majority of the Members present and by a distributed simple majority vote, be put to a vote again within 48 hours;

(b) if a distributed two-thirds majority vote is again not obtained because of the negative vote of two or less importing or two or less exporting Members, the proposal shall, if the Council so decides by a majority of the Members present and by a distributed simple majority vote, be put to a vote again within 24 hours;

(c) if a distributed two-thirds majority vote is not obtained in the third vote because of the negative vote of one exporting Member or one importing Member, the proposal shall be considered adopted;

(d) if the Council fails to put a proposal to a further vote, it shall be considered rejected.

(3) The Members undertake to accept as binding all decisions of the Council under the provisions of the Agreement.

## ARTICLE 15

### Composition of the Board

(1) The Executive Board shall consist of eight exporting Members and eight importing Members, elected for each coffee year in accordance with Article 16. Members may be re-elected.

(2) Each member of the Board shall appoint one representative and one or more alternates.

(3) The Chairman of the Board shall be appointed by the Council for each coffee year and may be reappointed. He shall not have the right to vote. If a representative is appointed Chairman, his alternate will have the right to vote in his place.

(4) The Board shall normally meet at the seat of the Organization, but may meet elsewhere.

## ARTICLE 16

### Election of the Board

(1) The exporting and the importing Members on the Board shall be elected in the Council by the exporting and the importing Members of the Organization respectively. The election within each category shall be held in accordance with the following paragraphs of this Article.

(2) Each Member shall cast all the votes to which it is entitled under Article 12 for a single candidate. A Member may cast for another candidate any votes which it exercises pursuant to paragraph (2) of Article 13.

(3) The eight candidates receiving the largest number of votes shall be elected; however, no candidate shall be elected on the first ballot unless it receives at least 75 votes.

(4) If under the provisions of paragraph (3) of this Article less than eight candidates are elected on the first ballot, further ballots shall be held in which only Members which did not vote for any of the candidates elected shall have the right to vote. In each further ballot, the minimum number of votes required for election shall be successively diminished by five until eight candidates are elected.

(5) Any Member who did not vote for any of the Members elected shall assign its votes to one of them, subject to paragraphs (6) and (7) of this Article.

(6) A Member shall be deemed to have received the number of votes originally cast for it when it was elected and, in addition, the number of votes assigned to it, provided that the total number of

votes shall not exceed 499 for any Member elected.

(7) If the votes deemed received by an elected Member would otherwise exceed 499, Members which voted for or assigned their votes to such elected Member shall arrange among themselves for one or more of them to withdraw their votes from that Member and assign or reassign them to another elected Member so that the votes received by each elected Member shall not exceed the limit of 499.

## ARTICLE 17

### Competence of the Board

(1) The Board shall be responsible to and work under the general direction of the Council.

(2) The Council by a distributed simple majority vote may delegate to the Board the exercise of any or all of its powers, other than the following:

(a) approval of the administrative budget and assessment of contributions under Article 24;

(b) determination of quotas under the Agreement with the exception of adjustments made under the provisions of Article 35 paragraph (3) and of Article 37;

(c) suspension of the voting rights of a Member under Articles 45 or 59;

(d) establishment or revision of individual country and world production goals under Article 48;

(e) establishment of a policy relative to stocks under Article 49;

(f) waiver of the obligations of a Member under Article 57;

(g) decision of disputes under Article 59;

(h) establishment of conditions for accession under Article 63;

(i)  a decision to require the withdrawal of a Member under Article 67;

(j)  extension or termination of the Agreement under Article 69; and

(k)  recommendation of amendments to Members under Article 70.

(3) The Council by a distributed simple majority vote may at any time revoke any delegation of powers to the Board.

## ARTICLE 18

### Voting Procedure of the Board

(1) Each member of the Board shall be entitled to cast the number of votes received by it under the provisions of paragraphs (6) and (7) of Article 16. Voting by proxy shall not be allowed. A member may not split its votes.

(2) Any action taken by the Board shall require the same majority as such action would require if taken by the Council.

## ARTICLE 19

### Quorum for the Council and the Board

(1) The quorum for any meeting of the Council shall be the presence of a majority of the Members representing a distributed two-thirds majority of the total votes. If there is no quorum on the day appointed for the opening of any Council session, or if in the course of any Council session there is no quorum at three successive meetings, the Council shall be convened seven days later; at that time and throughout the remainder of that session the quorum shall be the presence of a majority of the Members representing a distributed simple majority of the votes. Representation in accordance with paragraph (2) of Article 13 shall be considered as presence.

(2) The quorum for any meeting of the Board shall be the

presence of a majority of the members representing a distributed two-thirds majority of the total votes.

## ARTICLE 20

### The Executive Director and the Staff

(1) The Council shall appoint the Executive Director on the recommendation of the Board. The terms of appointment of the Executive Director shall be established by the Council and shall be comparable to those applying to corresponding officials of similar inter-governmental organizations.

(2) The Executive Director shall be the chief administrative officer of the Organization and shall be responsible for the performance of any duties devolving upon him in the administration of the Agreement.

(3) The Executive Director shall appoint the staff in accordance with regulations established by the Council.

(4) Neither the Executive Director nor any member of the staff shall have any financial interest in the coffee industry, coffee trade, or coffee transportation.

(5) In the performance of their duties, the Executive Director and the staff shall not seek or receive instructions from any Member or from any other authority external to the Organization. They shall refrain from any action which might reflect on their position as international officials responsible only to the Organization. Each Member undertakes to respect the exclusively international character of the responsibilities of the Executive Director and the staff and not to seek to influence them in the discharge of their responsibilities.

## ARTICLE 21

### Co-operation with other Organizations

The Council may make whatever arrangements are desirable for consultation and co-operation with the United Nations and its specialized agencies and with other appropriate inter-governmental organizations. The Council may invite these organizations and any organizations concerned with coffee to send observers to its meetings.

## CHAPTER V—PRIVILEGES AND IMMUNITIES

### ARTICLE 22

### Privileges and Immunities

(1) The Organization shall have legal personality. It shall in particular have the capacity to contract, acquire and dispose of movable and immovable property and to institute legal proceedings.

(2) The Government of the country in which the headquarters of the Organization is situated (hereinafter referred to as "the host Government") shall conclude with the Organization as soon as possible an agreement to be approved by the Council relating to the status, privileges and immunities of the Organization, of its Executive Director and its staff and of representatives of Members while in the territory of the host Government for the purpose of exercising their functions.

(3) The agreement envisaged in paragraph (2) of this Article shall be independent of the present Agreement and shall prescribe the conditions for its termination.

(4) Unless any other taxation arrangements are implemented under the agreement envisaged in paragraph (2) of this Article the host Government:

(a) shall grant exemption from taxation on the remuneration paid by the Organization to its employees, except that such exemption need not apply to nationals of that country; and

(b) shall grant exemption from taxation on the assets, income and other property of the Organization.

(5) Following the approval of the agreement envisaged in paragraph (2) of this Article, the Organization may conclude with one or more other Members agreements to be approved by the Council relating to such privileges and immunities as may be necessary for the proper functioning of the International Coffee Agreement.

## CHAPTER VI–FINANCE

### ARTICLE 23

### Finance

(1) The expenses of delegations to the Council, representatives on the Board, and representatives on any of the committees of the Council or the Board shall be met by their respective Governments.

(2) The other expenses necessary for the administration of the Agreement shall be met by annual contributions from the Members assessed in accordance with Article 24. However, the Council may levy fees for specific services.

(3) The financial year of the Organization shall be the same as the coffee year.

### ARTICLE 24

### Determination of the Budget and Assessment of Contributions

(1) During the second half of each financial year the Council shall approve the administrative budget of the Organization for the following financial year and shall assess the contribution of each Member to that budget.

(2) The contribution of each Member to the budget for each financial year shall be in the proportion which the number of its votes at the time the budget for that financial year is approved bears to the total votes of all the Members. However, if there is any change in the distribution of votes among Members in accordance with the provisions of paragraph (5) of Article 12 at the beginning of the financial year for which contributions are assessed, such contributions shall be correspondingly adjusted for that year. In determining contributions, the votes of each Member shall be calculated without regard to the suspension of any Member's voting rights or any redistribution of votes resulting therefrom.

(3) The initial contribution of any Member joining the Organization after the entry into force of the Agreement shall be assessed by the Council on the basis of the number of votes to be held by it and the period remaining in the current financial year, but the assessments made upon other Members for the current financial year shall not be altered.

## ARTICLE 25

### Payment of Contributions

(1) Contributions to the administrative budget for each financial year shall be payable in freely convertible currency, and shall become due on the first day of that financial year.

(2) If any Member fails to pay its full contribution to the administrative budget within six months of the date on which the contribution is due, both its voting rights in the Council and its right to have its votes cast in the Board shall be suspended until such contribution has been paid. However, unless the Council by a distributed two-thirds majority vote so decides, such Member shall not be deprived of any of its other rights nor relieved of any of its obligations under the Agreement.

(3) Any Member whose voting rights have been suspended,

either under paragraph (2) of this Article or under Articles 38, 45, 48, 54 or 59 shall nevertheless remain responsible for the payment of its contribution.

## ARTICLE 26

### Audit and Publication of Accounts

As soon as possible after the close of each financial year an independently audited statement of the Organization's receipts and expenditures during that financial year shall be presented to the Council for approval and publication.

## CHAPTER VII—REGULATION OF EXPORTS

## ARTICLE 27

### General Undertakings by Members

(1) The Members undertake to conduct their trade policy so that the objectives set forth in Article 1, and in particular paragraph (4) of that Article, may be achieved. They agree on the desirability of operating the Agreement in a manner such that the real income derived from the export of coffee could be progressively increased so as to make it consonant with their needs for foreign exchange to support their programmes for social and economic progress.

(2) To attain these purposes through the fixing of quotas as provided for in this Chapter and in other ways carrying out the provisions of the Agreement, the Members agree on the necessity of assuring that the general level of coffee prices does not decline below the general level of such prices in 1962.

(3) The Members further agree on the desirability of assuring to consumers prices which are equitable and which will not hamper a desirable increase in consumption.

# ARTICLE 28

## Basic Export Quotas

Beginning on 1 October 1968 the exporting countries shall have the basic export quotas specified in Annex A.

# ARTICLE 29

## Basic Export Quota of a Member Group

Where two or more countries listed in Annex A form a Member group in accordance with Article 5, the basic export quotas specified for those countries in Annex A shall be added together and the combined total treated as a single basic quota for the purposes of this Chapter.

# ARTICLE 30

## Fixing of Annual Export Quotas

(1) At least 30 days before the beginning of each coffee year the Council by a two-thirds majority vote shall adopt an estimate of total world imports and exports for the following coffee year and an estimate of probable exports from non-member countries.

(2) In the light of these estimates the Council shall forthwith fix annual export quotas for all exporting Members. Such annual export quotas shall be the same percentage of the basic export quotas specified in Annex A, save for those exporting Members whose annual quotas are subject to the provisions of paragraph (2) of Article 31.

# ARTICLE 31

## Additional Provisions Concerning
## Basic and Annual Export Quotas

(1) A basic quota shall not be allotted to an exporting Member

whose average annual authorized exports of coffee for the preceding three year period were less than 100,000 bags and its annual export quota shall be calculated in accordance with paragraph (2) of this Article. When the annual export quota of any such Member reaches 100,000 bags the Council shall establish a basic quota for the exporting Member concerned.

(2) Without prejudice to the provisions of footnote 2 of Annex A to the Agreement each exporting Member to which a basic quota has not been allotted shall have in the coffee year 1968-69 the quota indicated in footnote 1 of Annex A to the Agreement. In each of the subsequent years the quota, subject to the provisions of paragraph (3) of this Article, shall be increased by 10 percent of that initial quota until the maximum of 100,000 bags mentioned in paragraph (1) of this Article is reached.

(3) Not later than 31 July of each year, each Member concerned shall notify the Executive Director, for the information of the Council, of the amount of coffee likely to be available for export under quota during the next coffee year. The quota for the next coffee year shall be the amount thus indicated by the exporting Member provided that such amount is within the permissible limit defined in paragraph (2) of this Article.

(4) Exporting Members to which basis quotas have not been allotted shall be subject to the provisions of Articles 27, 29, 32, 34, 35, 38 and 40.

(5) Any Trust Territory, administered under a trusteeship agreement with the United Nations, whose annual exports to countries other than the Administering Authority do not exceed 100,000 bags shall not be subject to the quota provisions of the Agreement so long as its exports do not exceed that quantity.

## ARTICLE 32

### Fixing of Quarterly Export Quotas

(1) Immediately following the fixing of the annual export

quotas the Council shall fix quarterly export quotas for each exporting Member for the purpose of keeping supply in reasonable balance with estimated demand throughout the coffee year.

(2) These quotas shall be, as nearly as possible, 25 percent of the annual export quota of each Member during the coffee year. No Member shall be allowed to export more than 30 percent in the first quarter, 60 percent in the first two quarters, and 80 percent in the first three quarters of the coffee year. If exports by any Member in one quarter are less than its quota for that quarter, the outstanding balance shall be added to its quota for the following quarter of that coffee year.

## ARTICLE 33

### Adjustment of Annual Export Quotas

If market conditions so require, the Council may review the quota situation and may vary the percentage of basic export quotas fixed under paragraph (2) of Article 30. In so doing, the Council shall have regard to any likely shortfalls by Members.

## ARTICLE 34

### Notification of Shortfalls

(1) Exporting Members undertake to notify the Council as early in the coffee year as possible but not later than the end of the eighth month thereof, as well as at such later dates as the Council may require, whether they have sufficient coffee available to export the full amount of their quota for that year.

(2) The Council shall take into account these notifications in determining whether or not to adjust the level of export quotas in accordance with Article 33.

# ARTICLE 35

## Adjustment of Quarterly Export Quotas

(1) The Council shall in the circumstances set out in this Article vary the quarterly export quotas fixed for each Member under paragraph (1) of Article 32.

(2) If the Council varies the annual export quotas as provided in Article 33, then that change shall be reflected in the quotas for the current quarter, current and remaining quarters, or the remaining quarters of the coffee year.

(3) Apart from the adjustment provided for in the preceding paragraph, the Council may, if it finds the market situation so requires, make adjustments among the current and remaining quarterly export quotas for the same coffee year, without, however, altering the annual export quotas.

(4) If on account of exceptional circumstances an exporting Member considers that the limitations provided in paragraph (2) of Article 32 would be likely to cause harm to its economy, the Council may, at the request of that Member, take appropriate action under Article 57. The Member concerned must furnish evidence of harm and provide adequate guarantees concerning the maintenance of price stability. The Council shall not, however, in any event, authorize a Member to export more than 35 percent of its annual export quota in the first quarter, 65 percent in the first two quarters, and 85 percent in the first three quarters of the coffee year.

(5) All Members recognize that marked price rises or falls occurring within brief periods may unduly distort underlying trends in price, cause grave concern to both producers and consumers, and jeopardize the attainment of the objectives of the Agreement. Accordingly, if such movements in general price levels occur within brief periods, Members may request a meeting of the Council which, by a distributed simple majority vote, may revise the total level of the quarterly export quotas in effect.

(6) If the Council finds that a sharp and unusual increase or decrease in the general level of prices is due to artificial manipulation of the coffee market through agreements among importers or exporters or both, it shall then by a simple majority vote decide on what corrective measures should be applied to readjust the total level of the quarterly export quotas in effect.

## ARTICLE 36

### Procedure for Adjusting Export Quotas

(1) Except as provided for in Articles 31 and 37 annual export quotas shall be fixed and adjusted by altering the basic export quota of each Member by the same percentage.

(2) General changes in all quarterly export quotas, made pursuant to paragraphs (2), (3), (5) and (6) of Article 35, shall be applied *pro rata* to individual quarterly export quotas in accordance with appropriate rules established by the Council. Such rules shall take account of the different percentages of annual export quotas which the different Members have exported or are entitled to export in each quarter of the coffee year.

(3) All decisions by the Council on the fixing and adjustment of annual and quarterly export quotas under Articles 30, 32, 33 and 35 shall be taken, unless otherwise provided, by a distributed two-thirds majority vote.

## ARTICLE 37

### Additional Provisions for Adjusting Export Quotas

(1) In addition to fixing annual export quotas in accordance with estimated total world imports and exports as required by Article 30, the Council shall seek to ensure that:

    (a)   supplies of the types of coffee that consumers require are available to them;

(b) the prices for the different types of coffee are equitable; and

(c) sharp price fluctuations within brief periods do not occur.

(2) To achieve these objectives the Council may, notwithstanding the provisions of Article 36, adopt a system for the adjustment of annual and quarterly quotas in relation to the movement of the prices of the principal types of coffee. The Council shall annually set a limit not exceeding five percent by which annual quotas may be reduced under any system so established. For the purposes of such a system the Council may establish price differentials and price brackets for the various types of coffee. In so doing the Council shall take into consideration, among other things, price trends.

(3) Decisions of the Council under the provisions of paragraph (2) of this Article shall be taken by a distributed two-thirds majority vote.

## ARTICLE 38

### Compliance with Export Quotas

(1) Exporting Members subject to quotas shall adopt the measures required to ensure full compliance with all provisions of the Agreement relating to quotas. In addition to any measures it may itself take, the Council by a distributed two-thirds majority vote may require such Members to adopt additional measures for the effective implementation of the quota system provided for in the Agreement.

(2) Exporting Members shall not exceed the annual and quarterly export quotas allocated to them.

(3) If an exporting Member exceeds its quota for any quarter, the Council shall deduct from one or more of its subsequent quotas a quantity equal to 110 percent of that excess.

(4) If an exporting Member for the second time while the Agreement remains in force exceeds its quarterly quota, the Council shall deduct from one or more of its subsequent quotas a total amount equal to twice that excess.

(5) If an exporting Member for a third or subsequent time while the Agreement remains in force exceeds its quarterly quota, the Council shall make the same deduction as provided in paragraph (4) of this Article and the voting rights of the Member shall be suspended until such time as the Council decides whether to take action in accordance with Article 67 to require the withdrawal of such a Member from the Organization.

(6) In accordance with rules established by the Council the deductions in quotas provided for in paragraphs (3), (4) and (5) of this Article and the additional action required by paragraph (5) shall be effected by the Council as soon as the necessary information is received.


## ARTICLE 39

### Shipments of Coffee from Dependent Territories

(1) Subject to paragraph (2) of this Article, the shipment of coffee from any of the dependent territories of a Member to its metropolitan territory or to another of its dependent territories for domestic consumption therein or in any other of its dependent territories shall not be considered as the export of coffee, and shall not be subject to any export quota limitations, provided that the Member concerned enters into arrangements satisfactory to the Council with respect to the control of re-exports and such other matters as the Council may determine to be related to the operation of the Agreement and which arise out of the special relationship between the metropolitan territory of the Member and its dependent territories.

(2) The trade in coffee between a Member and any of its dependent territories which, in accordance with Article 4 or 5, is a

separate Member of the Organization or a party to a Member group, shall however be treated, for the purposes of the Agreement, as the export of coffee.

## ARTICLE 40

### Exports not Charged to Quotas

(1) To facilitate the increase of coffee consumption in certain areas .of the world having a low *per capita* consumption and considerable potential for expansion, exports to countries listed in Annex B shall not, subject to the provisions of sub-paragraph 2 (f) of this Article, be charged to quotas. The Council shall review Annex B annually to determine whether any country or countries should be deleted or added, and may, if it so decides, take action accordingly.

(2) The provisions of the following sub-paragraphs shall be applicable to exports to the countries listed in Annex B:

(a) The Council shall prepare annually an estimate of imports for internal consumption by the countries listed in Annex B after reviewing the results obtained in the previous year with regard to the increase of coffee consumption in those countries and taking into account the probable effect of promotion campaigns and trade arrangements. The Council may revise this estimate in the course of the year. Exporting Members shall not in the aggregate export to the countries listed in Annex B more than the quantity set by the Council and for that purpose the Organization shall keep Members informed of current exports to such countries. Exporting Members shall inform the Organization not later than thirty days after the end of each month of all exports made to each of the countries listed in Annex B during that month.

(b) Members shall supply such statistics and other

information as the Organization may require to assist it in controlling the flow of coffee to countries listed in Annex B and to ensure that it is consumed in such countries.

(c) Exporting Members shall endeavour to renegotiate existing trade agreements as soon as possible in order to include in them provisions designed to prevent re-exports of coffee from the countries listed in Annex B to traditional markets. Exporting Members shall also include such provisions in all new trade agreements and in all new sales contracts not covered by trade agreements, whether such contracts are negotiated with private traders or with government organizations.

(d) To maintain control at all times of exports to countries listed in Annex B, exporting Members shall clearly mark all coffee bags destined to those countries with the words "New Market" and shall require adequate guarantees to prevent re-exportation or diversion to countries not listed in Annex B. The Council may establish appropriate rules for this purpose. All Members other than those listed in Annex B, shall prohibit, without exception, the entry of all shipments of coffee consigned directly from, or diverted from, any country listed in Annex B, or which bear evidence on the bags or the export documents of having been originally destined to a country listed in Annex B, or which are accompanied by a Certificate showing a destination in a country listed in Annex B or marked "New Market."

(e) The Council shall annually prepare a comprehensive report on the results obtained in the development of coffee markets in the countries listed in Annex B.

(f) If coffee exported by a Member to a country listed in Annex B is re-exported, or diverted to any country not listed in Annex B, the Council shall charge the corresponding amount to the quota of that exporting

Member and in addition may, in accordance with rules established by the Council, apply the provisions of paragraph (4) of Article 38. Should there again be a re-exportation from the same country listed in Annex B, the Council shall investigate the case and, if it deems necessary, may at any time delete that country from Annex B.

(3) Exports of coffee beans as raw material for industrial processing for any purposes other than human consumption as a beverage or foodstuff shall not be charged to quotas, provided that the Council is satisfied from information supplied by the exporting Member that the coffee beans are in fact used for such other purposes.

(4) The Council may, upon application by an exporting Member, decide that coffee exports made by that Member for humanitarian or other non-commercial purposes shall not be charged to its quota.

## ARTICLE 41

### Regional and Inter-regional Price Arrangements

(1) Regional and inter-regional price arrangements among exporting Members shall be consistent with the general objectives of the Agreement and shall be registered with the Council. Such arrangements shall take into account the interests of both producers and consumers and the objectives of the Agreement. Any Member of the Organization which considers that any of these arrangements are likely to lead to results not in accordance with the objectives of the Agreement may request that the Council discuss them with the Members concerned at its next session.

(2) In consultation with Members and with any regional organization to which they belong, the Council may recommend a scale of price differentials for various grades and qualities of coffee which Members should strive to achieve through their pricing policies.

(3) Should sharp price fluctuations occur within brief periods in respect of those grades and qualities of coffee for which a scale of price differentials has been adopted as the result of recommendations made under paragraph (2) of this Article, the Council may recommend appropriate measures to correct the situation.

## ARTICLE 42

### Survey of Market Trends

The Council shall keep under constant survey the trends of the coffee market with a view to recommending price policies, taking into consideration the results achieved through the quota mechanism of the Agreement.

## CHAPTER VIII – CERTIFICATES OF ORIGIN AND RE-EXPORT

## ARTICLE 43

### Certificates of Origin and Re-export

(1) Every export of coffee from any Member in whose territory that coffee has been grown shall be accompanied by a valid Certificate of Origin in accordance with rules established by the Council and issued by a qualified agency chosen by that Member and approved by the Organization. Each Member shall determine the number of copies of the Certificate it will require and each original Certificate and all copies thereof shall bear a serial number. Unless the Council decides otherwise the original of the Certificate shall accompany the documents of export and a copy shall be furnished immediately to the Organization by the

Member, except that original Certificates issued to cover exports of coffee to non-member countries shall be despatched directly to the Organization by that Member.

(2) Every re-export of coffee from a Member shall be accompanied by a valid Certificate of Re-export, in accordance with the rules established by the Council, issued by a qualified agency chosen by that Member and approved by the Organization, certifying that the coffee in question was imported in accordance with the provisions of the Agreement. Each Member shall determine the number of copies of the Certificate it will require and each original Certificate and all copies thereof shall bear a serial number. Unless the Council decides otherwise, the original of the Certificate of Re-export shall accompany the documents of re-export and a copy shall be furnished immediately to the Organization by the re-exporting Member, except that original Certificates of Re-export issued to cover re-exports of coffee to a non-member country shall be despatched directly to the Organization.

(3) Each Member shall notify the Organization of the government or non-government agency which is to administer and perform the functions specified in paragraphs (1) and (2) of this Article. The Organization shall specifically approve any such non-government agency upon submission of satisfactory evidence by the Member country of the agency's ability and willingness to fulfill the Member's responsibilities in accordance with the rules and regulations established under the provisions of this Agreement. The Council may at any time, for cause, declare a particular non-government agency to be no longer acceptable to it. The Council shall, either directly or through an internationally recognized world-wide organization, take all necessary steps so that at any time it will be able to satisfy itself that Certificates of Origin and Certificates of Re-export are being issued and used correctly and to ascertain the quantities of coffee which have been exported by each Member.

(4) A non-government agency approved as a certifying agency under the provisions of paragraph (3) of this Article shall keep records of the Certificates issued and the basis for their issue, for a period of not less than two years. In order to obtain approval as a certifying agency under the provisions of paragraph (3) of this Article a non-government agency must previously agree to make the above records available for examination by the Organization.

(5) Members shall prohibit the entry of any shipment of coffee from any other Member, whether imported direct or via a non-member, which is not accompanied by a valid Certificate of Origin or of Re-export issued in accordance with the rules established by the Council.

(6) Small quantities of coffee in such forms as the Council may determine, or coffee for direct consumption on ships, aircraft and other international carriers, shall be exempt from the provisions of paragraphs (1) and (2) of this Article.

## CHAPTER IX – PROCESSED COFFEE

### ARTICLE 44

#### Measures relating to Processed Coffee

(1) No Member shall apply governmental measures affecting its exports and re-exports of coffee to another Member which, when taken as a whole in relation to that other Member, amount to discriminatory treatment in favour of processed coffee as compared with green coffee. In the application of this provision, Members may have due regard to:

    (a)   the special situation of markets listed in Annex B of the Agreement;

    (b)   differential treatment in an importing Member as far as imports of re-exports of the various forms of coffee are concerned;

(2) (a) If a Member considers that the provisions of paragraph (1) of this Article are not being complied with, it may notify the Executive Director in writing of its complaint with a detailed report of the reasons for its opinion together with a description of the measures it considers should be taken. The Executive Director shall forthwith inform the Member against which the complaint has been made and seek its views. He shall encourage the Members to reach a mutually satisfactory solution and as soon as possible make a full report to the Council including the measures the complaining Member considers should be taken and the views of the other party.

(b) If a solution has not been found within 30 days after receipt of the notification by the Executive Director, he shall not later than 40 days after the receipt of the notification establish an arbitration panel. The panel shall consist of:

(i) one person designated by the complaining Member;

(ii) one person designated by the Member against which the complaint has been made; and

(iii) a chairman mutually agreed upon by the Members involved or, failing such agreement, by the two persons designated under (i) and (ii).

(c) If the panel is not fully constituted within 45 days after the receipt of the notification by the Executive Director, the remaining arbitrators shall be appointed within 10 further days by the Chairman of the Council after consultation with the Members involved.

(d) None of the arbitrators shall be officials of any Government involved in the case or have any interest in its outcome.

(e) The Members concerned shall facilitate the work of the panel and make available all relevant information.

(f) The arbitration panel shall, on the basis of all the information at its disposal, determine, within three weeks after its establishment whether, and if so to what extent, there exists discriminatory treatment.

(g) Decisions of the panel on all questions, whether of substance or procedure, shall if necessary be by majority vote.

(h) The Executive Director shall forthwith notify the Members concerned and inform the Council of the panel's conclusions.

(i) The costs of the arbitration panel shall be charged to the administrative budget of the Organization.

(3) (a) If discriminatory treatment is found to exist the Member concerned will be given a period of 30 days after it has been notified of the conclusions of the arbitration panel, to correct the situation in accordance with the panel's conclusions. The Member shall inform the Council of the measures it intends to take.

(b) If after this period, the complaining Member considers that the situation has not been corrected it may, after informing the Council, take counter measures which shall not go beyond what is necessary to counteract the discriminatory treatment determined by the arbitration panel and shall last no longer than the discrimatory treatment exists.

(c) The Members concerned shall keep the Council informed of the measures being taken by them.

(4) In applying the counter measures Members undertake to have due regard to the need of developing countries to practice policies designed to broaden the base of their economies through, *inter alia,* industrialization and the export of manufactured products and to do what is necessary to ensure that the provisions of this Article are applied equitably to all Members in a like situation.

(5) None of the provisions of this Article shall be deemed to prevent a Member from raising in the Council an issue under this

Article or having recourse to Article 58 or 59, provided that any such action shall not interrupt any procedure that has been started under this Article without the consent of the Members concerned, nor prevent such procedure from being initiated unless a procedure under Article 59 in regard to the same issue has been completed.

(6) Any time limit in this Article may be varied by agreement of the Members concerned.

## CHAPTER X–REGULATION OF IMPORTS

### ARTICLE 45

### Regulation of Imports

(1) To prevent non-member exporting countries from increasing their exports at the expense of Members, each Member shall limit its annual imports of coffee produced in non-member exporting countries to a quantity not in excess of its average annual imports of coffee from those countries during the calendar years 1960, 1961 and 1962.

(2) The Council by a distributed two-thirds majority may suspend or vary these quantitative limitations if it finds such action necessary to further the purposes of the Agreement.

(3) The Council shall prepare annual reports of the quantity of permissible imports of coffee of non-member origin and quarterly reports of imports by each importing Member under the provisions of paragraph (1) of this Article.

(4) The obligations of the preceding paragraphs of this Article shall not derogate from any conflicting bilateral or multilateral obligations which importing Members entered into with non-member countries before 1 August 1962 provided that any importing Member which has such conflicting obligations shall

carry them out in such a way as to minimize the conflict with the obligations of the preceding paragraphs, take steps as soon as possible to bring its obligations into harmony with those paragraphs, and inform the Council of the details of the conflicting obligations and of the steps taken to minimize or eliminate the conflict.

(5) If an importing Member fails to comply with the provisions of this Article the Council by a distributed two-thirds majority may suspend both its voting rights in the Council and its right to have its votes cast in the Board.

## CHAPTER XI–INCREASE OF CONSUMPTION

### ARTICLE 46

### Promotion

(1) The Council shall sponsor the promotion of coffee consumption. To achieve this purpose it may maintain a separate committee with the objective of promoting consumption in importing countries by all appropriate means without regard to origin, type or brand of coffee and of striving to achieve and maintain the highest quality and purity of the beverage.

(2) The following provisions shall apply to such committee:

(a) The cost of the promotion programme shall be met by contributions from exporting Members.

(b) Importing Members may also contribute financially to the promotion programme.

(c) Membership in the committee shall be limited to Members contributing to the promotion programme.

(d) The size and cost of the promotion programme shall be reviewed by the Council.

(g)   The committee shall control all resources of promotion and approve all accounts related thereto.

(3)   The ordinary administrative expenses relating to the permanent staff of the organization employed directly on promotion activities, other than the costs of their travel or promotion purposes, shall be charged to the administrative budget of the Organization.

## ARTICLE 47

### Removal of Obstacles to Consumption

(1) The Members recognize the utmost importance of achieving the greatest possible increase of coffee consumption as rapidly as possible, in particular through the progressive removal of any obstacles which may hinder such increase.

(2) The Members recognize that there are presently in effect measures which may to a greater or lesser extent hinder the increase in consumption of coffee, in particular:

(a)   import arrangements applicable to coffee, including preferential and other tariffs, quotas, operations of Government import monopolies and official purchasing agencies, and other administrative rules and commercial practices;

(b)   export arrangements as regards direct or indirect subsidies and other administrative rules and commercial practices; and

(c)   internal trade conditions and domestic legal and administrative provisions which may affect consumption.

(3) Having regard to the objectives stated above and to the provisions of paragraph (4) of this Article, the Members shall endeavour to pursue tariff reductions on coffee or to take other action to remove obstacles to increased consumption.

(4) Taking into account their mutual interest and in the spirit of Annex A.II-1 of the Final Act of the First United Nations Conference on Trade and Development, the Members undertake to seek ways and means by which the obstacles to increased trade and consumption referred to in paragraph (2) of this Article could be progressively reduced and eventually wherever possible eliminated, or by which their effects could be substantially diminished.

(5) Members shall inform the Council of all measures adopted with a view to implementing the provisions of this Article.

(6) The Council may, in order to further the purposes of this Article, make any recommendations to Members, and shall examine the results achieved at the first session of the coffee year 1969-70.

## CHAPTER XII–PRODUCTION POLICY AND CONTROLS

### ARTICLE 48

### Production Policy and Controls

(1) Each producing Member undertakes to adjust its production of coffee to a level not exceeding that needed for domestic consumption, permitted exports and stocks as referred to in Article 49.

(2) Prior to 31 December 1968 each exporting Member shall submit to the Executive Board its proposed production goal for coffee year 1972-73, based on the elements set forth in paragraph (1) of this Article. Unless rejected by the Executive Board by a distributed simple majority vote prior to the first session of the Council after 31 December 1968 such goals shall be considered as approved. The Executive Board shall inform the Council of the production goals which have been approved in this manner. If the

production goal proposed by an exporting Member is rejected by the Executive Board, the Board shall recommend a production goal for that exporting Member. At its first session after 31 December 1968, which shall be not later than 31 March 1969, the Council by a distributed two-thirds majority vote and in the light of the Board's recommendations shall establish individual production goals for exporting Members whose own proposed goals have been rejected by the Board or who have not submitted proposed production goals.

(3) Until its production goal has been approved by the Organization or established by the Council, in accordance with paragraph (2) of this Article, no exporting Member shall enjoy any increase in its annual export entitlement above the level of its annual export entitlement in effect on 1 April 1969.

(4) The Council shall establish production goals for exporting Members acceding to the Agreement and may establish production goals for producing Members which are not exporting Members.

(5) The Council shall keep the production goals, established or approved under the terms of this Article, under constant review and shall revise them to the extent necessary to ensure that the aggregate of the individual goals is consistent with estimated world requirements.

(6) Members undertake to conform with the individual production goals established or approved under the terms of this Article and each producing Member shall apply whatever policies and procedures it deems necessary for this purpose. Individual production goals established or approved under the terms of this Article are not binding minima nor do they confer any entitlement to specific levels of exports.

(7) Producing Members shall submit to the Organization, in such form and at such times as the Council shall determine, periodic reports on the measures taken to control production and to conform with their individual production goals established or approved under the terms of this Article. In the light of its

appraisal of this and other relevant information the Council shall take such action, general or particular, as its deems necessary or appropriate.

(8) If the Council determines that any producing Member is not taking adequate steps to comply with the provisions of this Article such Member shall not enjoy any subsequent increase in its annual export entitlement and may have its voting rights suspended under the terms of paragraph (7) of Article 59 until the Council is satisfied that the Member is fulfilling its obligations in respect of this Article. If, however, after the elapse of such additional period as the Council shall determine it is established that the Member concerned has still not taken the steps necessary to implement a policy to conform with the objectives of this Article, the Council may require the withdrawal of such Member from the Organization under the terms of Article 67.

(9) The Organization shall, under such conditions as may be determined by the Council, extend to those Members so requesting it all possible assistance within its powers to further the purpose of this Article.

(10) Importing Members undertake to co-operate with exporting Members in their plans for adjusting the production of coffee in accordance with paragraph (1) above. In particular, Members shall refrain from offering directly financial or technical assistance or from supporting proposals for such assistance by any international body to which they belong, for the pursuit of production policies which are contrary to the objectives of this Article, whether the recipient country is a Member of the International Coffee Organization or not. The Organization shall maintain close contact with the international bodies concerned, with a view to securing their maximum co-operation in the implementation of this Article.

(11) Except as specified in paragraph (2) hereof, all decisions provided for in this Article shall be taken by a distributed two-thirds majority vote.

# CHAPTER XIII – REGULATION OF STOCKS

## ARTICLE 49

### Policy Relative to Coffee Stocks

(1) To complement the provisions of Article 48 the Council by a distributed two-thirds majority may establish a policy relating to coffee stocks in producing Member countries.

(2) The Council shall take measures to ascertain annually the volume of coffee stocks in the hands of individual exporting Members in accordance with procedures which it shall establish. Members concerned shall facilitate this annual survey.

(3) Producing Members shall ensure that adequate facilities exist in their respective countries for the proper storage of coffee stocks.

# CHAPTER XIV – MISCELLANEOUS OBLIGATIONS OF MEMBERS

## ARTICLE 50

### Consultation and Co-operation with the Trade

(1) The Organization shall maintain close liaison with appropriate non-governmental organizations concerned with international commerce in coffee and with experts in coffee matters.

(2) Members shall conduct their activities within the framework of the Agreement in a manner consonant with established trade channels. In carrying out these activities they shall endeavour to take due account of the legitimate interests of the coffee trade.

# ARTICLE 51

## Barter

In order to avoid jeopardizing the general price structure, Members shall refrain from engaging in direct and individually linked barter transactions involving the sale of coffee in the traditional markets.

# ARTICLE 52

## Mixtures and Substitutes

(1) Members shall not maintain any regulations requiring the mixing, processing or using of other products with coffee for commercial resale as coffee. Members shall endeavour to prohibit the sale and advertisement of products under the name of coffee if such products contain less than the equivalent of 90 percent green coffee as the basic raw material.

(2) The Executive Director shall submit to the Council an annual report on compliance with the provisions of this Article.

(3) The Council may recommend to any Member that it take the necessary steps to ensure observance of the provisions of this Article.

# CHAPTER XV—SEASONAL FINANCING

# ARTICLE 53

## Seasonal Financing

(1) The Council shall, upon the request of any Member who is also a party to any bilateral, multilateral, regional or inter-regional agreement in the field of seasonal financing, examine such agreement with a view to verifying its compatibility with the obligations of the Agreement.

(2) The Council may make recommendations to Members with a view to resolving any conflict of obligations which might arise.

(3) The Council may, on the basis of information obtained from the Members concerned, and if it deems appropriate and suitable, make general recommendations with a view to assisting Members which are in need of seasonal financing.

## CHAPTER XVI–DIVERSIFICATION FUND

### ARTICLE 54

#### Diversification Fund

(1) There is hereby established the Diversification Fund of the International Coffee Organization to further the objectives of limiting the production of coffee in order to bring supply into reasonable balance with world demand. The Fund shall be governed by Statutes to be approved by the Council not later than 31 December 1968.

(2) Participation in the Fund shall be compulsory for each Contracting Party that is not an importing Member and has an export entitlement of over 100,000 bags. Voluntary participation in the Fund by Contracting Parties to which this provision does not apply, and contributions from other sources, shall be under such conditions as may be agreed between the Fund and the parties concerned.

(3) An exporting Participant liable to compulsory participation shall contribute to the Fund in quarterly instalments an amount equivalent to US$0.60 times the number of bags it actually exports in excess of 100,000 bags each coffee year to quota markets. Contributions shall be made for five consecutive years commencing with coffee year 1968-69. The Fund by a two-thirds

majority vote may increase the rate of contribution to a level not exceeding US$1.00 per bag. The annual contribution of each exporting Participant shall be assessed initially on the basis of its export entitlement for the year of assessment as at 1 October. This initial assessment shall be revised on the basis of the actual quantity of coffee exported to quota markets by the Participant during the year of assessment and any necessary adjustment in contribution shall be effected during the ensuring coffee year. The first quarterly instalment of the annual contribution for coffee year 1968-69 becomes due on 1 January 1969 and shall be paid not later than 28 February 1969.

(4) The contribution of each exporting Participant shall be utilized for programmes or projects approved by the Fund carried out inside its territory, but in any case twenty percent of the contribution shall be payable in freely convertible currency for use in any programmes or projects approved by the Fund. In addition a percentage of the contribution within limits to be established in the Statutes shall be payable in freely convertible currency for the administrative expenses of the Fund.

(5) The percentage of the contribution to be made freely convertible currency in accordance with paragraph (4) may be increased by mutual agreement between the Fund and the exporting Participant concerned.

(6) At the commencement of the third year of operation of the Fund the Council shall review the results obtained in the first two years and may then revise the provisions of this Article with a view to improving them.

(7) The Statutes of the Fund shall provide for:

    (a)    the suspension of contributions in relation to stipulated changes in the level of coffee prices;

    (b)    the payment to the Fund in freely convertible currency of any part of the contribution which has not been utilized by the Participant concerned:

294

(c) arrangements that would permit the delegation of appropriate functions and activities of the Fund to one or more international financial institutions.

(8) Unless the Council decides otherwise, an exporting Participant which fails to meet its obligations under this Article shall have its voting rights in the Council suspended and shall not enjoy any increase in its export entitlement. If the exporting Participant fails to meet the obligations for a continuous period of one year, it shall cease to be a Party to the Agreement ninety days thereafter, unless the Council decides otherwise.

(9) Decisions of the Council under the provisions of this Article shall be taken by a distributed two-thirds majority vote.

# CHAPTER XVII–INFORMATION AND STUDIES

## ARTICLE 55

### Information

(1) The Organization shall act as a centre for the collection, exchange and publication of:

(a) statistical information on world production, prices, exports and imports, distribution and consumption of coffee; and

(b) in so far as is considered appropriate, technical information on the cultivation, processing and utilization of coffee.

(2) The Council may require Members to furnish such information as it considers necessary for its operations, including regular statistical reports on coffee production, exports and imports, distribution, consumption, stocks and taxation, but no information shall be published which might serve to identify the

operations of persons or companies producing, processing or marketing coffee. The Members shall furnish information requested in as detailed and accurate a manner as is practicable.

(3) If a Member fails to supply, or finds difficulty in supply, within a reasonable time, statistical and other information required by the Council for the proper functioning of the Organization, the Council may require the Member concerned to explain the reasons for non-compliance. If it is found that technical assistance is needed in the matter, the Council may take any necessary measures.

## ARTICLE 56

### Studies

(1) The Council may promote studies in the fields of the economics of coffee production and distribution, the impact of governmental measures in producing and consuming countries on the production and consumption of coffee, the opportunities for expansion of coffee consumption for traditional and possible new uses, and the effects of the operation of the Agreement on producers and consumers of coffee, including their terms of trade.

(2) The Organization may study the practicability of establishing minimum standards for exports of coffee from producing Members. Recommendations in this regard may be discussed by the Council.

## CHAPTER VXIII—WAIVER

## ARTICLE 57

### Waiver

(1) The Council by a distributed two-thirds majority vote may

relieve a Member of an obligation, on account of exceptional or emergency circumstances, *force majeure,* constitutional obligations, or international obligations under the United Nations Charter for territories administered under the trusteeship system.

(2) The Council, in granting a waiver to a Member, shall state explicitly the terms and conditions on which and the period for which the Member is relieved of such obligation.

(3) The Council shall not consider a request for a waiver of quota obligations on the basis of the existence in a Member country, in one or more years, of an exportable production in excess of its permitted exports, or which is the consequence of the Member having failed to comply with the provisions of Articles 48 and 49.


## CHAPTER XIX—CONSULTATIONS, DISPUTES AND COMPLAINTS

### ARTICLE 58

#### Consultations

Each Member shall accord sympathetic consideration to, and shall afford adequate opportunity for, consultation regarding such representations as may be made by another Member with respect to any matter relating to the Agreement. In the course of such consultation, on request by either party and with the consent of the other, the Executive Director shall establish an independent panel which shall use its good offices with a view to conciliating the parties. The costs of the panel shall not be chargeable to the Organization. If a party does not agree to the establishment of a panel by the Executive Director, or if the consultation does not lead to a solution, the matter may be referred to the Council in accordance with Article 59. If the consultation does lead to a solution, it shall be reported to the Executive Director who shall distribute the report to all Members.

## ARTICLE 59

### Disputes and Complaints

(1) Any dispute concerning the interpretation or application of the Agreement which is not settled by negotiation shall, at the request of any Member party to the dispute, be referred to the Council for decision.

(2) In any case where a dispute has been referred to the Council under paragraph (1) of this Article, a majority of Members, or Members holding not less than one-third of the total votes, may require the Council, after discussion, to seek the opinion of the advisory panel referred to in paragraph (3) of this Article on the issues in dispute before giving its decision.

(3)(a) Unless the Council unanimously agrees otherwise, the panel shall consist of:

    (i)    two persons, one having wide experience in matters of the kind in dispute and the other having legal standing and experience, nominated by the exporting Members;

    (ii)   two such persons nominated by the importing Members; and

    (iii)  a chairman selected unanimously by the four persons nominated under (i) and (ii) or, if they fail to agree, by the Chairman of the Council.

    (b)   Persons from countries whose Governments are Contracting Parties to this Agreement shall be eligible to serve on the advisory panel.

    (c)   Persons appointed to the advisory panel shall act in their personal capacities and without instructions from any Government.

    (d)   The expenses of the advisory panel shall be paid by the Organization.

(4) The opinion of the advisory panel and the reasons therefore shall be submitted to the Council which, after considering all the relevant information, shall decide the dispute.

(5) Any complaint that any Member has failed to fulfill its obligations under the Agreement shall, at the request of the Member making the complaint, be referred to the Council, which shall make a decision on the matter.

(6) No Member shall be found to have committed a breach of its obligations under the Agreement except by a distributed simple majority vote. Any finding that a Member is in breach of the Agreement shall specify the nature of the breach.

(7) If the Council finds that a Member has committed a breach of the Agreement, it may, without prejudice to other enforcement measures provided for in other Articles of the Agreement, by a distributed two-thirds majority vote, suspend that Member's voting rights in the Council and its right to have its votes cast in the Board until it fulfills its obligations, or the Council may take action requiring compulsory withdrawal under Article 67.

(8) A Member may seek the prior opinion of the Executive Board in a matter of dispute or complaint before the matter is discussed by the Council.

## CHAPTER XX – FINAL PROVISIONS

## ARTICLE 60

### Signature

The Agreement shall be open for signature at the United Nations Headquarters until and including 31 March 1968 by any Government which is a Contracting Party to the International Coffee Agreement, 1962.

# ARTICLE 61

## Ratification

The Agreement shall be subject to approval, ratification or acceptance by the signatory Governments or by any other Contracting Party to the International Coffee Agreement, 1962, in accordance with their respective constitutional procedures. Except as provided in paragraph (2) of Article 62 instruments of approval, ratification or acceptance shall be deposited with the Secretary-General of the United Nations not later than 30 September 1968.

# ARTICLE 62

## Entry into Force

(1) The Agreement shall enter into force definitively on 1 October 1968 among those Governments that have deposited instruments of approval, ratification or acceptance if, on that date, such Governments represent at least twenty exporting Members holding at least 80 percent of the votes of the exporting Members and at least ten importing Members holding at least 80 percent of the votes of the importing Members. The votes for this purpose shall be as distributed in Annex C. Alternatively, it shall enter into force definitively at any time after it is provisionally in force and the aforesaid requirements of this paragraph are satisfied. The Agreement shall enter into force definitively for any Government that deposits an instrument of approval, ratification, acceptance or accession subsequent to the definitive entry into force of the Agreement for other Governments on the date of such deposit.

(2) The Agreement may enter into force provisionally on 1 October 1968. For this purpose a notification by a signatory Government or by any other Contracting Party to the International Coffee Agreement, 1962, containing an undertaking to apply the Agreement provisionally and to seek approval, ratification or acceptance in accordance with its constitutional

procedures, as rapidly as possible, that is received by the Secretary-General of the United Nations not later than 30 September 1968, shall be regarded as equal in effect to an instrument of approval, ratification or acceptance. A Government that undertakes to apply the Agreement provisionally will be permitted to deposit an instrument of approval, ratification or acceptance and shall be provisionally regarded as a party thereto until either it deposits its instrument of approval, ratification or acceptance or up to and including 31 December 1968, whichever is the earlier.

(3) If the Agreement has not entered into force definitively or provisionally by 1 October 1968, those Governments that have deposited instruments of approval, ratification or acceptance or notifications containing an undertaking to apply the Agreement provisionally and to seek approval, ratification or acceptance may immediately after that date consult together to consider what action the situation requires and may, by mutual consent, decide that it shall enter into force among themselves. Likewise, if the Agreement has entered into force provisionally but has not entered into force definitively by 31 December 1968, those Governments that have deposited instruments of approval, ratification, acceptance or accession may consult together to consider what action the situation requires and may, by mutual consent, decide that it shall continue in force provisionally or enter into force definitively among themselves.

## ARTICLE 63

### Accession

(1) The Government of any State Member of the United Nations or of any of its specialized agencies may accede to this Agreement upon conditions that shall be established by the Council. In establishing such conditions the Council shall, if such country is an exporting country and is not named in Annex A, establish quota provisions for it. If such exporting country is

named in Annex A, the respective quota provisions specified therein shall be applied to that country unless the Council by a distributed two-thirds majority vote decides otherwise. Not later than 31 March 1969 or such other date as may be determined by the Council, any importing Member of the International Coffee Agreement, 1962, may accede to the Agreement on the same conditions under which it could have approved, ratified or accepted the Agreement and, if it applies the Agreement provisionally, it shall provisionally be regarded as a party thereto until either it deposits its instrument of accession or up to and including the above date, whichever is the earlier.

(2) Each Government depositing an instrument of accession shall, at the time of such deposit, indicate whether it is joining the Organization as an exporting Member or an importing Member, as defined in paragraphs (7) and (8) of Article 2.

## ARTICLE 64

### Reservations

Reservations may not be made with respect to any of the provisions of the Agreement.

## ARTICLE 65

### Notifications in respect of Dependent Territories

(1) Any Government may, at the time of signature or deposit of an instrument of approval, ratification, acceptance or accession, or at any time thereafter, by notification to the Secretary-General of the United Nations, declare that the Agreement shall extend to any of the territories for whose international relations it is responsible and the Agreement shall extend to the territories named therein from the date of such notification.

(2) Any Contracting Party which desires to exercise its rights under Article 4 in respect of any of its dependent territories, or which desires to authorize one of its dependent territories to

become part of a Member group formed under Article 5 or 6, may do so by making a notification to that effect to the Secretary-General of the United Nations, either at the time of the deposit of its instrument of approval, ratification, acceptance or accession, or at any later time.

(3) Any Contracting Party which has made a declaration under paragraph (1) of this Article may at any time thereafter, by notification to the Secretary-General of the United Nations, declare that the Agreement shall cease to extend to the territory named in the notification and the Agreement shall cease to extend to such territory from the date of such notification.

(4) The Government of a territory to which the Agreement has been extended under paragraph (1) of this Article and which has subsequently become independent may, within 90 days after the attainment of independence, declare by notification to the Secretary-General of the United Nations that it has assumed the rights and obligations of a Contracting Party to the Agreement. It shall, as from the date of such notification, become a party to the Agreement.

## ARTICLE 66

### Voluntary Withdrawal

Any Contracting Party may withdraw from the Agreement at any time by giving a written notice of withdrawal to the Secretary-General of the United Nations. Withdrawal shall become effective 90 days after the notice is received.

## ARTICLE 67

### Compulsory Withdrawal

If the Council determines that any Member has failed to carry out its obligations under the Agreement and that such failure significantly impairs the operations of the Agreement, it may by a distributed two-thirds majority vote require the withdrawal of such Member from the Organization. The Council shall immediately notify the Secretary-General of the United Nations of any such decision. Ninety days after the date of the Council's decision that Member shall cease to be a Member of the Organization and, if such Member is a Contracting Party, a party to the Agreement.

## ARTICLE 68

### Settlement of Accounts with Withdrawing Members

(1) The Council shall determine any settlement of accounts with a withdrawing Member. The Organization shall retain any amounts already paid by a withdrawing Member and such Member shall remain bound to pay any amounts due from it to the Organization at the time the withdrawal becomes effective; provided, however, that in the case of a Contracting Party which is unable to accept an amendment and consequently either withdraws or ceases to participate in the Agreement under the provisions of paragraph (2) of Article 70, the Council may determine any settlement of accounts which it finds equitable.

(2) A Member which has withdrawn or which has ceased to participate in the Agreement shall not be entitled to any share of the proceeds of liquidation or the other assets of the Organization upon termination of the Agreement under Article 69.

## ARTICLE 69

### Duration and Termination

(1) The Agreement shall remain in force until 30 September 1973 unless extended under paragraph (2) of this Article, or terminated earlier under paragraph (3).

(2) The Council after 30 September 1972 may, by a vote of a majority of the Members having not less than a distributed two-thirds majority of the total votes, either renegotiate the

Agreement or extend it, with or without modification, for such period as the Council shall determine. Any Contracting Party, or any dependent territory which is either a Member or a party to a Member group, on behalf of which notification of acceptance of such a renegotiated or extended Agreement has not been made by the date on which such renegotiated or extended Agreement becomes effective, shall as of that date cease to participate in the Agreement.

(3) The Council may at any time, by vote of a majority of the Members having not less that a distributed two-thirds majority of the total votes, decide to terminate the Agreement. Such termination shall take effect on such date as the Council shall decide.

(4) Notwithstanding termination of the Agreement, the Council shall remain in being for as long as necessary to carry out the liquidation of the Organization, settlement of its accounts and disposal of its assets, and shall have during that period such powers and functions as may be necessary for those purposes.

## ARTICLE 70

### Amendment

(1) The Council by a distributed two-thirds majority vote may recommend an amendment of the Agreement to the Contracting Parties. The amendment shall become effective 100 days after the Secretary-General of the United Nations has received notifications of acceptance from Contracting Parties representing at least 75 percent of the exporting countries holding at least 85 percent of the votes of the exporting Members, and from Contracting Parties representing at least 75 percent of the importing countries holding at least 80 percent of the votes of the importing Members. The Council may fix a time within which each Contracting Party shall notify the Secretary-General of the United Nations of its acceptance of the amendment and if the amendment has not become effective by such time, it shall be considered withdrawn.

The Council shall provide the Secretary-General with the information necessary to determine whether the amendment has become effective.

(2) Any Contracting Party, or any dependent territory which is either a Member or a party to a Member group, on behalf of which notification of acceptance of an amendment has not been made by the date on which such amendment becomes effective, shall as of that date cease to participate in the Agreement.

## ARTICLE 71

### Notifications by the Secretary-General

The Secretary-General of the United Nations shall notify all Contracting Parties to the International Coffee Agreement, 1962, and all other Governments of States Members of the United Nations or of any of its specialized agencies, of each deposit of an instrument of approval, ratification, acceptance or accession and of the dates on which the Agreement comes provisionally and definitively into force. The Secretary-General of the United Nations shall also notify all Contracting Parties of each notification under Articles 5, 62 paragraph (2), 65, 66 or 67; of the date to which the Agreement is extended or on which it is terminated under Article 69; and of the date on which an amendment becomes effective under Article 70.

## ARTICLE 72

### Supplementary and Transitional Provisions

(1) The present Agreement shall be considered as a continuation of the International Coffee Agreement, 1962.

(2) In order to facilitate the uninterrupted continuation of the 1962 Agreement:

    (a)    All acts by or on behalf of the Organization or any of its organs under the 1962 Agreement, in effect on 30

September 1968 and whose terms do not provide for expiry on that date, shall remain in effect unless changed under the provisions of the present Agreement.

(b) All decisions required to be taken by the Council during coffee year 1967-68 for application in coffee year 1968-69 shall be taken during the last regular session of the Council in coffee year 1967-68 and applied on a provisional basis as if the present Agreement had already entered into force.

IN WITNESS WHEREOF the undersigned, having been duly authorized to this effect by their respective Governments, have signed this Agreement on the dates appearing opposite their signatures.

The texts of this Agreement in the English, French, Portuguese, Russian and Spanish languages shall all be equally authentic. The originals shall be deposited in the archives of the United Nations and the Secretary-General of the United Nations shall transmit certified copies thereof to each signatory and acceding Government.

# ANNEX A

## Basic Export Quotas 1/

### (thousands of 60-kilo bags)

| | |
|---|---:|
| Brazil | 20,926 |
| Burundi 2/ | 233 |
| Cameroon | 1,000 |
| Central African Republic | 200 |
| Colombia | 7,000 |
| Congo (Democratic Republic) 2/ | 1,000 |
| Costa Rica | 1,100 |
| Dominican Republic | 520 |
| Ecuador | 750 |
| El Salvador | 1,900 |
| Ethiopia | 1,494 |
| Guatemala | 1,800 |
| Guinea (basic export quota to be established by the Council) | |
| Haiti | 490 |
| Honduras | 425 |
| India | 423 |
| Indonesia | 1,357 |
| Ivory Coast | 3,073 |
| Kenya | 860 |
| Malagasy Republic | 910 |
| Mexico | 1,760 |
| Nicaragua | 550 |
| Peru | 740 |
| Portugal | 2,776 |
| Rwanda 2/ | 150 |
| Tanzania | 700 |
| Togo | 200 |
| Uganda | 2,379 |
| Venezuela 2/ | 325 |
| **Grand Total** | **55,041** |

---

1/   According to the provisions of Article 31 (1), the following exporting countries do not have a basic export quota and shall receive in coffee year 1968-69 export quotas of: Bolivia 50,000 bags; Congo (Brazzaville) 25,000 bags; Cuba 50,000 bags; Dahomey 33,000 bags;

Gabon 25,000 bags; Ghana 51,000 bags; Jamaica 25,000 bags; Liberia 60,000 bags; Nigeria 52,000 bags; Panama 25,000 bags; Paraguay 70,000 bags; Sierra Leone 82,000 bags; Trinidad and Tobago 69,000 bags.

2/ Burundi, Congo (Democratic Republic), Cuba, Rwanda and Venezuela, after presentation to the Executive Board of acceptable evidence of an exportable production larger than 233,000; 1,000,000; 50,000; 150,000 and 325,000 bags respectively shall each be granted an annual export entitlement not exceeding the annual export entitlement it would receive with a basic quota of 350,000; 1,300,000; 200,000; 260,000 and 475,000 bags respectively. In no event, however, shall the increases allowed to these countries be taken into account for the purpose of calculating the distribution of votes.

# ANNEX B

## Non-quota countries of destination referred to in Article 40, Chapter VII

The geographical areas which are non-quota countries for the purposes of this Agreement are:

Bahrain
Botswana
Ceylon
China (Taiwan)
China (mainland)
Hungary
Iran
Iraq
Japan
Korea, Republic of
Kuwait
Lesotho
Malawi
Muscat and Oman
North Korea
Poland
Qatar
Romania
Saudi Arabia
Somalia
South-Africa, Republic of
Southern Rhodesia
South-West Africa
Sudan
Swaziland
Thailand
Trucial Oman
Union of Soviet Socialist Republics
Zambia

Note: The abbreviated names above are intended to be of purely geographical significance and to convey no political implications whatsoever.

# ANNEX C

## Distribution of Votes

| COUNTRY | EXPORTING | IMPORTING |
|---|---|---|
| Argentina | — | 16 |
| Australia | — | 9 |
| Austria | — | 11 |
| Belgium* | — | 28 |
| Bolivia | 4 | — |
| Brazil | 332 | — |
| Burundi | 8 | — |
| Canada | — | 32 |
| Colombia | 114 | — |
| Congo (Democratic Republic of) | 20 | — |
| Costa Rica | 21 | — |
| Cuba | 4 | — |
| Cyprus | — | 5 |
| Czechoslovakia | — | 9 |
| Denmark | — | 23 |
| Dominican Republic | 12 | — |
| Ecuador | 16 | — |
| El Salvador | 34 | — |
| Ethiopia | 27 | — |
| Federal Republic of Germany | — | 101 |
| Finland | — | 21 |
| France | — | 84 |
| Ghana | 4 | — |
| Guatemala | 32 | — |
| Guinea | 4 | — |
| Haiti | 12 | — |
| Honduras | 11 | — |
| India | 11 | — |
| Indonesia | 25 | — |
| Israel | — | 7 |
| Italy | — | 47 |
| Jamaica | 4 | — |
| Japan | — | 18 |
| Kenya | 17 | — |
| Liberia | 4 | — |
| Mexico | 32 | — |
| Netherlands | — | 35 |
| New Zealand | — | 6 |

| COUNTRY | EXPORTING | IMPORTING |
|---|---|---|
| Nicaragua | 13 | |
| Nigeria | 4 | |
| Norway | – | 16 |
| OAMCAF | (88) | – |
|    OAMCAF | ( 4) 1/ | – |
|    Cameroon | 15 | – |
|    Central African Republic | 3 | – |
|    Congo (Brazzaville) | 1 | – |
|    Dahomey | 1 | – |
|    Gabon | 1 | – |
|    Ivory Coast | 47 | – |
|    Malagasy Republic | 13 | – |
|    Togo | 3 | – |
| Panama | 4 | – |
| Peru | 16 | – |
| Portugal | 48 | – |
| Rwanda | 6 | – |
| Sierra Leone | 4 | – |
| Spain | – | 21 |
| Sweden | – | 38 |
| Switzerland | – | 19 |
| Tanzania | 15 | – |
| Trinidad & Tobago | 4 | – |
| Tunisia | – | 6 |
| Uganda | 41 | – |
| U.S.S.R. | – | 16 |
| United Kingdom | – | 32 |
| United States of America | – | 400 |
| Venezuela | 9 | – |
| **TOTAL** | **996** | **1,000** |

\* Includes Luxembourg

1/ Basic votes not attributable to individual contracting parties under Article 5 (4)(b).

# Bibliography

# BOOKS

Abbot, L. *Quality and Competition.* New York: Columbia University Press, 1955.

Baer, J., and O.G. Saxon. *Commodity Exchanges and Futures Trading.* New York: Harper and Brothers, 1949.

Bain, J.S. *Price Theory,* Rev. Ed., 1952: reprint. New York: Holt, Rinehart and Winston, 1963.

Baumol, W.J. *Business Behavior, Value and Growth.* New York: Macmillan, 1959.

Binder, A. *Internationale Regulierungen auf dem Weltweizenmarkt.* Kiel, 1952.

Brazilian Embassy. *Survey of the Brazilian Economy 1960.* Washington, D.C., 1960.

Carell, E. *Allgemeine Volkswirtschaftslehre,* 11. Aufl. Heidelberg, 1964.

Chamberlin, E.H. *The Theory of Monopolistic Competition,* 8th ed. Cambridge, Mass., 1962.

Curzon, S. *Multilateral Commercial Diplomacy.* London: Michael Joseph, 1965.

Davis, J.S. *International Commodity Agreements, Hope, Illusion or Menace.* New York: The Committee on International Economic Policy, 1947.

Edwards, C.D. *Maintaining Competition.* London: McGraw-Hill, 1st paperback ed., 1964.

Edwards, C.O., ed. *A Cartel Policy for the United Nations.* New York: Columbia University Press, 1946. Essay by Machlup.

Edwards, H.R. *Competition and Monopoly in the British Soap Industry.* Oxford: Clarendon Press, 1962.

Haarer, A.E. *Modern Coffee Production.* London: Leonhard Hill, 1962.

Her Majesty's Stationery Office (HMSO). International Coffee Agreement, Cmnd 1841. London, 1962.

Jöhr, V.W., and H.H. Singer. *The Role of the Economist to Official Advisor.* London: Allen and Unwin, 1955.

Kaysen, C., and D.F. Turner. *Antitrust Policy.* Cambridge, Mass: Harvard University Press, 1959.

Krelle, W. *Preistheorie.* Tübingen-Zürich, 1961.

League of Nations (Department of Economic Affairs). *International Cartels.* New York, 1945.

Lindahl, M.L., and W.A. Carter. *Corporate Concentration and Public Policy,* 3rd ed., Englewood Cliffs, N.J.: Prentice Hall, 1959.

Ludwig, M. *Internationale Rohstoffpolitik.* Zürich, 1957.

Macaron, P.M. *Price Formation in Natural Gas Fields.* New Haven: Yale University Press, 1962.

Machlup, E. *International Payments, Debts and Gold.* New York: Scribner's, 1964.

Machlup, E. *The Political Economy of Monopoly.* London: Wakefield, 1955.

McKie, James W. *Tin Cans and Tin Plate, A Study of Competition.* Cambridge, Mass: Harvard University Press, 1959.

Phillips, C.F. *Competition in the Synthetic Rubber Industry.* Chapel Hill: University of North Carolina Press, 1961.

Rowe, J.W. *Brazilian Coffee,* Royal Economic Society's Memorandum No. 34. London, 1932.

Rowe, J.W. *The World's Coffee.* Her Majesty's Stationery Office, London, 1963.

Ryan, W.J. *Price Theory.* London: Macmillan, 1961.

Schmitz, F. *Regulierungsprobleme auf den Weltrohstoffmärkten.* Diss. Köln, 1960.

Stackelberg, H.V. *Grundlagen der theoretischen Volkswirtschaftslehre.* Tübingen-Zürich, 1951.

Stocking, G.W., and M.W. Watkins. *Cartels or Competition.* New York: 20th Century Fund, 1948.

Weintraub, S. *Price Theory.* New York-London: Pitman Publishing Corporation, 1949.

Whittlesey, C.R. *National Interest and International Cartels.* New York: Macmillan, 1946.

Wickizer, V.D. *Coffee and Cocoa.* Stanford, California: Food Research Institute, Stanford University Press, 1945.

Wickizer, V.D. *Coffee, Tea and Cocoa, An Economic and Political Analysis.* Stanford, California: Food Research Institute, Stanford University Press, 1951.

Wilcox, C. *Public Policies Forward Business.* Chicago: Richard D. Irwin, 1955.

**316**

# ARTICLES

Adler, J. Comments on Prof. Nurkse's Paper, in *Kyklos,* Vol. XI (1958), p. 155.

American Economic Association (AEA). "Symposium: International Commodity Stabilization Schemes and the Export Problems of Developing Countries," in AER, *Papers and Proceedings,* Vol. LIII (1963), p. 65.

Anderson, O., Jr. "Trend," in HdSW, Vol. 10 (1961), p. 405.

Arndt, H. "Anpassung und Gleichgewicht am Markt," in J.N.St. 170 (1958).

Bain, J.S. "Theory of Monopolistic Competition after Thirty Years: The Impact on Industrial Organization," in AER, *Papers and Proceedings,* Vol. LIV (1964), p. 31.

Bilder, R.B. "The International Coffee Agreement: A Case History in Negotiation," in *Law and Contemporary Problems,* Vol. 28 (1963), p. 329.

Blau, G. "International Commodity Agreements," paper presented at the IER Congress on Economic Development, Vienna (Austria), 1962.

Chenery, H.B. "Comparative Advantage and Development Policy," in AER, Vol. LI, 1, (1961).

Clark, J.M. "Export Taxes on Tropical Products," in FAO, *Monthly Bulletin of Agricultural Economics and Statistics,* Vol. XII, No. 5 (1963), p. 11.

Ettori, O.T. "Fisica Du Agricultura Em Sao Paulo," in *Agricultura Em São Paulo,* Ans. XI, No. 7 (July 1964), p. 31.

Ezekiel, M. "The Cobweb Theorem," in QJE, 1938; reprinted in AEA, *Readings in Business, Cycle Theory,* London, 1950.

Gerhard, H.W. "Commodity Trade Stabilization Through International Agreements," in *Law and Contemporary Problems,* Vol. XXVIII, No. 2 (1963), p. 276.

Gray, R.W. "The Characteristic Bias in Some Thin Futures Markets," in *Food Research Studies* Vol. 1, No. 3, (1960), p. 296.

Haley, B.F. "The Relation between Cartel Policy and Commodity Agreement Policy," in AER, *Papers and Proceedings,* Vol. XXXVI (1946), p. 723.

Hoppmann, E. "Wettbewerbspolitik und Exportkartelle," in *Jahrbücher für National-Ökonomie und Statistik,* Bd. 173(4), 1961.

Houthakker, H.S. "The Scope and Limits of Futures Trading," in ed. T. Scitovsky, *The Allocation of Economic Resources,* Stanford University Press, Stanford, California, 1959.

Johnson, L.L. "Price Instability, Hedging and Trade Volume in the Coffee Futures Market" in *Journal of Political Economy,* Vol. 65, No. 4 (1957), p. 306.

Kindleberger, C.P. Discussion, in AER, *Papers and Proceedings,* Vol. LIII (1963), p. 106.

Kindleberger, C.P. "Flexible Exchange Rates," in eds. F.M. Tamagna et. al. *Monetary Management,* Englewood Cliffs, N.J.: Prentice Hall, 1963.

Kindleberger, C.P. "Terms of Trade for Primary Products" in ed. M. Clanson, *National and International Development,* Baltimore: John Hopkins, 1964.

Lovasy, G. Discussion, in AER, *Papers and Proceedings,* Vol. LIII (1963), p. 108.

Lovasy, G. "The International Coffee Market, A Note," in IMF *Staff Papers,* Vol. X (1962), p. 226.

Mason, E.S. Preface to Kaysen and Turner, *Antitrust Policy,* Cambridge, Mass.: Harvard University Press, 1959.

Mikesell, R.F. "International Commodity Stabilization Schemes and the Export Problems of Developing Countries," in AER, *Papers and Proceedings,* Vol. LIII, (1963).

Myint, H. "Economic Theory and the Underdeveloped Countries," in IPE, Vol. 73 (1965), p. 477.

Porter, R.S. "Buffer Stocks and Economic Stability," in *Oxford Economic Papers,* New Series, Vol. II (1950), pp. 95-118.

Roth, H. "Die Übererzeugung in der Welthandelsware Kaffee im Zeitraum von 1790-1929," in *Beitrage zur Erforschung der wirtschaftlichen Wechsellagen,* Aufschwung, Krise, Stockung, Jena, 1929, Heft 2.

Schneider, E. "Real Economics in Integration and Large-Scale Operation Versus Advantages of Domination," in ed. E.H. Chamberlin, *Monopoly and Competition and their Regulation,* London-New York: Macmillan, 1954, p. 205.

Sosnick, S.H. 'A Critique of Concepts of Workable Competition," QJE, Vol. LXXII (1958), p. 380.

Staley, E.E. "An Evaluation of Some Recent Contributions to the Political Economy of the Stabilization of International Price and Commodity Fluctuations," in *Weltwirtschaftliches Archiv,* Bd. 94 (1965), Heft 2, p. 337.

Stern, R.M. "Fluctuations in Commodity Trade," in IPE, Vol. LXXVII (1963), pp. 258-273.

Swerling, B.C. "Problems of International Commodity Stabilization," in Principles of Economic Policy, Consistent and Inconsistent: International Commodity Stabilization, AER, *Papers and Proceedings,* Vol. LIII (1963), p. 65.

Teutem, O. Van. "Coffee in Latin America: The Producers' Problem," in UN, *Economic Bulletin for Latin America,* Vol. IV, No. 1, (1959), p. 32.

Tyszinski, H. "Commodity Agreements and Price Fluctuations," in *The Economic Journal,* Vol. LXI (1951), p. 655.

Tyszinski, H. "Economics of the Wheat Agreement," in *Economica 1949,* p. 27.

Walker, H. "The International Law of Commodity Agreements," in *Law and Contemporary Problems,* Vol. 28 (1963).

Wickizer, V.D. "International Collaboration in the Coffee Market," in *Food Research Studies,* Stanford University Press, Vol. IV, No. 3, (1964), p. 301.

World First Coffee Congress. "5th Pan-American Coffee Conference, Curitiba, Panama, 18.-21.1.1954," in *Observatore Economico e Finansiero,* March 1954, No. 215, English Reprint p. 24.

Author Unknown. *The World Coffee and Tea, 1966-67 Guide,* April 1966, Vol. 6, No. 12.

# OFFICIAL PUBLICATIONS

Consello Nacional De Estatistica. Anuario Estatico Do Brasil, 1962.

Departmento Da Producao Vegetal. Agricultura Em São Paulo (Boletim Da Divisao De Economia Rural), Ano XI (1964), Ano I (1954).

FAO (Food and Agricultural Organization). *Coffee in Latin America: Productivity Problems and Future Prospects.*
I. Colombia and El Salvador.
II. Brazil, State of Sao Paulo,
Part 1: The State and Prospects of Production. A report prepared by the Joint Agriculture Division of the Economic Commission for Latin American and the FAO of the UN. Mexico, 1960.

FAO (Food and Agricultural Organization). "Coffee in the European Common Market," in FAO; *Monthly Bulletin of Agricultural Economics and Statistics,* Vol. 10, No. 11, (1961), p. 14.

FAO (Food and Agricultural Organization). *Commodity Review 1961, Rome, 1961.*

FAO (Food and Agricultural Organization). *Commodity Review 1962, Rome, 1962.*

FAO (Food and Agricultural Organization). *Commodity Review 1963, Rome, 1963.*

FAO (Food and Agricultural Organization). *Commodity Review 1965, Rome, 1965.*

FAO (Food and Agricultural Organization). *Commodity Stabilization in the French Area* (E/CN 13/51), papers of the Joint Session of the UN Commission on International Commodity Trade and FAO Committee on Commodity Problems, Rome, 1962.

FAO (Food and Agricultural Organization). "Recent Development in Coffee," in *Monthly Bulletin of Agricultural Economics and Statistics,* Vol. 7, No. 3 (1958), p. 13.

FAO (Food and Agricultural Organization). "The International Effects of National Grain Policies," Commodity Policy Studies No. 8, Rome, 1955.

FAO (Food and Agricultural Organization). The Role of Marketing Boards for Export Crops in Developing Countries (E/CN 13/50), agenda item 4: Joint Session of the UN Commission on International Trade and FAO Committee on Commodity Problems, Rome, 1962.

FAO (Food and Agricultural Organization). "The World Coffee Economy," *Commodity Bulletin Series No. 33 (CBS-33),* Rome, 1961.

General Agreement on Tariffs and Trade (GATT). Development Plan Study, March 16, 1965.

General Agreement on Tariffs and Trade (GATT). Report of Committee II on Consultations with Brazil on Agricultural Support Measures (Doc. L 1317), Geneva, 1960.

General Agreement on Tariffs and Trade (GATT). *The Impact of Commodity Problems on International Trade* (Doc. L 1656). Geneva, 1961.

General Agreement on Tariffs and Trade (GATT). *Trade in Tropical Products.* Geneva, 1963.

General Agreement on Tariffs and Trade (GATT). *Trends in International Trade, A Report by a Panel of Experts.* Geneva, 1958.

IBC (Instituto Brasileiro Do Cafe). Anuario Estatistico Do Cafe, 1964.

IBC (Instituto Brasileiro Do Cafe). Relatorio Da Diretoria, 1959.

IBC - GERCA (Grupo Executivo Da Racionalizacao Da Cafecultura). Programa De Racionalizacaa Da Cafecultura Brasileira, 1962.

IBC - GERCA (Grupo Executivo Da Racionalizacao Da Cafecultura). Relatorio 1964.

IBGE. Anuario Estatistico Do Brasil, 1964.

IBRD (International Bank for Reconstruction and Development). *History of Commodity Agreements.* Washington, D.C., July 1959.

IBRD (International Bank for Reconstruction and Development). *The Economic Development of Uganda.* Baltimore: John Hopkins, 1961.

ICCJCA. *Review of International Commodity Problems,* New York, 1954.

ICO (International Coffee Organization). *An Analysis of Coffee Prices 1953-1963/64* (ICC-EB 42), London, 1964.

ICO (International Coffee Organization). *Convention and Basic Documents,* Rio de Janeiro, 1958.

ICO (International Coffee Organization). ICC: *Mission to OMCAF Countries,* London, 1963.

ICO (International Coffee Organization). ICC-6-Res. 67, London, March 16, 1965.

ICO (International Coffee Organization). *Production Forecasts 1965-1970 and Their Implications* (staff paper), Vol. I and II (ICC-7-4), London, July 26, 1965.

IMF (International Monetary Fund). *Financial Statistics 1956,* Vol. IX, No. 1.

IMF (International Monetary Fund). *Financial Statistics,* Supplement 1962-63.

IMF (International Monetary Fund). *Financial Statistics,* March 1963.

PACB (Pan-American Coffee Bureau). *Annual Coffee Statistics,* 1960.

PACB (Pan-American Coffee Bureau). *Annual Coffee Statistics,* 1962.

PACB (Pan-American Coffee Bureau). *Annual Coffee Statistics,* 1964.

State of Paraná (Paulo Pimentel Administration). Investment Program 1966-1971.

United Nations (UN) *Economic Bulletin for Latin America,* Vol. IX, No. 2, Santiago, Chile, 1964.

United Nations (UN) *Economic Survey of Latin America 1955,* Economic Commission for Latin America, Mexico, 1956.

United Nations (UN) *Economic Survey of Latin America 1956,* Economic Commission for Latin America, Mexico, 1957.

United Nations (UN) *Economic Survey of Latin America 1957,* Economic Commission for Latin America, Mexico, 1958.

United Nations (UN) *Economic Survey of Latin America 1958,* Economic Commission for Latin America, Mexico, 1959.

United Nations (UN) *Economic Survey of Latin America 1963,* Economic Commission for Latin America, Mexico, 1964.

United Nations (UN) *Review of International Commodity Problems 1949,* New York, 1950.

UNCTAD (United Nations Conference on Trade and Development). *Stabilization of International Commodity Markets,* Geneva, March 1964 (E/ConF/46/8).

UNCTAD (United Nations Conference on Trade and Development). Doc. E/ConF/46/P/1/Rev. 1, Geneva June 15, 1964.

U.S. Department of Agriculture. *Coffee Situation, Programs and Policies in Producing Countries,* Foreign Agricultural Service (FAS-M-148), July 1963.

U.S. Senate. 83rd Congress, Special Subcommittee of the Committee on Banking and Currency, *Study of Coffee Prices: Hearing,* Part I, Washington, D.C., Government Printing Office, 1954.

U.S. Senate. 87th Congress, *Hearings before the Senate Commission on Foreign Relations on International Coffee Agreement 1962*, Washington, D.C., 1963.

U.S. Federal Trade Commission (FTC). *Economic Report of the Investigation of Coffee Prices*, Government Printing Office, Washington, D.C., July 30, 1954.

## JOURNALS, NEWSPAPERS, ETC.

Brasilian Institute of Economics (Center for Economic and Business Research). *Conjunctura Economica*, International Edition, Rio De Janeiro, Vol. VI-X.

Federation of British Industries. *Review*, June 1964.

Patton & Co., New York, 29, Pine Street. *Coffee Intelligence*, February 4, 1963 and October 5, 1965.

Patton & Co., New York, 29, Pine Street. *Deutsche Zeitung und Wirtschafts zeitung*, 13.4.1965 and 21.4.1965.

Patton & Co., New York, 29, Pine Street. *Financial Times*, March 6, 1964.

Patton & Co., New York, 29, Pine Street. *Neue Züricher Zeitung*, No. 299, 30.10.1964, p. 12. No. 19, 19. 1.1965, p. 12. No. 35, 5. 2.1965, p. 11.